CISTERCIAN STUDIES SERIES: NUMBER ONE HUNDRED FORTY-TWO

THE LETTERS OF SAINT ANSELM OF CANTERBURY
VOLUME THREE

CISTERCIAN STUDIES SERIES: NUMBER ONE HUNDRED FORTY-TWO

THE LETTERS
of
SAINT ANSELM
OF CANTERBURY

VOLUME THREE

Translated and annotated
by

Walter Fröhlich

α

Cistercian Publications
cistercianpublications.org

LITURGICAL PRESS
Collegeville, Minnesota
litpress.org

This translation is based on the text in volume four of the critical edition of F. S. Schmitt, OSB, *Anselmi Opera Omnia*, six volumes (Edinburgh, 1946–1963: rpt. Stuttgart, 1968).

A Cistercian Publications title published by Liturgical Press

Cistercian Publications
Editorial Offices
161 Grosvenor Street
Athens, Ohio 45701
cistercianpublications.org

The editors of Cistercian Publications express their great appreciation to John Leinenweber for his editorial help in bringing volumes two and three to completion.

© 1994 by Cistercian Publications © 2008 by Order of Saint Benedict, Collegeville, Minnesota. All rights reserved. No part of this book may be used or reproduced in any manner whatsoever, except brief quotations in reviews, without written permission of Liturgical Press, Saint John's Abbey, PO Box 7500, Collegeville, MN 56321-7500.

ISBN 978-0-87907-395-4

Library of Congress Cataloging-in-Publication Data
(Revised for volume 2)

Anselm, Saint, Archbishop of Canterbury, 1033–1109.
    The letters of Saint Anselm of Canterbury.
    (Cistercian studies series ; no. 96, 97, 142)
    Includes bibliographical references.
    1. Anselm, Saint, Archbishop of Canterbury, 1033–1109—Correspondence.   2. Catholic Church—England—Canterbury—Bishops—Correspondence.   I. Fröhlich, Walter, 1937–
II. Title.   III. Series: Cistercian studies series ; no. 96, etc.
BR754.A56A4 1990   282'.092 [B]   91-149193
ISBN 978-0-87907-742-6 (v. 1)

TABLE OF CONTENTS

Anselm as a Letter Writer 1
THE LETTERS OF ANSELM 7
    Letters 310–475
Selected Bibliography 271
Abbreviations 277
Errata, volume two 281
Indices to *The Letters of Saint Anselm* 283

FOREWORD

ANSELM AS A LETTER WRITER

THE ART OF WRITING LETTERS and preserving them in letter collections provided one of the major forms of literature between the fourth and the late seventh centuries. This period is characterized by the letters of Saint Augustine and various papal collections, the most important being the register of Gregory the Great, the administrative handbook of Cassiodorus, and the *Variae*.

During the Carolingian Renaissance of the eighth and ninth centuries the practice of writing and collecting letters for literary purposes was revived. This new interest was promoted by the improved communications within the Carolingian Empire and by renewed interest in classical literature and learning. Heralded by the letters of such Anglo-Saxon missionaries as Boniface and Lull, this revival involved almost every leading figure of the period including Alcuin, Lupus of Ferrière, Hincmar of Reims, and Rabanus Maurus.

The Golden Age of medieval epistolography was ushered in at the end of the tenth century by the letter collection of Gerbert of Aurillac. From the following two centuries, a few letters have survived from almost every literary figure of note and from many of no note at all. This prodigious flowering of the art of letter writing produced an abundance of letters of all types, furthered no doubt by improved communications and travel at that time. Medieval letter writing was governed by a definite epistolary form, the *ars dictaminis*. According to C.H. Haskins, a letter was to be constructed on certain definite lines. The proposed five parts were to be arranged in a logical sequence: the *salutation*, punctiliously observing the conventions of class, was followed by the *exordium*, designed to put the reader in the proper frame of mind for granting the request which followed. The *narration* explained the purpose of the letter, and was followed by a *petition*. Concluding phrases brought the letter to a graceful end.

The *modus epistolaris* imposed two further requirements on the letter writer: brevity and restriction to a single subject, the more important being brevity. In fact, there were no defined limits to the length of letters but this rule of thumb, often ignored, is perhaps best defined in a negative sense: a letter, depending on its subject matter, should not encroach on the patience of the reader. Brevity is often cited as a reason for omitting some additional argument or example. The second requirement, even less observed than the first, was that a letter should be restricted to a single subject. Sidonius of Lyon stated: 'As a rule, single subjects are dealt with in single letters'. *Ars dictaminis* later took up this point, emphasizing that the object of a letter should always be a specific request rather than a narrative or exposition.

Not only the writing of letters but also their preservation in letter collections became a significant feature of the intellectual atmosphere of the eleventh and twelfth centuries. The two most significant reasons for collecting and publishing letters were that letters offered a recognized form of literary production which provided the best way of expressing views on various matters not suited to other *genres* of literature, and that letters fulfilled a growing need for self-disclosure, much like the autobiography or memoirs of today.

Saint Anselm of Aosta, Bec, and Canterbury is recognized as the greatest mind between Saint Augustine and Saint Thomas Aquinas, and the most renowned theologian of his time. His fame rested on three major works and a number of tracts as well as a collection of prayers and meditations. In addition, he wrote many letters observing the requirements of *modus epistolaris*: brevity and the single subject. The literary aspect and character of his correspondence closely followed the literary fashion of the period.

Anselm wrote and received a great many letters. As literary *opuscula*, they were collected and copied into manuscripts. Some of the earliest manuscripts containing Anselm's letter collection were produced at monasteries with which Saint Anselm had close links. The Canterbury letter collection in MS L, (London, Lambeth Palace, MS 59) contains three hundred-eighty-six items, and sixteen additional letters in appendix La—a total of four hundred-two items. That of Bury Saint Edmunds in MS E (Cambridge, Corpus Christi College, MS 135) contains three hundred-forty-seven letters. Two hundred-ninety-three letters of the Bec collection are preserved in the Saint Victor MS V (Paris, Bibliothèque National, MS 14762). The most complete anselmian letter collection, in MS C (London; British Library, MS Cotton Claudius A.XI), consists of four hundred-sixteen letters.

F.S. Schmitt, the editor of the most recent critical edition of *Anselmi Opera Omnia*—which has provided the basis of this present translation—found four hundred-seventy-five items which he thought formed the total anselmian correspondence. Yet a close survey of these letters indicates the existence of a further one hundred-fifty letters. In my opinion, Anselm himself, excluded many of these from his collection. Through them we see Anselm at the center of an enormous correspondence network and understand that he edited his letters for a particular purpose.

Accepting the traditional framework of the *ars dictaminis*, Anselm reshaped the content matter and modified the style of his letters to suit his original ideas, keen intellect, and personal feelings. Anselm was a monk, a teacher, and an administrator, and the subject matter of his letters can be classified accordingly: spiritual, educational, and administrative.

Nearly sixty percent of Anselm's letters are addressed to monks and nuns. In these letters he offered *spiritual advice* as a pastor to his flock, dealing mainly with such themes as reading the Scripture and the Fathers for inspiration; the fleeting nature of transitory things; the constant need to progress towards perfection in the spiritual life and the importance of paying attention to little things; accepting suffering; showing compassion; expressing mutual charity and love; obeying superiors as God's representatives; and living a life of humility and prayer.

Anselm was called upon to resolve various problems affecting religious persons. These include such things as monks seeking permission to take part in the crusade, the treatment of renegade monks and nuns, the reception of new members into the monastery, the education of boys and young men, the relation of one monastery to another or to the ecclesiastical hierarchy, transfers from one monastery to another, the matter of exemption, interference of secular authorities in abbatial elections, and liturgical observances.

Anselm addressed numerous letters of encouragement and advice to the communities of religious women who came under his general protection and also letters to devout women living in the world. These letters and those in which he strove to recruit novices for the monastery treat themes that moved Anselm to fervent rhetoric. His attitude towards the recipient of his letters is that of a caring father and a pastor of souls seeking only the recipients' progress on their pilgrimage towards the celestial home. Anselm sincerely expressed the conviction of his inmost being, that monastic life is the closest approach to paradise one can achieve in this world. Anselm addressed with affectionate expressions those pursuing the same ideal as himself and those he wanted to encourage to do the same.

Anselm's role as *teacher*, his principles and method of education, the philosophical character of his learning, and the aesthetic bent that nurtured his interest in textual criticism all come to the fore at one time or another within his letters. The increasing number of students of the school of Bec put a great burden on Anselm as *magister scolae*. Since the teaching of grammar was not his favorite subject, he introduced others to teach it. This provided him with more time to pursue metaphysics and theology, which were more congenial to his talents as teacher.

He took his teaching role very seriously. Students were not driven to study by Anselm but attracted by his discretion and reason, gentleness and kindness. His work as spiritual father and teacher answered Anselm's inmost need to give of his talents to others, to give back to God the love of Christ through the souls it was his privilege to mould for time and eternity.

Beneath his gentleness and personal attractiveness, Anselm showed toughness of mind and will in *matters of administration*. His archiepiscopate was almost totally overshadowed by dissensions with his lords, King William II Rufus and King Henry I, over relations between the church and the crown. The letters connected with this relationship deal with all the urgent problems of his episcopacy. We find Anselm's disagreement over the royal *usus atque leges* as basic law of the Anglo-Norman realm and the consequent royal refusal to acknowledge Pope Urban II; the royal refusal to call a reforming council in England; the controversy between Pope Paschal II and Henry I over investiture; the crown's appointment of bishops and abbots; the marriage of the clergy; the administration of church property; and his fight to secure the primacy of Canterbury over York.

The brevity, the clarity of thought, and the seriousness of tone in these letters indicate Anselm's total commitment to the defense of *lex Dei* against *lex regis*. Anselm maintained that if the latter were not in harmony with the former the latter represented merely arbitrary human law. The letters dealing with this hotly contested matter display Anselm's shrewdness and competence, despite his own conventional disclaimer of any interest in public affairs or of any aptitude for politics.

The fact that Anselm worked hard to produce in writing the clarity and precision of his thoughts and that he also took pains over the clear and flawless transmission of the texts of his philosophical and theological works is borne out by the existence of a number of prayers and tracts in different stages of recension.

This care is also evident in the transmission of his literary work, his letter collection. A few years after becoming abbot of Bec, he started collecting his letters, asking for them to be returned by recipients and carefully editing the compiled material in three stages when leisure provided opportunity. In 1104, Anselm referred a novice inquiring about the first years of monastic life to a letter he had written on this very topic some thirty-one years previously. 'I advise you to look up the letter (AEp 37) which I wrote Dom Lanzo when he was a novice.' (AEp 335) It stands to reason that the novice was not to look for the original letter but for its copy within of the anselmian letter collection in a codex in the library of Christ Church monastery.

In late 1105 or early 1106, during a period of relative leisure, Anselm actively took part in editing the final version of his letter collection. These literary *opuscula* have an autobiographical touch. They display Anselm as a faithful monk, conscientious teacher, and ardent soldier of Christ who devoted his life totally to God and his service. He appears as a zealous laborer, creating a loving and truly Christian community of monks, as a compassionate teacher, and penetrating thinker, encouraging his students, and as an active reformer of the Church of God in unity with the pope and in agreement with papal ordinances. Thus he set the example of the impeccable Christian prelate whose faultless public conduct was to serve as a model and as a precedent for others. Thomas Becket was not unaware of the expectations he set. The image of his behavior was intended to create binding customs and eventually good laws. Anselm's letter collection was to be a manual of good examples for his own day and for the future. He conceived his letter collection to be a work of literature forming the complementary part of his philosophical and theological writings.

Munich   Walter Fröhlich

4 December 1993
900th anniversary of Anselm's consecration

Note:
I would like to thank Professor Giles Constable for his advice, assistance, and constant encouragement in my work on the Letters of Saint Anselm. This foreword owes much to his edition of *The Letters of Peter the Venerable* (Cambridge: Harvard 1967); J.D. Loughlin, *Saint Anselm as Letter Writer* (Washington, 1967); G. Constable, *Letters and Letter Collections* (Turnhout: Brepols, 1976); J. Wood, 'Letters and Letter-Collections from Antiquity to the Early Middle Ages: The Prose Works of Avitus of Vienne', in *The Culture of Christendom , Essays in Medieval History in Memory of Dennis L.T. Bethell* (London, 1993) 29 - 43; see also *The Letters of Saint Anselm*, I: 23 - 52.

310. FROM PRIOR ERNULF OF CANTERBURY.

A member of the community at Canterbury, most likely Prior Ernulf, blames Anselm for the increase of evils due to his absence from England. He tells him that his presence in England would be more useful than his absence and entreats him to return.

TO THE VENERABLE LORD AND HOLY FATHER ANSELM, ARCHBISHOP OF CANTERBURY: [ERNULF,] THE MOST DEVOTED SERVANT OF HIM AND OF THE WHOLE HOUSEHOLD OF THE LORD,[1] SENDING GREETING IN THE LORD.

HAVING CONSIDERED, HOLY FATHER, the poverty of our position and understanding, I could rightly have decided not to disturb again and again, with the words of my insignificant ability, the devotion of your holy mind, in which the sign of true piety shines and from which the companion of virtue, the brightness of wisdom, radiates. Nevertheless, the peaceful and blessed favor of your opinion raises me above myself to address our discourse to you, such as it is; not that I wish to teach you, who hardly need any human teaching, but to remember with you our grief and yours. At the beginning of our discourse I ask to come to this agreement with your reverence, that for the time being I be allowed to adopt the sweeter duty of chastising devoutly instead of the bitter deception of flattery.

I would wish your holiness to know that boundless sadness about your absence swallows up our souls, whose affection for you is the same as ever. If I am not mistaken, you would be more helpful in our danger[2] by showing yourself ready to share the plight of your sons than, absent and forgetful in some way of the wrongs done to us and the church, by allowing us to be harried by shameless and cruel enemies who spare neither our modesty nor our safety.[3] I consider you, holy father, to be unhappy because of this. For you, who were once a pledge of holy hope for your people, if you were now grieved because England is hard pressed by so unexpected an enemy, how you would lament, how you would strive to come to our help, to share with us these unprecedented forms of affliction! Of your own accord, with almost no one forcing you, you were snatched away from our dangers, perhaps in order that you might not feel what we are forced to endure and—what is more serious—forced to watch certain members of the court being raised to holy orders[4] without the consent of either canonical election or justice. There is no doubt that if the true doorkeeper[5] of the Church, that is Christ, were admitting them to the sacred offices, what we perceive daily in this province could not be committed, namely the unjust and pitiless tyranny of princes, the plundering of the poor, the despoiling of churches, to the point that even the place of the Lord's body and blood loses its immunity. Widows lament, old men weep over their misfortunes, seeing the hard-earned portion of their sustenance, which was scanty enough, being snatched from them. Virgins are seized and defiled by illicit intercourse and, what is the prime evil of all and brings disgrace upon our reputation, priests take wives. Apart from these evils there are many other shameful acts which it is wicked or impossible to remember or report.

If you had been eager to ponder on the rule of ecclesiastical administration and the order of ancient custom with anxious consideration, no reason would have deceived you into remaining in exile, nor would any others have incurred such grave danger because of your absence. Do you suppose that in this way you can turn aside the defiance of God's enemies who believe neither in God nor in truth unless forced to do so? I do not know by what reasoning your paternity reaches this conclusion. He who takes command of a ship must be all the more vigilant the more he fears the storms. But perhaps when you see choirs of souls being led before the judgement seat of Christ, those staunchest rams of the divine flock whom no wolf could harm, nor fear of anyone turn to flight, perhaps then you will feel ashamed of having fled solely according to the will of envious people. How blessed then will be the memory of our most holy father Ambrose, among all the others. As ecclesiastical history[6] relates he was not ashamed to resist the emperor Theodosius to his face[7] and to refuse him entry to the church because of his guilt.[8] What could such a disposition, such constancy, fail to achieve?

Holy father, even if someone, having imprisoned and ill-treated you, tore you to pieces, you should not have withdrawn in this way. How much more so when you experienced none of these things nor was your see denied to you! But you decided to flee because of a single word of a certain William,[9] and having left your opponent behind, you abandoned your sheep to be torn apart by the ungodly. It is shameful to think what has happened since all, or nearly all, of those to whom the churches in their present distress looked for comfort in their need, having admitted grounds for fear, chose rather to surrender with you than to resist in vain without you. What were they to do, whose father was absent and whose head gave them no help? Finally, your holiness is not to be instructed but admonished to hasten your arrival, to remove the disgrace of holy Mother Church and to bring speedy help against our enemies who are already pressing in upon our sanctuaries. The disease can still be cast out as long as the wound can be seen to be open on the surface. I know that if you wish to return to your see you will find many who are prepared, as they say, to defend God's cause bravely with you unless the desertion of your paternity weakens them.

If, as we have heard, you are intending to suspend or excommunicate England,[10] I ask you to deign to inform our brethren and myself, who have always been ready to obey you, what we are to do. Farewell.

1104, from Canterbury.

NOTES

1. The writer of this letter is a member of the community of Christ Church Canterbury, possibly Prior Ernulf, *VA* 130, or Osbern the precentor, *Epp* 39, 149, 152.
2. After Anselm failed to obtain the removal or even mitigation of the papal decrees on lay investiture and homage, *Ep* 306, King Henry banned him from his kingdom, *HN* 157, and 'ordered all the revenues of the archbishopric of Canterbury to be converted to his own uses', *HN* 159; *VA* 132.
3. Eadmer refutes accusations of this kind voiced in *Epp* 327, 330, 336, 355, 365, 366, saying that 'in their anxiety for his return [people] gave too little consideration to the true circumstances of the case', *HN* 160. Anselm himself wrote that he feared the precedent his example might set, see *Ep* 355.
4. This statement does not seem to agree with the facts, for during Anselm's second exile the King did not appoint any bishops: Osbern of Exeter died in autumn 1103 and the bishopric was vacant until 1107: on 1 August 1107 William de Warelwast witnessed a royal charter for the first time as Bishop of Exeter, *Reg.* II, 825. Abbeys whose abbots died were kept vacant: Battle 1102 - 1107; Cerne 1102 - 1114; Cher:sey 1102 - 1107; Gloucester 1104 - 1107; Milton 1102 - 1107; Peterborough 1103 - 1107. Thus this charge could only refer to Abbot Richard of Ely, see *Ep* 280, though there is some uncertainty concerning Evesham after the death of Abbot Walter in 1104, see *Heads.*
5. See Jn 10:3.
6. See Cassiodorus, *Historia Ecclesiastica tripartita*, 9, 30: *PL* 69:1144.
7. See Gal 2:11.
8. In 370 Emperor Theodosius, in a rage, had ordered a large number of people in Thessalonica to be killed.
9. William de Warelwast, the royal messenger, had given him to understand that he could only return to England if he abided by the royal *usus atque leges, HN* 10, as Lanfranc had done, *Epp* 305, 306.
10. This rumor seems to have been widespread, see *Ep* 349. Yet only in May or June 1105 did Anselm leave Lyon to put himself in a position from which he could effectively excommunicate King Henry, see Southern, *Anselm*, 176–177; M. Rule, II, 342 - 343.

311. TO PRIOR ERNULF OF CANTERBURY.

Writing to Prior Ernulf, Anselm defends himself against the charge that he gave up the archbishopric by not returning to England. He has been forbidden by the Pope to associate with those who are excommunicated. He denies that evils multiply because of his absence and that the King and bishop Robert of Lincoln were defamed by Eadmer and Alexander. He advises the monks to be careful in their contacts with those excommunicated by the Pope and to refuse to act in any way contrary to good order.

ANSELM THE ARCHBISHOP: TO HIS REVEREND AND DEAREST BROTHER, DOM PRIOR ERNULF, GREETING AND THE GRACE OF GOD.

YOUR LOVE BRINGS IT ABOUT that you and our friends are grieved that I did not come back to England after my return from Rome,[1] but that I appear to be relinquishing my pastoral care without any reason, but the wise religious men[2] to whom I explain the matter do not think so, nor do I understand it so either. As far as I am concerned, I am not relinquishing my office but I cannot live in the place where I ought to be carrying it out, as you can perceive if you consider the matter carefully. You have heard that according to an Apostolic decision I cannot, without danger to my soul, communicate[3] with those people whose communion I cannot avoid whenever I communicate with the King, as long as he communicates with them. Just consider what I could do if I came to crown the King and celebrated Mass and they were around me! It is certain that I could not send them away but I dare not pray with them. I ought not to deny the King the customary service, since the lord Pope conceded this to him and ordered me to do it if I were present.

If it is said to me that I should stay at home and not go to court, and thus while performing the other good deeds of my office I abstain from communion with bad people, then the King with all his bishops and nobles would complain that, by refusing to crown him I am taking away from him the honor of his crown which the primate of his kingdom owes him by custom.[4] Thus it would seem right to them and they would complete the act of transferring the dignity of our church to another church. If this took place while I was living in the kingdom I would be unable to prevent it either personally or through anybody else, and an intolerable diminution of our church would be confirmed.

If however they say that it is not fitting for a man who ought to shed his blood for his sheep and for the Church of God to flee at a single word, then I say that this word, in which such serious evils are contained, should not be underestimated. As I have already said, under no circumstances can I deal with these evils without danger to my soul and without detriment to the church entrusted to me. Moreover I do not fear the shedding of my blood or even the destruction of my body or the loss of my possessions. If these things happened to my person I would suffer them willingly for the sake of asserting the truth. But none of this would happen to me; rather, if I should come into conflict with the King in England grave oppression would lay waste to our church and the people who belong to it to no purpose and a multitude of those tormented would turn on me, cursing me as the cause of their afflictions. Therefore it seems better to me that during my absence tribulation should continue to rage in England if it cannot be avoided, than that any evil custom should be confirmed for the future by my presence and toleration, or that a great number of people should lament that they are suffering tribulation because of me with me looking on.

If the objection is raised that the loss of souls which is seen to happen because of my absence is greater than the temporal evil which would be caused by my presence, and therefore the former should be rejected for the sake of the latter: I have already said that if it should come upon me I would maintain unshaken patience. But since we ought not to do evil in order that good may come, so I ought not to bring any evil on any innocent people so that good may come to the souls of others. In any case, I said last year when they threatened to expel[5] me, that I did not want to leave on account of the pastoral care and obedience laid upon me, but I said this because of those who were threatening this lest I would be leaving merely because of their words, and not because I believed that it would be any use for me to remain. For as soon as discord and rivalry should appear between the King and myself, in like manner bodily evils would boil up and spiritual goods freeze to the core.

The charge has been laid upon me that I have, cunningly as it were, defamed the King and his kingdom and the bishop of Lincoln,[6] not openly myself, but secretly through our monks. This is certainly untrue because no one has been advised to do this by me. Our brothers Eadmer and Alexander, who above all are being accused of this, do not know that such things are being said about them and you know that denouncers, adding great things to little things, tend to be liars. Moreover, before we reached Rome, much was being said about England inside and outside of Rome. In all these matters, neither by myself nor through those wiser than myself can I follow better advice than to await the providence of God and commit the matter to his judgement. You should know, however, that it is my intention that with the assistance of God I shall never belong to any mortal man, nor bind myself by oath of allegiance to anyone.

You asked our advice as to what you ought to do among and with those people with whom the lord Pope has forbidden me to communicate. This matter is very delicate and it is extremely difficult not to communicate with those people with whom the King communicates, especially as this communion was forbidden to me alone by the Pope in Rome and I do not dare to order that you should communicate with those with whom I do not communicate.[7] But if you continue in the way in which I left you, you are not to be reprimanded in any way. For you cannot cut yourself off from the whole kingdom nor do you have any share in their wickedness. If anyone asks anything of you which is not fitting to your honor and your religion, be on your guard that neither threats nor blandishments nor any other trick persuade you to do anything you would later regret. Whatever happens, for the sake of God and charity towards your neighbor, do not give up the guidance and care of the brothers lest violence should expel you from the church. If adversities and tribulations should increase, then grow in strength and do not desert your brothers in temptation. If anyone should demand of any monk of our church any oath, any pledge of loyalty or any agreement which is against good order so as to gain some power which we call 'obedience', then deliberate on the matter and avert the evil as far as possible according to your understanding.[8]

Whatever may happen in the future I commend you and all our brothers, together with everything which belongs to our church, to the protection of God.

1104 from Lyon.

NOTES

1. See *Ep* 305.
2. Anselm seems to be referring to Archbishop Hugh of Lyon, with whom he spent the greater part of his second exile.
3. See *Epp* 308 and 280, also *HN* 148.
4. It was customary for the King to wear his crown three times a year, at Christmas, Easter and Whitsun, besides on the day of his coronation, see E.A. Freeman, *History of the Norman Conquest* (Oxford, 1871) 3:329; F. Barlow, *The Feudal Kingdom of England* (London, 1955) 169, 395; D.C. Douglas, *William the Conqueror* (London, 1964) 225; J. LePatourel, *The Norman Empire* (Oxford, 1976) 125–6, 138, 240–1.
5. The Lent meeting with the King at Canterbury in 1103, *HN* 146–7.

6. Robert Bloet had been chancellor of William II before he was appointed to the see of Lincoln in March 1093, see Fröhlich, 'Bischöfliche Kollegen', *AA* 1 (1969) 259–261.
7. See *Codex Iuris Canonici*, E. Eichmann, K. Mörsdorf, Kirchenrecht (Paderborn, 1960) 3:384.
8. See *Ep* 312.

312. TO THE MONKS OF CANTERBURY.

Anselm consoles the monks of Christ Church Canterbury since he is unable to return as they wish. He commits the care of their souls to Prior Ernulf as they requested.

ANSELM THE ARCHBISHOP: TO HIS DEAREST FELLOW-MONKS, BROTHERS AND SONS, LIVING AT CHRIST CHURCH CANTERBURY, SENDING THE GREETING AND BLESSING OF GOD AND HIS OWN, AS FAR AS HE CAN.

I GRATEFULLY ACKNOWLEDGE, love and approve your kind desire concerning our return since it proceeds from the kindness of love, even if God has wished to ordain otherwise than my desire to be with you. For God often arranges the lives of his servants in a manner different from what the human mind, although it has the best of intentions, desires. Just as gold is tested in a furnace,[1] so does he test the minds of his elect in the fire of tribulation. If this happens to you by his paternal correction or testing do not give way, but like sons strive to make progress out of this very tribulation. It is not unusual for God's servants to be struck by many kinds of adversities on this pilgrimage since they are not of this world.[2] The more they are troubled here, the more they perceive the world and desire to pass from this world to their rest. For this reason I admonish you, I beseech you as my dearest sons that if the matter requires it you should strive to bind yourselves more closely to the service of God with the same degree of diligence as the enemy of mankind will use to attempt to draw you away from your religious life. Thus you will fight more bravely against the enemy and will obtain God's help more efficaciously. It is not necessary for me to write at any length to you on these matters because by the grace of God you know it already and the testimony of the Scriptures is present to you and the wisdom of Dom Prior will be able to advise and comfort you if you are willing to trust him.

Your petition that I should commit the entire care of your souls to Dom Prior both privately and publicly until I return to you, this I have done and do, as if to myself so that according to the wisdom God has given him and the zeal for the house of God[3] which he has in his heart, he may judge and dispose, punish and spare, so that souls may be nourished in innocence and that vices, as far as possible, with the help of God, may be totally eradicated and excluded from the house of God.[4]

I know that some of you long for our absolution, but because it is not possible for me to do this individually now, as far as I am able, I desire, pray for and impart God's and our absolution and benediction to you all. Always love the discipline of your order; maintain peace among yourselves and obedience to the Prior unharmed. May the Lord be always with you. Amen.

1104 from Lyon.

NOTES

1. See Wi 3:6.
2. See Jn 15:19.
3. See Ps 68:10.
4. See Ep 311.

313. TO ANTONY, SUBPRIOR OF CANTERBURY.

Anselm praises subprior Antony of Christ Church Canterbury for his zeal in the observance of the Rule but admonishes him to have more confidence in the truth of confessions made to him.

ANSELM THE ARCHBISHOP: TO HIS DEAREST BROTHER AND SON ANTONY,[1] SUBPRIOR, GREETING AND BLESSING.

I REJOICE AND GIVE THANKS TO GOD and to you for the good zeal[2] which you have and because you willingly observe your rule and strive fervently that others observe it as well. I beseech you, as I have often done before, to persevere in this good intention because it is pleasing to God and you will earn a good reward from him.

But there is one thing which I once heard some people complaining about. They say that sometimes, when a confession of certain negligences which can be seen to have been committed without evil intent and can be regarded merely as sins of carelessness is made before you, your love judges them with improper suspicion while listening to them. Looks and such things are like signs in which no certainty of malice can be detected. I admonish you, therefore, as my beloved friend and advise you as my dearest son not to do this except when the case is so clear that it cannot be excused on the grounds of malice. This causes much harm. You can only punish severely a fault which is a violation of the Rule, and you should banish every base suspicion when it cannot be proved. Thus your brothers will love you and will correct themselves without any feeling of shame. Farewell.

1104 from Lyon.

NOTES

1. See *Ep* 182, *HN* 197.
2. See RB 72:2.

314. TO GUNDULF, BISHOP OF ROCHESTER.

Anselm writes to Bishop Gundulf of Rochester that he can promise nothing about his return to England and that he will not do anything which might detract from his episcopal honor. He encourages him to be firm even if no agreement is reached between the King and himself.

ANSELM, BY THE PROVIDENCE OF GOD, ARCHBISHOP: TO HIS REVEREND AND DEAREST FELLOW BISHOP GUNDULF, SENDING HIM GREETING AND WISHING HIM WHAT HE KNOWS BETTER AND IS ABLE TO DO BETTER.

I GIVE YOU THANKS for your great generosity but even more for your goodwill which always wants to do more than it can. I cherish and praise your good desire concerning our return and the advice proceeding from your true love, but I dare not promise anything certain regarding the outcome of this wish and commend myself and everything concerning me to God's providence to which everything is subject. I pray him and I ask all my friends to pray that he may dispose of me in his goodness and never permit my will to entreat anything deviating from his will. You should know, however, that I hope in God, and it is my intention never knowingly to do anything against episcopal honor for the sake of my return to England. For I prefer not to agree with men rather than by agreeing with them to disagree with God.

The advice you sought about what you should do if my lord the King and I do not come to an agreement I gave you briefly in an earlier letter.[1] This only I say at the moment: do not let any threats, any promise or any trick extort any homage, any oath or any pledge of loyalty from your piety. If anyone demands one of these from you let this be your answer: 'I am a Christian, I am a monk, I am a bishop and therefore I want to remain loyal to everyone according to what I owe each one.' Whatever else may be said to you, do not add anything to these words or detract anything from them which might change their meaning. I say the same about myself, and with the help of God I do not want to add anything to it or take anything away from it.

Greet your sons and daughters[2] and ours as you know how, and pray that they may remember us. Farewell.

1104 from Lyon.

NOTES

1. See *Ep* 306.
2. This seems to refer to the nuns of the Benedictine convent at Malling, see *Life of Gundulf*, ed. R. Thomson (Toronto, 1977); translated by the nuns of Malling Abbey (Malling Abbey, 1984) iv.

315. TO POPE PASCHAL.

Anselm commends Archbishop Leger of Bourges to Pope Paschal II. He reports his conversation with William de Warelwast and tells him that the King has not yet answered him. Anselm had not sent on the letters the Pope had given him for the King and the Queen because the Pope had later given another letter for them to William de Warelwast.

TO HIS LORD AND FATHER, PASCHAL, THE SUPREME PONTIFF: ANSELM, SERVANT OF THE CHURCH OF CANTERBURY, SENDING DUE SUBJECTION WITH PRAYERS.

YOUR MAJESTY WILL REMEMBER, I think, how I interceded with you for our beloved brother, the archbishop of Bourges,[1] and how favorably you answered. Now that he is going to present himself to you I presume to pray with all possible fervor that he may rejoice to find Apostolic loving-kindness.

After I had left your presence, William,[2] the ambassador of the King of England, who caught up with me before I reached Lyon,[3] told me on behalf of the King that I should act in such a way that I could live in England just as my predecessor Lanfranc had lived with his father. From this I understood that he did not wish for my return to England unless I should become his liege man, swear fealty to him and consecrate those on whom he would confer investitures of churches. Therefore I told[4] the King that I could not do these things and that you had ordered me not to associate with those who accepted investitures from him; but that if he would allow me to live in England according to my rank and the obedience I owe you I would be prepared to serve God and him and the people entrusted to me according to my office. Furthermore, I asked him to give me a reply about his will in this matter, but this he has not yet done. Since William returned to England I have not been able to obtain anything from the revenues of my bishopric.[5]

With regard to the letters which you ordered me to send on your behalf to the King and to the Queen, William was told in Rome that they had been written at my direction and, as I heard, the same William received others[6] given out by your Holiness which I consider not in agreement with those drawn up by me. I am certain, however, that if they had been drawn up by me they would either not have been seen at all or held in contempt and derision, for the King says, as I hear, that I am his only adversary.

On all these matters I await the advice of your authority, and am prepared, with God's grace, to suffer for truth anything which is not unseemly for a Christian. May God long preserve your paternity unharmed for us. Amen.

1104 while at Lyon.

NOTES

1. Archbishop Leger of Bourges, 1097 - 1120.
2. William de Warelwast, see *Epp* 305, 306, 308.
3. See *HN* 155–157.
4. See *Ep* 308.

5. See *HN* 159.
6. See *Ep* 305; the papal letters of differing contents to King Henry and Queen Matilda are not preserved.

316. TO GUNDULF, BISHOP OF ROCHESTER.

Anselm instructs Bishop Gundulf of Rochester to remind the King of the answer he had promised him after the meeting of the court. If he was repossessed of his estates so that he could make use of his revenues, Anselm would accept a delay of this answer. If the King did not answer him he would consider himself as a bishop unjustly disseised.

ANSELM THE ARCHBISHOP: TO THE
REVEREND BISHOP GUNDULF, GREETING.

I HAVE RECEIVED THE LETTER OF OUR LORD THE KING[1] in which, as you know, he promised me that he would reply to me after the meeting of the court.[2] I instruct your charity therefore, to go to him on our behalf and speak thus: 'My Lord, the Archbishop of Canterbury offers his faithful service to you as his lord and King and has instructed me to recall to your mind that you should answer him as you said you would'. If he wishes to send me his reply under his seal, well and good. If however, he does not wish to answer by a letter of his, inform me by a letter of yours what he answered. If he still wishes to postpone his answer to a later date, I accept the delay and a later date for the reply, provided that in the meantime he leaves me in possession of the archbishopric as I was when I left England, so that you can send me out of our possessions whatever I now ask for and shall in future ask for. If, however, he dispossesses me so that I have no control over what is mine, tell him that I shall accept no delay but shall consider myself as a bishop disseised,[3] without the due process of law by which a bishop is to be dispossessed. If he wants to answer me and yet does not allow me to have lawful possession of the see, do not refuse to reply, do not keep silent but tell him what I just said: that I shall consider myself as a bishop disseised without lawful judgement.[4] Greet the Queen kindly as my dearest lady and daughter.

Spring 1104 while at Lyon.

NOTES

1. This letter from King Henry to Anselm is not preserved.
2. Possibly the Easter court, 9 April 1104, at Winchester.
3. 'Disseise' is a legal term meaning to put someone out of possession, usually wrongfully or by force; see Anselm's demand *Epp* 319, 321; B. Golding, 'Tribulationes Ecclesiae Christi: The Disruption caused at Canterbury by Royal Confiscations in the time of Anselm', *Spicilegium Beccense* II (Paris, 1984) 283–298.
4. For Henry's reply to Gundulf's intervention on Anselm's behalf, see *Ep* 318.

317. FROM MATILDA, QUEEN OF THE ENGLISH.

Queen Matilda of the English beseeches Anselm to return to England.

TO HER TRULY EMINENT LORD AND FATHER ANSELM, BY THE GRACE OF GOD ARCHBISHOP OF CANTERBURY: MATILDA, QUEEN OF THE ENGLISH, HIS HUMBLE HANDMAID, WITH THE ASSURANCE OF DEEP DEVOTION AND SERVICE.

TURN, HOLY LORD AND MERCIFUL FATHER, *my mourning into joy* and *gird me with happiness.*[1] See, lord, your humble handmaid throws herself on her knees before your mercy and, stretching suppliant hands towards you, begs you for the fervor of your accustomed kindness. Come, lord, come and visit your servant. Come, I beg, father, appease my groans, dry my tears, lessen my pains, put an end to my sorrow. Fulfill my desires, grant my request.

But you will say: 'I am prohibited by law and bound by the restraints of certain obligations and dare not transgress the decrees of the Fathers.'[2] How is it father, that *the teacher of the gentiles*,[3] *the chosen vessel*,[4] put all his efforts into the annulling of the laws? Did he not offer sacrifice in the temple[5] for fear of scandalizing those of the circumcision who still believed [in the Jewish laws]? Did not he who condemned circumcision circumcise Timothy[6] so that he became *all things to all men*?[7] What indeed should a child of mercy do, a disciple of him who gave himself up to death in order to redeem slaves? You see, yes, you see your brothers, your fellow-servants, the people of your Lord, now undergoing shipwreck, now slipping into the deep,[8] and you do not come to their aid, you do not extend your right hand to them, you do not expose yourself to danger! Did not the Apostle choose *to be accursed by Christ for the sake of his brothers*?[9]

My good lord, tender father, bend this severity a little and soften—let me say it with your leave—your heart of iron. Come and visit your people,[10] and among them your handmaid who yearns for you from the depths of her heart. Find a way by which neither you, the shepherd who leads the way, may give offence, nor the rights of royal majesty be diminished.[11] If these cannot be reconciled, at least let the father come to his daughter, the lord to his handmaid, and let him teach her what she should do. Let him come to her before she departs from this world. Indeed if I should die before being able to see you again—I speak shamelessly—I fear that even *in the land of the living*[12] and every joyful occasion of exulting would be cut off. You are *my joy*,[13] *my hope*,[14] *my refuge*.[15] *My soul [thirsts] for you like a land without water*.[16] Therefore I even *stretch out my hands to you*,[17] so that you may drench its dryness with the oil of gladness[18] and water it with the dew of your natural sweetness. If neither my weeping nor the wish of the people can move you, putting aside my royal dignity, giving up my insignia, putting off my honors, spurning my crown, I will trample the purple and the linen and will come to you, *overcome with grief.*[19] I will embrace your knees and kiss your feet, and even if Giezi came[20] he would not move me until the greatest of my desires had been achieved.

May the peace of God which surpasses all understanding guard your heart and your mind[21] and cause you to abound with tender mercy.[22]

1104.

NOTES

1. See Ps 29:12.
2. Matilda is referring to the papal decrees prohibiting lay investiture and homage of clerics to laymen, HN 144.
3. 1 Tm 2:7.
4. Ac 9:15.
5. See Ac 21:26.
6. See Ac 16:3.
7. 1 Co 9:22.
8. See *Ep* 310 and *HN* 159–160.
9. Rm 9:3.
10. See Lk 1:68, 7:16.
11. The royal *usus atque leges*, see HN 10.
12. Ps 26:13; 141:6.
13. Ph 4:1.
14. Ps 141:6.
15. Ps 30:4.
16. Ps 142:6.
17. Ps 87:10.
18. Ps 44:8.
19. Lam 1:13.
20. See 4(2) K 4:27.
21. Ph 4:7.
22. See Lk 1:78.

318. FROM HENRY, KING OF THE ENGLISH.

King Henry of the English is grieved that Anselm cannot live in agreement with him as his predecessor had lived with his father. He informs Anselm that he will send legates to Rome and on their return he will let him know his decision. Meanwhile he grants Anselm the use of his benefice.

HENRY, KING OF THE ENGLISH: TO ANSELM, ARCHBISHOP OF CANTERBURY, GREETING AND FRIENDSHIP.

YOU INFORMED ME that you were not able to come to me and live with me as Lanfranc, your predecessor, lived with my father for many years.[1] I suffer greatly because you are unwilling to do this. If you had been willing to do this I would gladly have received you and shown you all those honors and privileges and friendship which my father showed to your predecessor.

Indeed, in his letter the Apostolic lord sent me his requests and admonitions about the matters in question.[2] Wherefore, I intend to send my ambassadors to Rome[3] and, according to the counsel of God and my barons, reply there to the lord Pope and seek what I have to seek. When I have received the Pope's reply, I shall inform you what God has conceded to me. In the meantime I agree that you may have what is fitting of the benefice of the church of Canterbury[4] although I do this unwillingly because, if it did not rest with you, there is no mortal man whom I would rather have in my kingdom with me than you. Witnessed by Robert,[5] bishop of Lincoln, and William.[6]

Spring 1104.

NOTES

1. See *Ep* 308.
2. See *Ep* 305.
3. See *HN* 162; they did not achieve any success in the matter.
4. See *Ep* 316.

5. Robert Bloet, Bishop of Lincoln, see *Ep* 311.
6. William de Warelwast.

319. TO HENRY, KING OF THE ENGLISH.

Anselm replies to King Henry of the English that at his baptism and on receiving holy orders he promised to obey the law of God alone and not the customs of the King's father and Lanfranc. If the King can accept this and restores his possessions, he is prepared to return to England.

TO HENRY, BY THE GRACE OF GOD KING OF THE ENGLISH AND HIS LORD: ANSELM, ARCHBISHOP OF CANTERBURY, SENDING FAITHFUL SERVICE AND PRAYERS.

IN THE LETTER OF YOUR HIGHNESS[1] which I recently received your Honor assured me of your friendship and that there was no mortal man whom you would more gladly have in your kingdom than me if I were willing to live with you as Archbishop Lanfranc lived with your father.

I give thanks for your friendship and your goodwill. With regard to what you say about your father and Archbishop Lanfranc I reply that neither at my baptism nor at any of my ordinations did I promise to observe the law or custom of your father or of Archbishop Lanfranc but rather the law of God and of all the orders which I received. Wherefore, if you wish me to be with you in such a way that I may be able to live according to the law of God and my rank, and if you reinvest me according to that same law of God with everything which you have received from my archbishopric since I left you, and which, had I been present, you would not have received without my consent: if you promise me this I am prepared to come back to you in England and, with God's help, to serve God and you and all those entrusted to me according to the office laid upon me by God. Indeed, there is no other mortal king or prince with whom I would rather live or whom I would rather serve. However, if you absolutely refuse to accept this, then you will be doing what pleases you; I indeed, by the grace of God, shall never deny his law.

I dare not—because I ought not—omit to tell you that God will not merely demand of you whatever royal power owes him but also whatever pertains to the office of the Primate of England.[2] This burden is too much for you. Nor ought you to be displeased at what I say. No man subjects himself to God's law with greater advantage than the King, and no man disregards his law at greater risk. For it is not I but Holy Scripture that says: *The mighty will suffer mightier torments*[3] and: *The stronger pains threaten the more powerful;*[4] may God avert this from you!

In the reply which you have already given me twice[5] I perceive nothing except—if I dare to say so—a certain postponement which is not good either for your soul or for the Church of God. Therefore, if in answer to this you continue putting off a clear statement of your intention I am afraid that, since the cause is not mine but entrusted to me by God himself, I will no longer be able to delay making my appeal to God.[6] For this reason I beseech and entreat you not to force me to cry with sorrow, against my will: *Arise, O God, decide your own cause.*[7]

May almighty God speedily turn your heart towards his will so that after this life he may lead you into his glory.

Spring 1104 at Lyon.

NOTES

1. See *Ep* 318.
2. See *HN* 159, *VA* 132 and *Ep* 310.
3. Wi 6:7.
4. Wi 6:9.
5. These letters are not preserved; they are mentioned in *Ep* 316 and *HN* 159.

6. See *Ep* 316.
7. Ps 73:22.

320. FROM MATILDA, QUEEN OF THE ENGLISH.

Queen Matilda of the English tells Anselm what joy his letter had given her. With regard to his nephew Anselm, she considers him to be her relative by adoption. She assures Anselm that her husband is kindly disposed towards him and will in future grant him the revenues he asked for.

TO HER PIOUSLY ESTEEMED FATHER AND DEVOUTLY REVERED LORD, ARCHBISHOP ANSELM: MATILDA, BY THE GRACE OF GOD QUEEN OF THE ENGLISH, LOWLIEST HANDMAID OF HIS HOLINESS, SENDING PERPETUAL GREETING IN CHRIST.

I RENDER COUNTLESS THANKS to your unceasing goodness which has not forgotten me but has deigned to show the presence of your present absence through a letter of yours.[1] Indeed, after the clouds of sadness in which I was wrapped were driven away, the stream of your words broke through to me like a ray of new light. I embrace the parchment sent by you in place of a father, I press it to my breast, I move it as near to my heart as I can, I reread with my mouth the words flowing from the sweet fountain of your goodness, I go over them in my mind, I ponder them again in my heart and when I have pondered over them I place them in the sanctuary of my heart.

Where everything is worthy of praise I only wonder at what the excellency of your judgement has added about your nephew.[2] For myself I do not consider that I make any distinction between what is yours and what is mine; that means of course between what is mine and what is mine. Indeed what is yours by kinship is mine by adoption and love.

Truly, the consolation of your writing strengthens my patience, gives me hope and maintains it, lifts me up as I fall, sustains me when I am slipping, gives me joy when I grieve, mitigates my anger and calms my weeping.[3] Frequently and secretly it wisely assures me of the return of the father to his daughter, the lord to his handmaid, the shepherd to his sheep. In the same way however, the confidence which I have in the prayers of good men and the benevolence which, after careful investigation, I consider comes from the heart of my lord,[4] gives me assurance. For he is more kindly disposed towards you than most people might think. With God's help and my suggestions, as far as I am able, he may become more welcoming and compromising towards you. What he now permits to be done concerning your revenues,[5] he will permit to be done better and more abundantly in future when you ask for it in the right way and at the right time. Although he considers himself more than a fair judge, nevertheless I beg the abundance of your loving-kindness that, having excluded the rancor of human bitterness which is not usually found in you, you may not turn away the sweetness of your love from him. May you rather show yourself before God as a devoted intercessor for him and for me, as well as for our child[6] and the state of our kingdom. May your holiness always prosper.

1104.

NOTES

1. This letter is not preserved.
2. See *Ep* 309.
3. Matilda's letter is remarkable for its style which in some of the repetitions and puns seems to be imitating Anselm's own style. Who was writing these letters? See also *Epp* 242, 317, 323, 395, 400.
4. Her husband King Henry I; Matilda refers to Henry and Anselm by the same word, *Dominus*, Lord.
5. See *Ep* 318.
6. William, their first-born son, see *Ep* 305.

321. TO MATILDA, QUEEN OF THE ENGLISH.

Anselm thanks Queen Matilda of the English for the love she showed him and his kin in her letter. He praises her for trying to soften her husband's heart and is grateful for what has been promised him about his revenues, but states that they are totally his by right. He assures her that he bears no rancor towards the King and will pray for her and her children.

TO HIS REVEREND LADY, HIS DEAREST DAUGHTER MATILDA, BY THE GRACE OF GOD QUEEN OF THE ENGLISH: ANSELM, ARCHBISHOP OF CANTERBURY, SENDING HIS FAITHFUL SERVICE, HIS PRAYERS AND THE BLESSING OF GOD AND HIS OWN, IF IT IS WORTH ANYTHING.

I GIVE BOUNDLESS THANKS to your Highness by loving and praying for you for the magnitude of your holy love towards my humble self which I perceived in your letter.[1] In it you clearly displayed with what affection you love me when you received and treated my parchment in the way you describe. Your dignity raised my spirits so much by declaring that what nature denies me your grace bestows, that those who are mine by kinship are yours by adoption and love.[2]

By trying to soften the heart of my lord the King towards me because of your desire for my return I perceive that you are doing what is fitting for you and advantageous for him. For if he has any bitterness of heart towards me I am not aware of ever having deserved it in any way at all, as far as I can see. If at any time I served him he knows it, and I think he will not consign it to oblivion. If in some respects he dislikes me without cause it would be advantageous for him to drive this rancor away from him lest he sin before God.

You promise me that the King will in future grant me better and more abundant access to our revenues, of which at present he allows me a small amount.[3] I should not be ungrateful to your benevolence because you are doing this, as far as you are able through your goodwill. But it should not be necessary to make me such a promise because no confiscation or decrease of them should take place against my will. Whoever advised him to appropriate any of these revenues advised him to commit a sin which is no slight one, nor one that should ever be tolerated. For whoever despoils a bishop of his goods can in no way be reconciled to God unless he restores to him all his goods intact. You should know that however small a part of these goods I am deprived of, it is as if I were deprived of everything. I do not say this for love of money but for the love of God's justice.

Your kindness prays me not to take my love away from my lord the King but to intercede for him, for yourself, for your offspring and for your realm. I have always done this up to now. But as to the future I commit myself to the providence of God, with whom *the son does not bear the iniquity of the father*[4] nor the wife that of her husband. I hope in God that I may not harbor any rancor against anybody in my heart which could separate me from God. May almighty God guard you and your offspring[5] forever in his grace.

1104.

NOTES

1. See *Ep* 320.
2. Anselm repeats Matilda's words, see *Ep* 320.
3. See *Epp* 319, 320, also *HN* 159 and *VA* 132.
4. Ezk 18:20.
5. See *Epp* 305, 319, 320, 424.

322. TO WILLIAM, BISHOP-ELECT OF WINCHESTER.

Anselm writes to William, bishop-elect of Winchester, on behalf of himself and Archbishop Hugh of Lyon that he should not hand over a castle belonging to Duke Robert to King Henry lest he appear to be buying the King's favor and his bishopric.

ANSELM, ARCHBISHOP OF CANTERBURY: TO WILLIAM, HIS BELOVED FRIEND, BISHOP-ELECT OF WINCHESTER, SENDING HIM THE GREETING AND THE BLESSING OF GOD AND HIS OWN, FOR WHAT IT IS WORTH, AND WISHING THAT HE MAY ALWAYS BE RULED BY DIVINE COUNSEL AND PROTECTED BY DIVINE HELP.

YOUR MESSENGER WHO WAS SENT TO US for this purpose presented your case to our reverend lord and father Hugh, Archbishop of Lyon, and to me at the same time, as you ordered,[1] and I have shown the letter you sent to me to this father of ours. At his command I am replying in this letter on his behalf as well as on mine.

We rejoice and give thanks to God for your constancy in truth and that you only seek counsel that is pleasing to God and fitting to your honor and to the rank to which you have been elected.[2] We discussed the whole case as your messenger explained it to us as diligently as we could, enlisting other prudent and religious men, and invoking God to guide us, we considered with a single mind the advice which you sought. The essence of the case on which you sought advice, as far as we understand it, is this: whether you can rightly give the castle you hold from Duke Robert to his brother, King Henry, against the will of the Duke, because of the injustices which the Duke has committed against you as you reported.[3]

We consider before God and before all just men that you cannot rightly do this. For even if the Duke freed you from what you owe him by your oath of allegiance and through the faith you have promised him or through any common custom, he could not free you from what you owe to God and your neighbor for the sake of God and on account of the Christian religion. For this reason we consider that you should not disinherit the aforesaid Duke of what you hold from him and hand his inheritance over to his enemy.

In this matter it is very important that your love take care not to receive episcopal consecration yet; if you should do what the King is demanding of you no one would ever be able to blot out the execrable rumor that this was done in order to buy the bishopric which you feared to lose. Therefore, since we must take care for *what is good not only before God but also before men,*[4] may God avert this from you and may he never permit such an evil example to be spread about you through any gossip. With regard to the fact that you received the aforesaid castle from the King, as if you were his man:[5] if you swore him this oath of allegiance merely to obtain the office, we think that you are in no way bound to it, so that you may allow him the use of this castle against the Duke. Moreover, just as no man should promise anything against the will of God, so he should not perform what he has so promised under any circumstances, nor can anyone rightly demand this of him.[6]

We are ordering other matters to be reported to you by word of mouth through your messenger. Our aforesaid lord and father, [Archbishop Hugh,] greets you as friend to friend. Farewell.

1104–1105 while at Lyon.

NOTES

1. This letter is not preserved.
2. Compare Anselm's praise with Eadmer's description of William's motivation for withdrawing from his consecration at Christmas 1102, HN 145–146.
3. He seems to have held a strategic position around Dieppe, see G.H. Williams, *The Norman Anonymous of 1100* (Harvard, 1951) 91.

4. Rm 12:17 Vulg.
5. The castle was held by the Giffard family from the Duke. William wanted to turn it over to the King and receive it back and hold it as the King's man, not the Duke's man, see G.H. Williams, *The Norman Anonymous of 1100* (Harvard, 1951) 91, note 296.
6. William, bishop-elect of Winchester, took Anselm's advice to heart as *Ep* 344 shows.

323. MATILDA, QUEEN OF THE ENGLISH, TO POPE PASCHAL.

Matilda, Queen of the English, thanks Pope Paschal II for the instructions given to her and the King through messengers and letters. She demonstrates how desperately the English people need Anselm and asks him to bring about a just settlement so that Anselm may soon be able to return.

TO THE SUPREME PONTIFF AND UNIVERSAL POPE, PASCHAL: MATILDA, BY THE GRACE OF GOD QUEEN OF THE ENGLISH, WISHING HIM SO TO DISPENSE THE RIGHTS OF APOSTOLIC DIGNITY IN TEMPORAL MATTERS THAT WITH THE VESTMENT OF JUSTICE HE MAY MERIT TO BE ETERNALLY COUNTED TO THE APOSTOLIC GATHERING IN THE JOYS OF PERPETUAL PEACE.

I GIVE THANKS AND PRAISE AS FAR AS I CAN to your sublime holiness, O Apostolic man, for those things which your paternal charity has frequently deigned to convey with such devout admonition to my lord the King and myself by word of mouth through your legates and your own letters. I approach the threshold of the most holy Roman Apostolic See and embrace the feet of my holy father, the Apostolic Pope, as far as it is allowed and I am able, with my whole heart and my whole soul and my whole mind.[1] Having cast myself at your paternal knees I request and beg with unseasonable and seasonable[2] petitions, without ceasing or desisting, until I feel that either my modest humility or rather the persevering importunity of my knocking has been heard by you.[3]

May your excellency, however, not be enraged at this audacity of mine by which I presume to speak in this manner, nor the prudence of the clerics and people of the Roman senate be amazed. There was, I say, there was under your Apostolic dignity, a disciple of the Holy Spirit, Archbishop Anselm, with us and the English people, happy as we then were. He was our wisest counselor and the most loving father of the aforesaid people. What he received abundantly from the exceedingly rich treasury of his Lord, whose key-bearer we recognized him to be, this he bestowed more abundantly on us, particularly when the Lord's *faithful minister*[4] *and prudent steward*[5] flavored what he was bestowing with the strong brine of wisdom, softened it with the sweetness of eloquence and adorned it with the wonderful charm of his speech. So it came about that a great abundance of milk was available for the Lord's tender lambs, a most rich richness of pasture for the sheep, and an exceeding fullness of nourishment for the shepherds.[6]

Since all these things have ceased, there is nothing left except the shepherd seeking nourishment, the flock seeking pasture, the young seeking the breast, crying out loud with many groans. During the absence of a great shepherd, particularly Anselm, something is withheld from each of the aforesaid individuals, or rather everything is withheld from everybody. In the sorrow of such mourning, in the scandal of such grief, in the mockery of such a loss, for such a deformation of our kingdom, there remains nothing for me to do in my bewilderment than to flee bearing my dismay, to the holy Apostle Peter and his vicar, the Apostolic man. And so I flee to your kindness, o lord, and ask that we and the people of the kingdom of the English should not slip into such failure and decline. For *what profit is there in our blood* when we descend *into corruption*?[7]

May your paternity therefore advise favorably in what concerns us and, within a set time, about what my lord the King asks your goodness,[8] so deign to open your paternal heart to us that we may rejoice about the return of our dearest father, Archbishop Anselm, and may keep unblemished the subjection which we owe to the holy Apostolic See.

I, however, instructed by your most salutary and beloved admonitions, as far as it is possible for the strength of a woman, and having asked for the help of competent men, will strive with my whole strength that my humility may fulfill, as far as it can, what your sublimity has advised. May your paternity prosper happily.

1104.

NOTES

1. See Mt 22:37.
2. See 2 Tm 4:2.
3. See Lk 11:8.
4. Eph 6:21.
5. Lk 12:42.
6. For Anselm's way of speaking, see *Epp* 30, 207, 285.
7. Ps 29:10.
8. King Henry sent messengers to Rome in the spring of 1104, see *HN* 162.

324. TO BALDWIN, KING OF JERUSALEM.

Anselm tells King Baldwin of Jerusalem what an honor it is to be king of that city and encourages him to reign in such a way as to be a shining example for the other kings of the world.

TO HIS DEAREST LORD BALDWIN, BY THE GRACE OF GOD KING OF JERUSALEM: ANSELM, THOUGH UNWORTHY, ARCHBISHOP OF CANTERBURY, WISHING THAT HE MAY SO REIGN OVER THE EARTHLY JERUSALEM IN THIS LIFE THAT HE MAY REIGN IN THE HEAVENLY JERUSALEM IN THE LIFE TO COME.[1]

ALTHOUGH BY THE GIFT OF GOD you have the knowledge which, with God's help, should be enough to enable you to live a good life, and although I know that your intention is good, yet the abundance of love which I feel for you induces me to write something to your Highness from such a distance. For just as a burning fire is fanned into greater flame by the wind, so goodwill is aroused by friendly admonition to burn more fervently.

You know, my dearest lord, that God chose out of the whole world the city of Jerusalem as his very own special place both before the coming of the Lord and at his coming. From it came the first kings whom God loved, from it came the prophets, in it was God's own house and his sanctuary; there our redemption took place, there the *King of kings*[2] lived, and from there the salvation of the human race was spread throughout the world. May your Highness consider therefore, how eminent is God's grace that wishes you to be king in this city, and with what desire and zeal the king whom God has placed there should devote himself to the will and service of God. I beseech, therefore, I entreat and admonish you as my lord and friend that you strive to govern yourself and all those subject to you according to the law and will of God so that you may set a bright example by your life to all the kings of the earth.[3]

May our Lord Jesus Christ so reign in your heart and in your deeds that you, with your predecessor King David, may reign for ever in heaven. Amen.

Know that I pray for you daily, no matter how poor my prayers may be.

1104 or 1105.

NOTES

1. For Baldwin, see *Ep* 235. Anselm's reason for sending this letter is uncertain—it could have been Baldwin's conflict with the Patriarch Daimbert, hostile gossip about Baldwin through his rival Bohemond of Antioch, Baldwin's treatment of his second wife or just the chance of a messenger travelling to Jerusalem. Thus it is difficult to date it: J. F. A. Mason, 'St Anselm's Relations with Laymen', *Spicilegium Beccense* 1 (Paris, 1959) 558–559, suggests 1102–1108.

2. 1 Tm 6:15.
3. For Anselm's concept of kingship, see *Epp* 248, 249 and W. Fröhlich, 'Anselm's Weltbild as conveyed in his letters', Anselm Studies 2 (1988) 483–525; W. Fröhlich, 'Anselm's von Canterbury *imago regis* dargestellt aus seinen Briefen', Universität und Bildung, FS for L. Boehm (Munich, 1991) 13–24; W. Fröhlich, 'Anselm's concept of kingship', *Spicilegium Beccense* 3 (Paris, 1992). Perhaps Anselm is here thinking of King Henry, whom he considers to be opposing the law of God and of the Church. This would point to the early period of Anselm's second exile, hence 1104 or 1105. This date is further supported by the position of this letter in MS L.

325. TO MATILDA, COUNTESS OF TUSCANY.

Anselm thanks Countess Matilda of Tuscany for having protected him from his enemies by the safe conduct she had provided. Since worldly duties for the Church prevent her from becoming a nun, Anselm advises her to carry a veil with her secretly so that she can put it on if she should be in danger of death. He sends her his Prayers and Meditations.

ANSELM, SERVANT OF THE CHURCH OF CANTERBURY: TO HIS LADY AND MOTHER IN GOD, THE TRULY BELOVED AND REVEREND COUNTESS MATILDA,[1] WISHING HER TO REJOICE IN CONTINUED AND LONG-LASTING PROSPERITY IN THIS LIFE AND ETERNAL FELICITY IN THE LIFE TO COME.

I WISH TO GIVE THANKS TO YOUR HIGHNESS but I cannot find words to write worthy of your merit. I realize that it was a great blessing that through you God delivered me not once but many times from the power of my enemies[2] just when they expected me to fall into their hands. But when I consider with what kind, loving and maternal affection this was carried out I realize that it is much more than I can express.

I cannot forget with what anxious prayer and entreaty you instructed me through our brother and son Alexander[3] not to expose my body to any danger at all, and with what zeal you instructed your people to receive me with not less care, indeed if possible with even more, than your own person, telling them not to lead me by the shorter but by the safer route to a place of safety.[4] They faithfully carried this out according to what they perceived to be your will. There is no lack of feeling in my heart to give you thanks, but mouth and pen are not capable of expressing what my heart feels. What therefore I cannot do, I pray God that he may reward you, protect you from all the enemies of body and soul and lead you to a blessed and eternal place of safety.

I always preserve in my heart the memory of your holy desire through which your heart yearns to hold the world in contempt; but the holy and unwavering love which you have for mother Church lovingly holds you back. From this it is evident that your reverence is pleasing to God in every way and therefore, while calmly awaiting a definite sign from God, you should patiently bear the burden which you are carrying in tribulation with good hope. Nevertheless I presume to give you a word of advice: if you see yourself threatened by certain danger of death—which God avert!—give yourself totally to God before you leave this life, and for this purpose you should always have secretly in your possession a veil which you have prepared. Whatever I may say, I pray and desire for you that God may entrust you to nothing save his providence and advice.

Your Highness has informed me through our aforesaid son Alexander that you do not have the *Prayers and Meditations*[5] which I myself wrote and which I thought you had, so I am sending them to you.[6] May almighty God rule and protect you always with his blessing.

1104.

NOTES

1. Matilda, born about 1046, in San Miniato, near Florence, was daughter of Count Boniface III of Tuscany. After his death in 1052 her

mother married Geoffrey, Duke of Lorraine, in 1054 and thus she was related via Countess Ida, *Ep* 82, to Count Eustace II of Boulogne and their sons, among whom was Baldwin, King of Jerusalem, *Epp* 235, 324. She was also related through her stepfather to his brother, Frederic of Lorraine, Abbot (Desiderius) of Monte Cassino, later Pope Stephen IX from 1057–1058, see H.E.J. Cowdrey, 'The Age of Abbot Desiderius' (Oxford, 1983). Drawn in such a way into the papal reforming party she became one of the most persistent opponents of the German Kings and Roman Emperors, Henry IV and Henry V. In 1069 she married her stepfather's son, from whom she separated in 1071. From then on, as his only heir, she ruled her imperial fiefs and property in Tuscany, Emilia and Lombardy. She revered Pope Gregory VII and supported his plans for the reform of the Church. On 28 January 1077, Gregory VII received Emperor Henry IV, who had crossed the Alps to beg to be freed from excommunication, in her castle at Canossa. Having acted as a mediator with Abbot Hugh of Cluny, *Ep* 259, Matilda became a fervent supporter of the liberty of the Church. In 1079 she bequeathed her property to the Church, which led to open conflict with Henry IV, who banished her and confiscated her fiefs in 1082. She was successful, however, in fighting off an imperial army; by supporting Henry IV's son, Conrad, against his father, she tried to weaken her opponent even more. In 1089, aged 43, she married the seventeen year old Welf V, Duke of Bavaria, an opponent of the Emperor; she left her second husband in 1095. Having been relieved of the imperial ban and appointed imperial representative in northern Italy, she renewed the donation of her property in 1102; in 1111 she reached an agreement with Henry V, who was to be her heir. The ensuing quarrel concerning Matilda's property lasted over a century and was decided in the reign of Emperor Frederick II in favor of the Church. Matilda died on 24 July 1115, in Bondeno, near Ferrara, and was buried in the Abbey of St Benedetto di Polirone. Pope Urban VIII had her remains translated to St Peter's in Rome in 1634; see P. Maccarini, 'Anselme de Canterbury et Mathilde de Canossa dans le cadre de l'influence bénédictine au tournant des XIe-XIIe siècles', *Spicilegium Beccense 2*, (Paris, 1984) 331–340.

2. For the danger of a journey to Rome, see *VA* 103, 104; *HN* 89–90, 91, 93, 94, 95, 133, 151–152.
3. Alexander, a monk of Canterbury, was a member of Anselm's household. For his growing importance, see Southern, *Anselm*, 199–200.
4. In late summer or autumn 1103 Anselm passed through Countess Matilda's territory on his way to and from Rome, *Ep* 301; *VA* 128–130, and Itinerary, vol. 1:341.

5. *Anselmi Orationes sive Meditationes* AOO III:3–91; ET by Benedicta Ward (Penguin Classics, 1973); T. Bestul, 'The Collection of Private Prayers in the "Portiforium" of Wulfstan of Worcester and the "Orationes sive Meditationes" of St Anselm, *Spicilegium Beccense* 2, (Paris, 1984) 355–364.
6. There is a picture of Anselm handing Countess Matilda a copy of his *Prayers and Meditations* in Codex 289 in the library of the Benedictine monastery at Admont, Austria. For a reproduction of the illumination see *Spicilegium Beccense* 2, (Paris, 1984) facing p. 331, and the cover of these translated letters.

326. FROM GERARD, ARCHBISHOP OF YORK.

Archbishop Gerard of York tells Anselm that evil people are trying to come between them. He confesses that in the past he had been rather slack in the cause of God and in supporting Anselm and promises to assist him in future. He asks him to reply without mentioning their names.

TO HIS BELOVED FATHER: THE SON
OFFERING SERVICE AND OBEDIENCE.[1]

A MIND THAT IS A FRIEND OF TRUTH must take care not to yield easily to the opinion of those whom either hatred, or love, or a certain vain and idle inclination towards untruth impels to lie. They are people whose inactivity, since it does not lead to anything honorable, kindles in them the fire of envy against those who live honorably. I know that people of that kind are trying to make the sweetness of your soul bitter for me.[2] Added to this is the fact that our efforts have sometimes been weaker than would have been fitting for God's cause and yours.[3]

But far be it from me, far be it from the love which binds me to you, that in future you should not have me as an assistant of the word of God for which you worked until your exile.[4] If you know how to show me the warmth of your love, which I often experienced in you on many important occasions, then you will have in me both a faithful servant and fellow servant in Christ and a fellow worker in his word. However, it made me more negligent than was proper in this cause because I heard that you were more negligent than was fitting in compassion towards me in my tribulation.[5] The great love I bear towards you is apparent everywhere among my friends and yours, and frequently in the hearing of the King and the nobles of the kingdom.

Do not hesitate to write to me,[6] refraining from mentioning our names,[7] what your attitude is towards me.

1104.

NOTES

1. The names Anselm and Gerard are inserted in MS 1 fol. 117v, 1.19.
2. See *Epp* 250, 253, 283 and *HN* 137–138.
3. He had previously supported the Kings in the various stages of the conflict between Anselm and William II and Henry I. This policy culminated in his obeying King Henry by agreeing to consecrate the bishops-elect William Giffard of Winchester and Roger of Salisbury at Christmas 1102 in London, against the will of Anselm, see *Epp* 200, 261, 273, 280, 283, 308, and *HN* 145–146.
4. Anselm left England for Rome on 27 April 1103, *HN* 149. His 2nd exile began shortly before Christmas outside Lyon when William de Warelwast informed him of the King's will; see *Ep* 306; also *HN* 157, *VA* 130.
5. Gerard became involved in the quarrel about the primacy of Canterbury when he was requested to make a profession of obedience to the Archbishop of Canterbury on being translated from Hereford to York on 6 January 1101, see *Epp* 283, 354; *HN* 186–187; *HC* 33. In 1102 he was one of the royal messengers who asked Pope Paschal to remove or mitigate the papal decrees on investiture and homage. The differing reports of the royal messengers and Anselm's messengers caused a great scandal, *HN* 137–139; *Ep* 250. When informed about this the Pope excommunicated Gerard, see *Epp* 281, 283.
6. This is letter 262 in MS L, which suggests that it was written in 1104.
7. See *Ep* 363; *Ep* 362 proves that it was written by Gerard.

327. TO ORDWY, A MONK OF CANTERBURY.

Anselm, writing to Ordwy, a monk of Christ Church Canterbury, denies the false statements people are spreading about him regarding investitures.

ANSELM, ARCHBISHOP OF CANTERBURY: TO HIS DEAREST BROTHER AND SON ORDWY,[1] GREETING AND THE BLESSING OF GOD.

I GIVE THANKS TO YOUR LOVE for being anxious about my reputation and for asking how you should reply to the false accusers who seek occasion to attack me. They say, as you write me, that I forbid the King to grant investitures and, what is worse, that I permit evil and wicked clerics to usurp and ravage churches, and that I do not rise up against them. They also say that I give churches to laymen.

Tell them that they lie. For I do not forbid the King to grant investitures of churches by my own authority, but since in a great Council I heard the Pope excommunicate laymen who give and those who accept such investitures as well as those who consecrate those who receive them, I do not want to associate with those who are excommunicated, nor be excommunicated myself.[2] Indeed I do not tolerate willingly, but sorrowfully clerics who oppress the churches, and I rise up against this to such an extent that I am in exile and despoiled of my episcopal possessions for that reason.[3] The objections they raise concerning the clerics would not occur if the investitures which I rise up against did not take place. I do not give churches to laymen when I give them my manors to farm, but I grant them so that they may care for them, not that they may appoint or remove a cleric except by my order or that of our archdeacon[4] or by the prior in the manors of our church. They accuse me most wickedly of minding other people's business and of neglecting my own,[5] but they do not say this for love of the truth but in order to silence my voice which speaks for truth. Farewell.

c. 1104 while at Lyon.

NOTES

1. Ordwy or Ordion was a monk of Canterbury who became prior of St Andrew's Cathedral Priory, Rochester, about 1108, where he died in 1125; see *Heads*, 64; also *Epp* 336, 355.
2. Lenten synod, Rome 1099, *HN* 144.
3. See *Epp* 280, 310, 311; also *HN* 141, 142, 144–146.
4. William the Archdeacon, see *Epp* 208, 257.
5. A frequent charge raised at that time, see *Epp* 310, 330, 336, 355, 365, 366. It is refuted by Eadmer in *HN* 160; *VA* 130.

328. TO ANSELM, HIS NEPHEW.

Anselm informs his nephew that he had tried to have Richeza, his sister and young Anselm's mother, admitted to the convent of Marcigny. The Abbot of Chiusa had opposed this intention. He urges him to progress in his studies and in his virtues, and asks him to greet his teacher, Dom Walter.

ANSELM THE ARCHBISHOP: TO HIS BELOVED NEPHEW ANSELM,[1] GREETING AND BLESSING.

THE ANXIETY AND SORROW WHICH YOU FEEL for your mother[2] I also bear. For this reason I have begged the lord Abbot of Cluny to receive her into the monastery of the handmaid of the Lord at Marcigny.[3] He gladly granted this with his grace and for love of us, and the handmaids of God also wished this greatly. Therefore, by a letter and by our messenger I begged the abbot of Chiusa[4] and his monks, as humbly and as earnestly as I could, to concede this to our sister because of me, but they did not want to give their consent at all. Rather they were very angry at me and thought that I had done them a great dishonor. But I shall not yet give up trying to achieve, by whatever means

I can, what I have begun. If I am not able to do so we must not, you and I, be overcome with inconsolable sadness but patiently commit ourselves and her to the providence of God. I trust in God that he will not allow her to be tempted by any troubles beyond what she is able to bear but that he will lead her through the many tribulations which she has suffered since her infancy and which, if God so disposes, she will bear unto the end, and make her enter into his rest. As to myself, as far as I am able, I shall not cease to help her in every way as long as I live.

Now with regard to yourself, I instruct and order you not to be idle on any account but to strive to progress daily in that purpose for which I left you in England. Strive to understand the value of correct grammar and accustom yourself to writing daily, chiefly in prose. Do not be fond of writing in a difficult style but in a plain and clear one. Always speak in Latin except when you are obliged to do otherwise.[5] Above all, aim at a good character and sober habits. Avoid chatter.[6] For a man gains more by being silent and listening, and from considering how he can profit by other people's example and words, than by displaying his own knowledge by verbosity without being forced to do so.

Greet your teacher[7] in a friendly way from me; I would really like to be of some use to him if God gives me the opportunity, both for your sake and that of the other brothers he teaches, and on account of his excellent character. In the meantime, however, I have put this before Dom Prior[8] and asked him earnestly to treat him so kindly that he will not regret having attached himself to us. Farewell.

c. 1104–1105 while at Lyon.

NOTES

1. See *Epp* 211, 264, 268, 289, 290, 291, 292, 309, 320.
2. Anselm's only sister, Richeza. Her husband, Burgundius, seems to have died, see *Epp* 211, 258, 264, 268.

3. Marcigny was a Cluniac foundation for nuns about seventy-five kilometers west of Cluny, see *VA* 123 and N. Hunt, *Cluny under St Hugh 1049–1109* (London, 1967) 187–194.
4. The monastery of St Michael the Archangel at Chiusa, some thirty kilometers west of Turin, where Burgundius and Richeza had offered their first-born son Anselm to God, see *Ep* 211; *VA* 104. The abbot of Chiusa possibly feared the loss of young Anselm's inheritance if his mother entered Marcigny as a nun, see Southern, *Anselm*, 10.
5. See *Epp* 290, 291.
6. See Si 19:5; RB 49:7.
7. Dom Walter and his assistant Theodor, see *Ep* 309.
8. Archbishop Anselm had entrusted the care and charge of the monks to Prior Ernulf, see *Ep* 312.

329. TO MATILDA, QUEEN OF THE ENGLISH.

Anselm thanks Queen Matilda of the English for her generosity and defends himself against the charge that he had obstructed his return to England by his excessive demands in his letter to the King.

TO MATILDA, HIS REVEREND LADY AND DEAREST DAUGHTER, GLORIOUS QUEEN OF THE ENGLISH: ANSELM THE ARCHBISHOP, SENDING THE GREETING AND BLESSING OF GOD AND HIS OWN, IF IT IS WORTH ANYTHING, AND HIS SERVICE AND LOVING PRAYERS.

MY HEART GIVES AS MUCH THANKS as it can engender for the great generosity of your Highness, and what it cannot achieve it does not cease to desire. May he who inspires it himself repay. Indeed, the pious and sweet affection you feel towards me through the inspiration of God you express most clearly when you write[1] to me about the bitterness, sadness and solicitude which you feel on account of my absence. This absence of mine, as far as I and those who consider the case carefully understand it, has not been extended for so long through any fault of mine.

With devout affection your excellency complains that my lack of moderation has disturbed the peace of mind of my lord the King and his nobles, and that this has prevented the good, begun by your efforts, from being brought to an end. Indeed, in our letter[2] which is said to contain that lack of moderation, nothing indiscriminate, nothing unreasonable, although this was imputed to me in the King's letter, can be found if what is written there and the prohibition which I heard and which everybody knows about is examined with an unbiased judgement and a calm mind. I uttered nothing against the King's father and Archbishop Lanfranc, men of great and religious renown, when I showed that I had not promised either in baptism or in my ordinations to obey their law and customs, and stated that I was not going to disobey the law of God. What is now required of me on the grounds that those men acted as they did I cannot do without committing a most serious offence because of what I heard with my own ears in Rome. If I were to scorn that, I should certainly be acting against the law of God. Therefore, in order to show with what reasons I refused to do what was required of me according to their customs, I showed how I would much rather be under obligation to observe the Apostolic and ecclesiastical decree known to everybody. In this the law of God can be perceived without doubt, since it was promulgated to strengthen the Christian religion. I need not say here how dangerous it would be to despise this law, since Christians who have ears to hear[3] may daily learn it from divine utterances.

That distorted interpretation of my utterances, according to which I am said to have spoken unreasonably, I do not ascribe to the King's mind or yours. The King received our letter kindly at first, according to what I heard, but later someone with a spiteful and insincere intention, I know not who, incited him against me by a distorted interpretation through no fault of mine. Who that may be I do not know;

but I do not doubt that either he does not love, or does not know how to love, his lord.

May almighty God so favor you and your children with prosperity in this life that he may lead you to the happiness of the life to come. Amen.

August 1104, while at Lyon.

NOTES

1. Matilda's letter to Anselm is not preserved.
2. See *Ep* 319.
3. See Mt 11:15 et al.

330. TO GUNDULF, BISHOP OF ROCHESTER.

Anselm thanks Bishop Gundulf of Rochester for his careful dealings as administrator of the widowed archdiocese. He is not in exile because of the words of a silly cleric as he told Prior Ernulf. He asks Gundulf to send him the King's reply of 29 September as quickly as possible and commends Robert's possessions and family to him once more.

ANSELM THE ARCHBISHOP: TO HIS OLD AND EVER NEW AND TRUE FRIEND, BELOVED IN GOD, THE REVEREND BISHOP GUNDULF, GREETING.

ALTHOUGH YOUR CONSTANCY does not need to receive frequent expressions of thanks for the good deeds which you have begun, yet lest others should think that I do not value the kindness and solicitude which you certainly display in your great labors for my sake,[1] or that I do not esteem them as I should, I give your reverence thanks in heart and word and writing. In everything which concerns me and our affairs I perceive that you speak and act as you should as prudently and as vigorously as you can, and with the most true love. Moreover I am certain that with God's help your good will towards me, as it has never failed since it first began, so it will never fail as long as you live.

Your charity complains that, because of the contemptible words of one cleric,[2] I have not returned to England,[3] but this is not the case. Read the letter[4] about this matter which I sent in another way to our deputy, Dom Prior Ernulf, which I thought you had seen. There I think you will find some good reasons why I should not have, nor, as things now stand, should I now return to England. However, I do not wish these reasons to be made public.

As to the reply[5] which the King said he would give me on the feast of St Michael,[6] I am certain that neither Dom Everard[7] nor any other of our messengers can receive it on that day because it has not been sent to me so that it can arrive on that day. Therefore, if you do not receive the answer on that day I beg you to ask for it as speedily and as earnestly as you can, and have the King's letter sent to me whatever it may contain. If he does not wish to give any answer, or wishes to put it off any longer, inform me of that without delay by your letter. Since this cannot conveniently be done so quickly by Dom Everard, send it by my servant Vulgarus of Lyminge with some companion, or by some other messenger on foot. On no account will I grant or accept a further postponement before beginning to take counsel of God and his Church about what should be done in such a case. I trust in God, whose cause it is that is in question, that it will be concluded to his honor at some time or other, and that his Church will not always be afflicted as it is now.

I do not know[8] who the spiteful people are who out of the wickedness of their hearts interpreted the letter I sent to the King as if I were boasting that I had always obeyed the law of God, and had accused his father and Archbishop Lanfranc of having lived outside the law of God. Certainly those who say this must either have very distorted or very little understanding. For the King's father and Archbishop Lanfranc, men of great and holy renown, did certain things in their time which, according to the will of God, I am now unable to do without incurring the damnation of my soul. You have done well, and I am grateful that you told me the whole thing plainly in your letter just as it happened.

It is not enough for me to have frequently recommended to your care the possessions and the family of Robert,[9] who is here with me. Once more, on account of the great goodwill which I have for him, I entrust them to your charge and beg you to guard them in peace, as far as you can.

I greet your sons and daughters[10] and mine, and particularly Dom Ernulf, your chaplain. May almighty God protect you always and everywhere. Amen.

August 1104 while at Lyon.

NOTES

1. Bishop Gundulf of Rochester acted as administrator of the archdiocese during Anselm's absence from 27 April 1103 to early September 1106.
2. William de Warelwast spoke on behalf of the King, see *Ep* 306; *HN* 157; *VA* 130.
3. See *Ep* 327.
4. See *Ep* 311.
5. Anselm had asked King Henry to allow him to live according to the law of God and his rank, to reinvest him with the archbishopric and to restore everything which had been alienated, see *Ep* 319. There are further requests for an answer from the King in *Epp* 321, 329.
6. 29 September 1104.
7. At the end of January 1104 Dom Everard had come to Lyon with a letter from the King, *HN* 159, which is not preserved; he returned to England with *Epp* 306, 307, 308, 309.
8. For the following see *Ep* 329.
9. See *Epp* 299, 331.
10. See *Ep* 314.

331. TO ERNULF, PRIOR OF CANTERBURY.

Anselm writes to Prior Ernulf at Christ Church Canterbury that he cannot follow his advice completely since Dom Everard cannot return to England for Michaelmas. He informs him that an agreement between the Archbishop of York and the Bishop of London is invalid if the Archbishop of Canterbury is not part of it and he answers a number of queries about monastic business. He is waiting for the King's answer to his request to be reinvested.

ANSELM THE ARCHBISHOP: TO THE REVEREND PRIOR, DOM ERNULF, SENDING THE GREETING AND BLESSING OF GOD AND HIS OWN, IF IT IS WORTH ANYTHING.

I RECEIVED THE LETTER[1] of your reverend affection abounding with prudent counsel, charitable care for my cause, a feeling of sincere love and a violent complaint about the tribulations which are afflicting your heart and our church.[2] I have not been able to follow the advice partly because Dom Everard[3] did not come to me in time to be able to return to England for the feast of St Michael.[4] On the other matters I shall try to carry out what you advise if I can, with the help of God. As I have said, I thank God and you for your care and love. With regard to the tribulations, you do not need our consolation except in those matters which can be mitigated by our advice or power. For you know that we have to go through many tribulations and through water and fire in order to obtain refreshment.[5] There are many other things which are not hidden from your wisdom which encourage us to rejoice in tribulation. I do not doubt that you are doing this with God's consolation and that you will continue to do it until the end.

Concerning the matters about which you asked for a reply from us: first of all I say that the agreement which the Archbishop of York and the Bishop of London reached should neither be established nor carried out without the

Archbishop of Canterbury. If the church of Canterbury should have no living bishop, they should wait for one. Therefore, if anything has been done by this agreement it ought not stand and I shall nullify it.

I cannot give you any advice about the loss which you suffered either through the reeves or through the cellarer because the matter has passed. However, if you are able to get anything back by any means, I rejoice. For the future I approve your advice about the companions of the reeves. Concerning Geoffrey I advise you and instruct the lord bishop of Rochester[6] that he should be treated with justice lest he complain to the King or anybody else, slandering you, that he was unjustly treated. He should either satisfy you as is just concerning what he owes you, or return the house for which he is in your debt. Concerning Dom Joseph, I am instructing[7] the aforesaid bishop that if there is need he should help you so that you may be able to discuss with him the debts and the lands which he holds according to your disposition, and this I commit to you to arrange.

With regard to accepting boys and young men[8] I support your judgement for the many sensible reasons which you wrote about until, God willing, I return and we shall be able to consider these and other matters together. This however I wish and ask, that wherever I may be, if any of this age are to be accepted, those should first be accepted to whom permission has been given. About the matter for which certain people criticize both me and you, namely about people of our church, you know why it had to be done. Hardly anyone comes to us except those we willingly accept. About the layman whom you received: God disposed mercifully with him because you showed charity to him and his friends, and he came to rest by a good end; may God absolve him from all his sins. About the cleric of Beauvais whom God in his clemency brought to you: I rejoice, and I advise that he be often edified by your discourse about contempt for the glory of the world, the uncertainty of human life and the danger to souls who are passing from this world while loving worldliness, although I believe you do this anyway. About the cleric of London whom you received: I approve what you did. About Robert, the servant of the poor: carry out what you suggested to me. For if he regains his health I believe that he will be useful in some service to the church for the salvation of his soul; and if he dies he will be saved. About Robert of Lyminge, this is my judgement: if by this time he has become a monk I grant to his wife, as long as she lives, the lands which he holds from me; and if anyone receives them from anyone else except from the Archbishop of Canterbury, either myself or whoever canonically succeeds me, may he be subjected to the excommunication which I can inflict upon him and the anger of God which I can call down upon him. Therefore, whenever he enters the monastery, or if he should end his life without having entered, what I have said about the lands should remain valid.

About the brothers who left the monastery irregularly and who were brought back by the ordinance of God:[9] I praise everything you have done. About those who remained: if they are of good will I give thanks to God. But about the one who has proved to be completely incorrigible: I consider him handed over to satan[10] because of his wickedness, and I do not think you should accept him in your company any more. About the evil rumor which the people in their folly cry out about you: you should be consoled by your wisdom. It is not censure but rather praise of a monastery when certain people flee from it because they are not seeking a better life, nor can they in any way endure the good way of life which is demanded of them.

Dom Cornelius asked me about his father to whom, as you know, you and I gave the hope of being accepted. I think it good, if it seems right to you, that he be accepted, since he comes from a great distance solely for love of the holy monastic life and has already reached the dignity of old age.

About the priests who returned to the wives they had dismissed,[11] I have sought advice from our venerable father, the Archbishop of Lyon.[12] He wished to advise that they are under no circumstances to be admitted any longer to the churches, but rather that infants should be baptized by some other clerics or laymen. Nor does he recommend that they be received for any necessity whatsoever, which can frequently arise in the absence of priests. However, consider what I say and the needs which you see and, having acknowledged the bishop's advice, do what you would advise if I were present.

With regard to the celebration of feasts about which you wrote to me, I commit this to your judgement. What you thus decide I confirm and let it be ratified. Concerning the octave of the Nativity of holy Mary,[13] the mother of God, which many of our brothers ask to have observed in our church because it is observed in many churches: also do what seems best to you.[14]

On our behalf tell Dom Robert,[15] the monk, our beloved son, who usually takes care of our possessions, that if it is in his power he should permit Robert the cleric,[16] who is with me, to hold the house which he has in Canterbury just as peacefully as Roger Puntel held it.

You ask me to suffer with you in your tribulations and to pray for you; I do both, and know that you always do the same for us. May almighty God always give you his consolation.

If the King's reply[17] has not been given to the bishop by the appointed day,[18] I have told him that he should demand it as swiftly as he can and that he should send it to me through Vulgarus of Lyminge with some companion, or by two other messengers on foot because this cannot be done so quickly by Dom Everard.

August 1104 while at Lyon.

NOTES

1. This letter is not preserved.
2. See *Ep* 310; *HN* 159 and *VA* 132: 'King Henry at once took the archbishopric into his own hands and deprived Anselm of all his possessions. There were many negotiations between them over this, and the King's anger was not appeased for a year and a half.' According to *Ep* 359 William fitz Rodulf was the royal keeper of the archbishop's revenues.
3. See *Epp* 306, 307, 308, 309, 330; *HN* 159.
4. See *Ep* 330.
5. See Ps 65:12.
6. Bishop Gundulf of Rochester acted as Anselm's deputy during his exile, see *Epp* 287, 299, 300, 359.
7. Anselm is referring to a letter to Gundulf which is not preserved.
8. For Anselm's regard for the young, see *Ep* 291.
9. See *Ep* 333.
10. See 1 Co 5:5.
11. See canons 4, 5, 6, of the Council of Westminster, *HN* 142.
12. Archbishop Hugh of Lyon was Anselm's host from December 1103 to April 1105.
13. 8–15 September.
14. Anselm had delegated the charge of the community of Christ Church Canterbury to Prior Ernulf, see *Ep* 312.
15. See *Ep* 289.
16. See *Ep* 330.
17. See *Epp* 319, 321, 329, 330.
18. Michaelmas, 29 September, 1104, see *Ep* 330.

332. TO THE MONKS OF CANTERBURY.

Anselm consoles the monks of Christ Church Canterbury in their troubles and encourages them to live a truly monastic life. He informs them that he does not yet know anything about his return.

ANSELM THE ARCHBISHOP: TO HIS BROTHERS AND DEAREST SONS SERVING GOD AT CHRIST CHURCH CANTERBURY, SENDING THE GREETING AND BLESSING OF GOD AND HIS OWN, AS FAR AS HE CAN.

I KNOW YOUR DESIRE and the tribulation which you are enduring at the moment, and that you fear even greater ones in the future. For this reason no better counsel can be given to you than that you should direct your thoughts completely to the service of God. Whether God tests you by tribulation, whether he punishes you or harasses you, you should always respond to this by your perseverance in living a holy life. In this way you show how courageous you are and how truly you love him, and in this way you appease him; trained in this way you advance towards greater things and, purified, you merit even greater gifts. Therefore let idle chatter among you come to an end, all slander be torn out by the root, muttering be suppressed, impatience be curbed, vain curiosity disappear, idleness be expelled, grumbling be banned, displeasure and unfitting anger on account of any mental offence be laid aside, negligence be eliminated and envy be wiped out. Let anything which is out of harmony with your intention be held in abomination and whatever harmonizes with monastic institutions be held in love. May obedience and zeal and diligence towards all the virtues which fight against the above-mentioned vices, and all the others, burn brightly. Let each one examine diligently his private and public life, and let whoever finds a fault there hasten to offer worthy satisfaction lest God punish the whole community for his guilt. Divine judgement often does this so that a great number of people are thrown into confusion for the guilt of one alone. If it were not exceedingly long, many examples could be quoted. I must put an end to our exhortation because many of you have knowledge of the Scriptures, and you have our most beloved brother, Dom Prior Ernulf, who knows and can speak to you about these things and others.[1]

May almighty God deign to cleanse you from all evils, make you abound in all good things and rejoice after this life in his kingdom. May the blessing of God rest upon you and may he grant you the remission of all your sins. Amen.

At present I do not know when I shall be able to return to you,[2] but I trust in God that your prayer will not be in vain.

c. August 1104 while at Lyon.

NOTES

1. See *Ep* 312.
2. Anselm was eagerly awaiting the reply from King Henry to his request to allow him to live according to the law of God and his rank, to be reinvested with his archbishopric and have everything belonging to it restored to him, see *Epp* 319, 321, 329, 331.

333. TO ULFRIC, PHILIP AND WILLIAM, MONKS OF CANTERBURY.[1]

Anselm admonishes the monks Ulfric, Philip and William, who had run away from the cloister and have now returned, not to be ashamed to do penance.

ANSELM THE ARCHBISHOP: TO HIS DEAREST BROTHERS
AND SONS ULFRIC, PHILIP AND WILLIAM, SENDING
THE GREETING AND BLESSING OF GOD AND HIS OWN.

I HAVE HEARD[2] that through the persuasion of the ancient serpent[3] whose cunning drove our first parents out of paradise, you have in your turn abandoned the paradise of the cloister and the religious way of life, and for this I am deeply grieved. But I was consoled and gladdened because God did not shut the gate of paradise to you so that you could not enter it later but rather mercifully forced you to return to the peace which you had left behind. If you give him thanks for this mercy which he showed you against your will, and if you promise improvement not only by word of mouth before men but also in your hearts in the face of God, then I shall give thanks to God with you and shall expel from my heart all the rancor which I conceived because of your guilt.

Therefore I admonish you as my sons to expel completely from your hearts, by doing penance before God, those vicious and diabolic desires which you had, and not bewilder your minds indiscriminately by indulging in any shame after God has called you back to himself. But putting your trust in the fact that God receives repentant sinners kindly, you should be at peace in your good intentions and in the love of your order. For it sometimes comes to pass that the devil cannot complete what he has started because God has mercy on his servant and defends him, and so he turns to another ruse: the man whom he could not bring to a fall as he had intended may now fall through his unwillingness to bear excessive shame. Only in the sight of God be amazed that you could have wished this and be ashamed, but before men take comfort in your good conscience and be confident. By your good way of life show that all wicked desires are foreign to you and thus you will bring it about that nobody remembers what you did and there will be no wicked suspicion about you.

May almighty God absolve you from all past sins and protect you in future from every sin for ever. Amen.

c. August 1104 at Lyon.

NOTES

1. Referred to in *Ep* 331.
2. See *Ep* 331.
3. See Rev 12:9.

334. TO THIDRICUS, MONK OF CANTERBURY.

Anselm assures Thidricus, monk and scribe at Christ Church Canterbury, of their mutual love and instructs him to insert words of St Paul into chapter four of De conceptu virginali.

ANSELM THE ARCHBISHOP: TO HIS DEAREST SON THIDRICUS,[1] SENDING GREETING AND BLESSING.

I GIVE YOU THANKS FOR THE VISIT of your letter[2] full of the delightful charm of overflowing love. I do not doubt that, even when you are silent, it keeps on burning in your heart. I do not need to say much about my love for you because you are aware of it.

In the sentence of the fourth Chapter of the book *De conceptu virginali*[3] write the words of the Apostle exactly as you find them here,[4] for the Apostle says there *is no condemnation for those who live in Christ Jesus, who do not walk according to the flesh.*[5] Farewell, my son.

August 1104, while at Lyon.

NOTES

1. Thidricus was librarian and scribe at Christ Church Canterbury, see *Ep* 379 and Introduction, vol. 1, p. 36.
2. Thidricus' letter is not preserved.
3. *AOO* II, 135–173; ET J. Hopkins and H. Richardson, *Complete Treatises*, 3:139–179.

4. Thidricus was copying Anselm's *De conceptu virginali*. In MS Oxford Bodleian, Bodley 271, attributed to Thidricus, there is a scribal irregularity at this very place. For a full discussion of this problem see *AOO* 226*–237* and Southern, *Anselm*, 238.

5. Rm 8:1.

335. TO WARNER, MONK OF CANTERBURY.

Anselm encourages the novice Warner of Christ Church Canterbury to take the final steps towards becoming a monk. He advises him to entrust himself to Prior Ernulf, and recommends to him the letter he had written to the novice Lanzo many years ago.

ANSELM THE ARCHBISHOP: TO WARNER,[1] SENDING THE GREETING AND BLESSING OF GOD AND HIS OWN, AND WISHING THAT A PERFECT END MAY FOLLOW THE GOOD BEGINNING.

BLESSED BE GOD IN HIS GIFTS *and holy in all his works,*[2] who visited you with his grace, dearest son, when your body and soul were in danger of death, and mercifully called both back to life. Think and consider how great a sign of his love God gave you when, with paternal care, he forced you to return to him and to wish to serve him when you were not only fleeing from him but also despising and resisting him even to the point of death. Never think that what you undertook is of less value to you because you were forced to do it by the fear of death and not attracted to it by your own free will. For God does not so much weigh by what beginning or for what reason a man starts to do good but rather with how much resolution and devotion he retains the grace of God given to him. Paul, the apostle, was converted to the Christian faith by force, but since he kept the faith with his whole heart and finished the race in it,[3] he joyfully gave us to understand in his own words that a crown of righteousness was reserved for him.[4]

You have with you my dearest brother Dom Prior Ernulf, who is no less able than I to advise you by his knowledge and goodwill and to absolve you by my authority.[5] I commit you to God and to him, and you should commit yourself to him after God, according to our advice and our command. By the grace of God you are well educated. Direct the knowledge which God permitted you to acquire while loving the world towards the love of God, from whom you have whatever you have, so that in place of the worldly glory for which you were longing with your learning you may attain the eternal glory which you either scorned or only feebly desired. Zealously observe the customs of our order into which you have entered as though they were decreed by God, because not one is useless, not one is superfluous.

I advise you to ask for the letter which I wrote to Dom Lanzo when he was a novice.[6] There you will find how you should behave at the beginning of your monastic life and how to meet with the temptations which assail a novice.

I pray as much as I can that God may give you absolution and remission of all your sins and so strengthen you at the start of your resolution that he may lead you to eternal glory. Amen.

August 1104 while at Lyon.

NOTES

1. Warner is probably the cleric of Beauvais about whom Anselm rejoiced in *Ep* 331. In 1125 he became Abbot of Battle, from where he retired in his fourteenth year to Lewes Priory, see *Heads*, 29.
2. Ps. 144:13.
3. See 2 Tm 4:7.
4. See 2 Tm 4:9.
5. See *Ep* 312.
6. See *Ep* 37, which is quoted in *Epp* 35, 51, and *VA* 32–34. On these early letters of friendship see Southern, *Anselm*, 67–76; B. McGuire, 'Love, friendship and sex in the eleventh century: the experience of Anselm', *Studia Theologica* 28 (1974) 111–152.

336. TO ORDWY, MONK OF CANTERBURY.

Anselm answers the calumnies about which Ordwy, a monk of Christ Church Canterbury, had informed him. He assures him that he did not command that laymen take over the offices of clerics in his churches after the clerics were expelled nor is he evading the duties of his office by staying abroad voluntarily.

ANSELM THE ARCHBISHOP: TO HIS DEAREST BROTHER AND SON ORDWY, SENDING THE GREETING AND BLESSING OF GOD.

MAY THE LORD TAKE CARE OF YOU because you are concerned about my reputation, and for this I give you thanks. I replied[1] to you some time ago concerning those things which those who prefer to lie by speaking evil of me rather than to speak the truth by telling good things, if there are any in me, chatter against me. But you are still asking with charitable solicitude that I should reply to those who say that they have frequently seen laymen standing at the altars in the churches belonging to my special care since the priests have been expelled,[2] collecting alms from the altar and audaciously usurping the offices of burial and whatever else belonged to the right of priests. When you inquired about these matters you discovered from the evidence of our archdeacon worse things,[3] as you say, than you had heard before. You have also heard the clerics of these churches saying that they often complained to me about these offenses, privately and publicly in the synod,[4] but that they had received no help.

Therefore I tell you that these things have never been done by my command, by my will or with my consent. If at any time I heard a complaint about them—which I cannot recall—I never dismissed it without what I believed to be a sufficient rebuke. Finally I think that this does not take place in any of our churches at all. If, indeed, it ever was or is being done in other churches I am completely unaware of it; and as far as I am concerned I never wished nor do I now wish it. For that reason it does not worry me at all that I should *be judged*[5] by those who make these discoveries not for love of truth but by the incitement of malice.

As to what you say you have heard about my not being greatly concerned about returning to you,[6] I reply that since I left England I have not been able to perceive how I could reasonably return. Certainly I neither wish nor ought to scorn the charge laid upon me by God or forget the love of the brothers and sons entrusted to me. Farewell.

August 1104 while at Lyon.

NOTES

1. See *Ep* 327.
2. See *Ep* 331.
3. William the Archdeacon, see *Epp* 208, 257, 327.
4. At Westminster, Michaelmas 1102, *HN* 141-144.
5. See 1 Co 4:3.
6. For this frequent charge see *Epp* 310, 327.

337. TO EULALIA, ABBESS OF ST EDWARD, SHAFTESBURY, AND HER NUNS.

Anselm tells Abbess Eulalia and her nuns at Shaftesbury that he knows that they want a letter from him to refresh their memory of him. He encourages them to live as if they were always in the presence of their guardian angels. He cannot yet say anything definite about his return.

ANSELM THE ARCHBISHOP: TO HIS DEAREST SISTERS IN CHRIST, TO THE LADY ABBESS OF ST EDWARD, EULALIA,[1] AND ALL HER AND HIS DAUGHTERS, SENDING THE GREETING AND BLESSING OF GOD, AND HIS OWN, FOR WHAT IT IS WORTH.

THROUGH A CERTAIN SERVANT OF THE KING who brought me the King's seal your love has asked, as he said, to be greeted by a letter from us. I preferred to do this by a messenger of mine whom I knew I would soon be sending to England. I know that the abundance of true and pious love makes you eagerly wish to see my letter. As you cannot have my presence, which you long for with pious affection according to your will, you can at least display it to some extent to yourself through my letter, and perhaps refresh your memory of me so that it may not fade away. All this I impute to the greatness of your sincere affection. Since you ask for a letter of mine so that in it you may in some way see me and refresh your memory of me, I recognize that you have a true memory of me. Moreover, just as I know that your goodwill and sincere love for me is not growing cold, so you should know that mine for you is not growing cool.

Indeed, I desire most of all that you remember me and love me as you do so that, as you know my desire, you should all strive to burn increasingly in the love of God and that you who are subject to your mother should endeavour to display obedience, not to the eye but in the inmost heart. I know that you are putting up with adversities and tribulations from every side but under these circumstances you should be especially zealous in guarding your order and your way of life because you obtain the consolation of God better by leading a good life than if for the sake of some worldly impediment you slacken the fervor of your intention. In whatever secluded place you may be, be certain and have no doubt at all that each one of you has her own angel who sees and notes every thought and action and reports it to God the judge.[2] I advise you therefore, dearest daughters, that both in secret and in public each one should so guard all the movements of her heart and body as if she sees her guardian angel present to her bodily eyes. May almighty God protect you with his blessing and lead you to the sight of his glory. Amen.

I know that you want to know something about our return but at present I cannot write you anything certain.

Pray that it may come about according to God's good pleasure and will.

August 1104 while at Lyon.

NOTES

1. See *Epp* 183, 403.
2. See RB 7:28.

338. TO POPE PASCHAL.

Anselm informs Pope Paschal II that he is sending Baldwin to discuss with him the case between himself and the King of the English. He reminds him that he has been exiled from his bishopric and robbed of its property because of his obedience to the Holy See and for the freedom of the Church.

TO PASCHAL, HIS LORD AND FATHER, THE SUPREME PONTIFF, WITH RESPECTFUL LOVE AND LOVING RESPECT: ANSELM, CALLED BISHOP OF THE CHURCH OF CANTERBURY, SENDING HIS DUE SUBJECTION WITH PRAYERS.

SINCE THE CASE BETWEEN the King of the English and myself, for which I once came into your presence,[1] is for the most part known to your Highness, and what is still to be reported can be told by your faithful servant, our dearest brother Baldwin,[2] the bearer of this letter, I do not need to dwell on it in writing. This brother, the confidant of my affairs and a friend of the freedom of the Church of God I send to your feet as if he were myself and I commit him to listening and speaking in my place. I write this because, due to my obedience to you and your predecessors and for the freedom of the Church, which I do not wish to disavow, I am an exile from my bishopric and despoiled of its possessions.[3] In this matter your prudence has no need of our prayers or of our advice.

May almighty God long preserve your Holiness unharmed for us in prosperity. Amen.

Autumn 1104 while at Lyon.

NOTES

1. Anselm had been in Rome from early October until 18 November 1103, see *HN* 152-155; *VA* 128; *Ep* 303.
2. See *Epp* 124, 151.
3. *HN* 157, 159; *VA* 132; *Epp* 303, 310, 331. The fact that the King gave no answer to Anselm, see *Ep* 319, on the appointed date—originally Easter 1104 (see *Ep* 316) and then Michaelmas, 29 September 1104 (see *Ep* 330 and the letters which were sent at the same time, *Epp* 329, 331, 332, 333, 334, 335, 336, 337)—may have prompted this letter.

339. TO JOHN, BISHOP OF TUSCULUM AND JOHN THE CARDINAL.

Anselm informs both John, Cardinal Bishop of Tusculum, and Cardinal John that he is sending Baldwin to the Pope because of the dispute between himself and the King of the English. He asks for their assistance and reminds them that he is once more in exile.

TO HIS REVEREND LORDS AND DEAREST FRIENDS JOHN, BISHOP OF TUSCULUM,[1] AND CARDINAL JOHN:[2] ANSELM, CALLED BISHOP OF CANTERBURY, WISHING THEM WHAT A FAITHFUL FRIEND WISHES FRIENDS IN WHOM HE TRUSTS.

I AM SENDING DOM BALDWIN,[3] our dearest brother and son who truly loves you, to the feet of the lord Pope on account of the case which exists between the King of the English and me, or rather between him and the freedom of the Church of God, for which I am an exile from my bishopric and despoiled of all its possessions.[4] I beg your holiness to assist him in the presence of the lord Pope in everything concerning this matter as friends of the truth and supporters of the aforesaid freedom, and to defend me lest the stability of church doctrine and Apostolic authority ever be weakened in any way by me or because of me. I would prefer to die and to be weighed down by complete penury in exile as long as I live rather than to see the honor of the Church of God harmed in any way because of me or through my example. Farewell.

Autumn 1104 while at Lyon.

NOTES

1. See *Epp* 125, 128, 129, 213. As bishop of a suburbicarian diocese, Tusculum, today Frascati, John was Cardinal Bishop.
2. See *Ep* 284.
3. See *Ep* 338.
4. See *HN* 157, 159; *VA* 130.

340. TO POPE PASCHAL.

Anselm asks Pope Paschal II to put an end to the dispute between the church of Chartres and Countess Adela of Chartres. He blames the clerics and praises the Countess for her loyalty to the Church.

TO PASCAL, THE SUPREME PONTIFF, TO BE LOVED WITH REVERENCE AND TO BE REVERED WITH LOVE: ANSELM, SERVANT OF THE CHURCH OF CANTERBURY, SENDING FAITHFUL PRAYERS WITH DUE SUBJECTION.

YOUR PRUDENCE HAS NO NEED OF OUR ADVICE in the case which stands between the church of Chartres[1] and the Countess of Chartres[2] about which I spoke to your Highness in Rome.[3] As far as I can see, the urgency of the matter requires that we and all those who love the peace and good of that church should direct our prayers to your Holiness so that, since it is recognized that grave scandal has been caused by the clerics, it may be brought to a peaceful solution by a decision of your Apostolic wisdom. How intolerable the evil will become, unless it is put right, you can learn from the things you will hear from the bearers[4] of this letter who know the facts of the matter. The fact that the Countess respects your legates more than the princes of Gaul and receives your commands I believe is so well known to your Holiness that you do not need any information from us. Wherefore, if the prayers of my humility are strong enough to rise up to the ears of such great Highness I beg you as much as I can that it may please you to bring about a harmonious end to so harmful a discord as the matter demands and as befits you. In the same way it clearly rests with you to strengthen what has been established for the good of God's Church and to correct anything which dissipates peace and charity as far as possible.

May almighty God long keep your paternity unharmed for us in his grace. Amen.

Autumn 1104 while at Lyon.

NOTES

1. Ivo was Bishop of Chartres from 1090–1116, see *Ep* 181.
2. Adela, Countess of Chartres and Blois, a sister of Henry I, King of the English, see *Ep* 286. She brought about the reconciliation between Anselm and King Henry at l'Aigle, 21–22 July 1105, *HN* 165–167; *Ep* 364.
3. Anselm was in Rome from early October until 18 November 1103, see *Ep* 338.
4. One of them was Baldwin, see *Epp* 338, 339.

341. FROM PHILIP, KING OF THE FRENCH.

King Philip I shows concern about the unjust treatment Anselm is receiving and invites him to leave the unhealthy place where he is staying and come to France.

PHILIP,[1] BY THE GRACE OF GOD, KING OF THE FRENCH: TO ANSELM, VENERABLE ARCHBISHOP OF CANTERBURY, GREETING.

BECAUSE, REVEREND PASTOR, I have heard that you are being unjustly oppressed,[2] I do not wish to hide from you that I am greatly saddened. If your oppression could in any way be alleviated by any help from us we would not delay in giving it. Moreover, since you are in exile in a place which is detrimental to physical health, we ask you to deign to visit our Gaul with your presence,[3] and there you will experience the affection of my mind and be taking care of your health. Farewell.

c. 1104 or 1105, sent to Lyon.

NOTES

1. King Philip I of the French, 1060–1108.
2. Philip is referring to Anselm's second exile, see *Epp* 306, 310, 331, and *HN* 157–159; *VA* 130.
3. Anselm spent the first part of his second exile with his friend, Archbishop Hugh of Lyon, from Christmas 1103 to April 1105. Lyon, on the western border of the kingdom of Burgundy, had become part of the Holy Roman Empire in 1032 on the death of King Rudolf III who bequeathed his kingdom to King Conrad II of Germany by sending him his diadem and insignia.

342. FROM LOUIS, DESIGNATED KING OF THE FRENCH.

King Louis IV, joint regent of the French, grieves at Anselm's situation and invites him to the royal court, since the place where he is staying is detrimental to his health.

TO ANSELM, VENERABLE ARCHBISHOP OF CANTERBURY: FROM LOUIS,[1] THE DESIGNATED KING OF THE FRENCH, GREETING.

MOST HOLY FATHER, I suffer with you in your distress[2] and if you could be relieved of it in any way through our office I would try with most willing concern to restore your former tranquillity. However, an even deeper pain pierces our bosom because the wisdom which is in you sojourns so far from our realm. Added to this as an additional burden to your banishment is the fact that you have chosen to live in a place which is more likely to bring about sickness than health, and neglect to preserve your life which should be kept for the whole world. Therefore we beg you to deign to come to our region so that if it appears agreeable to you to live here you will bear your exile more easily. Farewell.

c. 1104 or 1105, sent to Lyon.

NOTES

1. Louis IV, son of King Philip, became joint regent in ruling France in 1098. He succeeded his father in 1108 and ruled until 1137.
2. The letter from Louis is similar to his father's, see *Ep* 341.

343. TO RAINALM, RESIGNED BISHOP OF HEREFORD.

Anselm consoles Rainalm who was invested by the King with the bishopric of Hereford and had resigned it out of love of virtue and truth. Due to his own uncertain position, Anselm cannot promise him any help.

ANSELM, ARCHBISHOP OF CANTERBURY: TO RAINALM,[1]
WHO WISELY PREFERS TRUTH TO VANITY, BRAVELY
DESPISES TRANSITORY GLORY FOR THE SAKE OF HONOR
AND MANFULLY ACCEPTS POVERTY, WISHING THAT
HE MAY ALWAYS BE PROTECTED AND CONSOLED
BY THE GREETING AND THE GRACE OF GOD.

YOUR LOVE ASKED ME TO SEND you some consolation. This I willingly do in the manner which I think to be most suitable for you and most profitable for you before God. May your conscience, your virtue and your perseverance be the consolation of your heart in the sight of God. You acted bravely when, for the sake of truth, you rejected the bishopric into which you had been thrust against the will of God. Do not let your heart yearn that God may grant you as a reward for virtue what you scorned for the sake of virtue. The virtue which you preserved is far more precious than what you rejected for its sake. You would greatly tarnish the beauty of your virtue in the eyes of God if you expected anything paltry and transitory as a reward and consolation from him. I do not say that you ought not have the bishopric or that you do not deserve it but I admonish you to rejoice in your conscience about the grace in which God has caused you to stand firm, and to commit your recompense and consolation to the providence of God alone. Remember what the Holy Spirit says to you: *Wait on the Lord; act manfully, let your heart be strengthened and wait for the Lord.*[2] When you feel want and poverty growing around you, you can be sure that the Lord is increasing his grace in you in many ways.

This I desire to be your consolation, in this I desire you to strengthen your hope. Then the Lord *will make your righteousness like the dawn, and the justice of your cause like the noonday sun.*[3] Since I do not know what God is going to do with me I dare not promise anything from myself for your consolation but I can show the goodwill which God has given me and which you have deserved. Certainly, if I have the opportunity at any time, by the grace of God, I desire to be useful to you in body and soul.

May almighty God, my dearest brother, make you rejoice by his continuing protection and consolation. Amen.

c. 1104 or 1105 while at Lyon.

NOTES

1. Rainalm or Reinelm, chancellor of Queen Matilda, was appointed by the King to succeed Roger (see *Epp* 280, 261) as bishop of Hereford. When Anselm refused to consecrate him he returned his ring and staff to the King, (*HN* 145) lost his bishopric and was banished from the

court for some time (*Reg* II 613). After the settlement of the dispute about investiture Rainalm was reinvested with the bishopric and consecrated by Anselm together with William of Winchester, Roger of Salisbury and William de Warelwast of Exeter on 11 August 1107, see *Ep* 261 and Fröhlich, 'Bischöfliche Kollegen', *AA* 2 (1970) 147–148; W. Fröhlich, 'Anselm and the Bishops of the Province of Canterbury', *Spicilegium Beccense* 2 (Paris, 1984) 125–145. Reinelm died in 1115.
2. Ps 26:14.
3. Ps 36:6.

344. TO WILLIAM, BISHOP-ELECT OF WINCHESTER.

Anselm encourages William Giffard, the bishop-elect of Winchester, to persevere in rectitude and to reject the counsel of evil men.

ANSELM THE ARCHBISHOP: TO HIS BELOVED FRIEND WILLIAM, BISHOP-ELECT OF WINCHESTER,[1] SENDING HIM GREETING AND WISHING HIM TO BE PROTECTED IN EVERYTHING BY THE GRACE OF GOD.

ALTHOUGH BY THE GRACE OF GOD I can trust in your constancy, yet since I desire unceasingly that you should never turn aside from rectitude but always progress towards what is better, I take pleasure in encouraging your love out of the fullness of my heart.[2]

All those who prompt you against the sincerity of integrity and justice are poisonous serpents and children of the ancient serpent.[3] I ask you therefore as a beloved friend and advise you as my dearest son that if anyone wishes to advise you in any way against the counsel of God he may never so whisper in your ear by promising, threatening, flattering and begging that he poison your mind by his persuasion. You know that *the Lord brings the counsel of princes to nothing but the counsel of the Lord stands forever.*[4] I say this because I do not doubt that the ancient enemy, whom you have confounded by bravely persevering in rectitude, will seek with tricks of every sort to destroy the state and reputation of your integrity and change the praise which you have received with the help of God into mockery—which God avert! I do not name anything specifically that you should guard against because I think that in the sight of God nothing that in any way disfigures integrity should be taken lightly.

May almighty God so guard and protect your life always and everywhere in everything that no enemy of yours may laugh at any disfigurement of your excellence. Amen.

1104 or 1105 while at Lyon.

NOTES

1. See *Epp* 212, 229, 236, 265, 273, 274, 275, 276, 322, 343, 386, 404.
2. See Mt 12:34; Lk 6:45.
3. See Rev 12:9, 20:2.
4. Ps 32:10–11.

345. TO GUNTHER, CANON OF ST QUENTIN OF BEAUVAIS.

Anselm advises Gunther, canon of St Quentin of Beauvais, whom his fellow canons want to elect in place of the intruded Provost Odo, not to resist the will of the majority of the community and the advice of the former provosts, Bishops Ivo of Chartres and Walo of Paris.

ANSELM, SERVANT OF THE CHURCH OF CANTERBURY: TO HIS BELOVED BROTHER AND FRIEND GUNTHER,[1] CANON OF ST QUENTIN, SENDING HIM GREETING AND WISHING THAT HE MAY ALWAYS BE RULED BY THE COUNSEL OF GOD.

I HEAR THAT YOUR BROTHERS OF BEAUVAIS, the canons of the church of St Quentin, not rashly but for many reasons wish to remove Dom O[do],[2] who is only called your abbot, from that dignity and to put your fraternity in his place. They fear, however, that for the love of the peace your piety enjoys at present, you may not readily wish to consent to their intention. Since they know that you love my humble self and hope that you will trust my advice more than that of anyone else, they ask me to let your charity know what I think about it.

If in the body of Christ we are *members one of another*[3] and even more so in a single church made up of religious persons, then whoever does not permit, nor wish that the other members, and even the whole body, make use of him as their own member, I do not see how he can prove himself a member of that body; and if that body is the body of Christ, how he can show himself to be a member of Christ. There is another point: no one who acts rightly wishes to live for himself alone,[4] but just as he desires and believes that, if he is a member of God, all the advantages of the other members will be his in the life to come, in the same way, if there is any good in him he ought to wish that it should belong to others in this life.

Therefore I advise you as far as I can, and beseech you, dearest brother and friend, that if your whole community, or the better part of it,[5] on the advice of the reverend bishops of Chartres[6] and Paris,[7] who were your fathers and who brought you up, should pressingly elect you to what I named above, you should not by any means flee it or be obstinate. I consider it more advantageous for you to preserve the peace of contemplation by love in your mind and the obedience of brotherly charity in your actions than to wish to choose contemplation alone by despising the prayers and the need of others.[8] Farewell.

1104 or 1105 while at Lyon.

NOTES

1. Gunter or Gunther was also encouraged by Ivo of Chartres, see letters 11 and 140 of Ivo, PL 162:24, 147; FT in *Correspondence*, ed. et trans.

J. Leclercq (Paris, 1949) I:48–51. He evidently did not take office at St Quentin for Odo was succeeded by Ralph who was elected 4 October 1105, GC IX, 820.
2. Odo had been forced upon the abbey, see GC IX, 820.
3. Rm 12:5.
4. See Rm 14:7.
5. See RB 64:1.
6. Ivo of Chartres, see *Ep* 181.
7. Walo of Paris, see *Ep* 272; *VA* 132; *HN* 162–163.
8. Compare Anselm's advice in *Ep* 52.

346. TO MATILDA, QUEEN OF THE ENGLISH.

Anselm admonishes Queen Matilda of the English to give up investitures in the churches in her care and encourages her to assist the other churches of England.

TO MATILDA, GLORIOUS QUEEN OF THE ENGLISH, REVEREND LADY, MOST BELOVED DAUGHTER: ANSELM, ARCHBISHOP OF CANTERBURY, SENDING THE BLESSING OF GOD AND HIS FAITHFUL SERVICE WITH PRAYERS.

LET ME SPEAK BRIEFLY, but from the heart, as to that person whom I desire to advance from an earthly kingdom to a heavenly one. When I hear anything about you which is not pleasing to God or advantageous for you, and if I then neglected to admonish you, I would neither fear God nor would I love you as I should.

After I left England I heard that you were dealing with the churches in your hands otherwise than is expedient for them or for your own soul. I do not wish to say here how you are acting—according to what I have been told—because to no one is it better known than to yourself.[1] Therefore, I beseech you as my lady, advise you as my queen and admonish you as my daughter—as I have done before[2]—that the churches of God which are in your power should know you as mother, as nurse, as kind lady and queen. I do not say this concerning those churches alone but about all the churches in England to which your help can be extended. For he who says that *each one will receive according to what he has done in his body whether good or evil*[3] does not exclude anyone.

Again I beg, advise and admonish you, my dearest lady and daughter, not to consider these things heedlessly in your mind, but, if your conscience testifies that you have anything to correct in this matter, hasten to correct it so that in future you will not offend God, as far as this is possible for you through his grace. Concerning the past, if you see that you have failed in your duty, you should make him favorable towards you.[4] Surely, it is not enough for someone to desist from evil unless he takes care, if possible, to make amends for what he has done.

May almighty God always guide you so that he may repay you with eternal life.

1104 or 1105 while at Lyon.

NOTES

1. Anselm is referring to the papal decrees of Lent 1099 forbidding lay investiture and homage of clerics to laymen. Anyone breaking these decrees was threatened with excommunication, *HN* 114. Anselm had published these decrees when he returned to England after his first exile in September 1100.
2. See *Ep* 288.
3. 2 Co 5:10.
4. See Gen 43:14.

347. TO MATILDA, QUEEN OF THE ENGLISH.

Anselm rejoices that Queen Matilda of the English has taken his admonition to heart and advises her to follow her conscience always. He cannot return to England as long as the King disregards the will of God.

TO HIS LADY AND DAUGHTER BELOVED IN GOD, MATILDA, QUEEN OF THE ENGLISH: ANSELM, ARCHBISHOP OF CANTERBURY, SENDING THE GREETING AND BLESSING OF GOD, AND HIS OWN, AS FAR AS HE CAN, AND FAITHFUL PRAYERS WITH SERVICE.

YOUR HIGHNESS GAVE ME GREAT JOY with your letter[1] insofar as you have given me good hope about yourself. For the humble acceptance of disapproval and admonition is usually followed by hope of improvement.[2] Therefore I give thanks to God who gives you the good will you indicated in your reply to me, and I give thanks to you that you maintain it with sweet affection. Wherefore I pray God that what he himself inspires in you in his mercy he may preserve and increase so that when your soul leaves your body it may be brought before his sight and receive from him the reward of eternal felicity.

If your prudence needed to be taught how you ought to live in order to please God I would strive to demonstrate this according to my ability. But since I am fully aware that by the grace of God, you can distinguish between good and evil through the understanding of your mind, this I ask, this I beseech, this I admonish: that the unfailing intention of your heart be that in all your actions, great and small, you rather choose what you consider pleases God more.

In that letter you demonstrated sufficiently with holy and sweet affection that you desire my return to England. But I do not see that he[3] in whose power my return chiefly rests—as far as it depends on a man—agrees in this matter with the will of God, and it would not be good for my soul to disagree with God's will. I fear that he may realize too late that he has gone astray from the right path, having despised God's counsel and having followed the advice of princes, which the Lord brings to nothing.[4] I am certain, however, that he will realize this one day.

May almighty God gladden your excellency and my lowliness one day by the sight of one another, according to his will, and may he multiply the gifts of his grace in you. Amen.

1104 or 1105 while at Lyon.

NOTES

1. This letter is not preserved.
2. Anselm may be referring to his admonition in *Ep 346*.
3. Henry I, King of the English.
4. Ps 32:10, Anselm is referring to members of the *curia regis*, see *Epp* 344, 348, 351, 352, 353, 430.

348. POPE PASCHAL TO HENRY, KING OF THE ENGLISH.

Pope Paschal II assures King Henry I that he is interested only in his salvation and is keeping the King's messengers until the Lenten synod so that the King's requests may be answered according to the will of God. He is very concerned that Anselm is in exile once more and that he has been despoiled of his possessions. He is pleased that the decrees of the Council of Westminster are being carried out.

PASCHAL, THE BISHOP, SERVANT OF THE SERVANTS OF GOD: TO HIS DEAREST SON HENRY, KING OF THE ENGLISH, GREETING AND APOSTOLIC BLESSING.

SINCE WE EMBRACE YOU with more fervent love, so much the more do we ask those things which pertain to your salvation. We demand nothing else from you except what serves your salvation, your honor and your victory. All these are yours through your subjection to the Lord and your obedience to the Church. Furthermore, those who suggest anything else to your solicitude either love you less or love you falsely because they try to make you hateful to God.[1] For it is written: *Whoever turns a deaf ear so as not to hear the law, his prayer shall be an abomination.*[2] Therefore we wish you to listen to us in matters concerning God so that we may be listened to by God on your behalf. We seek you and not your possessions.[3] You yourself can see, and anybody who thinks reasonably can also see, that in the matter of our claim and command we gain no advantage and your power is not diminished in any way.

Since we long for you with the tenderness of Christ[4] and wish you to become and remain a member of Christ, for this reason we are still[5] showing paternal patience with you. We are holding back your messengers until the next Lenten synod[6] solely with the intention and hope that such answers will be given which will be in accordance with your salvation and the will of God. Otherwise it will be necessary for us to implement the decision of this synod concerning those people, so that those who do not wish to have the grace of Christ may feel the sword of Christ.[7]

As regards the person of the Archbishop we are not able to meet with your petition[8] because your power will not allow him to live in England unless he offends against the power of the Lord. Furthermore we are unable either to let him go to England or to send him there at the risk of his salvation. We are amazed that you not only made him an exile but also despoiled him of the possessions of his church. Clearly the charity of the Church cannot suffer this any longer. Concerning all these matters, dearest son, do not listen to any of your enemies but direct your path[9] towards the will of the Lord. Ask for advice in this way, reply in this way, so that you may delight in us and we in you in the Lord.[10]

It is pleasing that the decrees to stop the spreading of evil, which were promulgated with the consent of the synod[11] in your presence, are being made public according to accepted practice by the mother churches, and are being observed for the correction of offenders.

May almighty God snatch you away from all evil and guard you in his will. Amen.

Given at the Lateran on December twenty third.

23 December 1104 at the Lateran.

NOTES

1. The Pope is referring to King Henry's advisors who support him in his demands, see *Ep* 346. These advisors (Count Robert of Meulan and others) were excommunicated by the Lenten synod in 1105, see *Ep* 353.
2. Pr 28:9.
3. See 2 Co 12:14.
4. See Ph 1:8.
5. Negotiations had taken place since late 1100. William de Warelwast went to Rome in late 1100, intending to return at Easter 1101 but he was delayed until September. Bishops Gerard, Herbert and Robert and the monks Baldwin and Alexander, see *Ep* 217, went to Rome in late 1101 or early 1102, and returned in August 1102, see *Epp* 250, 265. Anselm went to Rome in April 1103, see *Ep* 286. After Christmas 1103, when Anselm was forbidden to return to England, King Henry sent messengers to Rome on his own account, see *Ep* 323, to make every possible effort to induce the Pope to instruct Anselm to return to England and in all matters to bow to the King's wishes and obey his bidding, *HN* 162. At the same time Anselm sent Baldwin to Rome, see *Epp* 338, 339, 349.
6. Lent 1105 was from 22 February to 9 April.
7. The Pope is threatening excommunication, see *Ep* 353.
8. None of the King's letters to the Pope, and only two of the Pope's to the King (*Epp* 348, 351) during these negotiations are preserved, see *Ep* 379.
9. See Si 2:6.
10. The tone of this letter is conciliatory, but firm as far as the issue is concerned. It is noteworthy that homage of clerics to laymen is not mentioned, see *Ep* 351; Southern, *Anselm*, 174–175. Negotiations

between Pope and King had probably already begun. They led to the compromise of l'Aigle in July 1105 (*HN* 165–167; *VA* 134) and to the solution of the investiture controversy in the Anglo-Norman kingdom; see *Epp* 181, 222, 351, 389, 390, 397; *HN* 186; *HC* 13–14.
11. Council of Westminster, Michaelmas, 1102; *HN* 141–144.

349. TO PRIOR ERNULF AND THE MONKS OF CANTERBURY.

Anselm forbids Prior Ernulf and the monks of Christ Church Canterbury to give the King any money from his revenues as long as he is not reinvested with the archbishopric. He informs them that Baldwin has returned from Rome with the news that the Pope is going to have this discussed at the following Lenten synod and has informed the King of this. Anselm asks for a new copy of Cur Deus Homo *and of* De Conceptu Virginali *to be made for the Pope.*

ANSELM THE ARCHBISHOP: TO DOM PRIOR ERNULF AND THE BROTHERS LIVING UNDER HIM AT CHRIST CHURCH CANTERBURY, SENDING GREETING AND BLESSING, AND FROM GOD THE ABSOLUTION OF THEIR SINS.

YOUR FRATERNITY ASKS ME FOR ADVICE about your tribulation, and particularly about the money which was exacted from you by the King. You know how he has despoiled me of the possessions of the archbishopric.[1] Therefore on no account shall he receive anything from all the money of the whole archbishopric through me unless he first reinvests me according to the canons and restores to me what he took away;[2] neither should you give him any money of your own accord without my orders. But if he should force you to give it either for fear that he might do still worse to you or through any other compulsion, I shall cry out to God equally for what he has taken and what he is about to take from me and you—for what is yours is mine—and invoke his judgement.

Do not let the present tribulations greatly terrify or upset you for *God is faithful who will not allow you to be tempted* beyond what you can bear.³ *Be strong in the Lord and in the power of his might.*⁴ God, *who does not abandon those who trust in him,*⁵ will put an end to these evils.

Dom Baldwin, when he returned from Rome,⁶ brought word from the lord Pope that at the Council which is to meet next Lent⁷ he will act with regard to our business on the advice which he receives from that Council, and this he has told the King.⁸

I ask you to have the books *Cur Deus Homo* and *De Conceptu Virginali*⁹ written out for me in one volume because I wish to send them to the lord Pope.¹⁰ I also ask that whoever copies them should be one who writes clearly and legibly. Farewell. Do this as quickly as you conveniently can and send it to me.

January or February 1105 while at Lyon.

NOTES

1. See *Epp* 310, 331.
2. For Anselm's reiteration that no demands are to be made of him until he is reinvested, see *Ep* 316 and also *Epp* 223, 225.
3. 1 Co 10:13.
4. Eph 6:10.
5. Jdt 13:17.
6. See *Epp* 338, 339.
7. Feb/Mar 1105.
8. See *Ep* 348.
9. *AOO* II, 39–133, 137–173.
10. Pope Paschal II.

350. MATILDA, MARCHIONESS OF TUSCANY, TO POPE PASCHAL.

Matilda, Marchioness of Tuscany, intercedes with Pope Paschal on behalf of Anselm since it is unbecoming for such a prominent member of the Church to be cut off from his office for such a long time.

TO THE MOST HOLY AND VENERABLE FATHER AND LORD IN CHRIST, PASCHAL, BISHOP OF THE PRIME SEE: FROM MATILDA,[1] BY THE GRACE OF GOD MARCHIONESS, SENDING, IF IT IS WORTH ANYTHING, THE ALLEGIANCE OF TOTAL SUBJECTION, AS MUCH DUE AS IT IS FAITHFUL.

AMONG OTHER THINGS which we presume to ask of your paternity we particularly entreat your clemency with regard to the expulsion of our father and lord Anselm, the venerable Archbishop of Canterbury.[2] Therefore, following the due judgement of your see,[3] may you as a pious father and lord faithfully take heed of the tribulations and wretchedness which that holy and reverend father bears for the catholic faith and the holy Roman church. May you have pity on this lamentable complaint, and by your holy activities may you most kindly stretch out the hand of your advice and help. It is improper that such a prominent member of the holy Roman church should be cast out as an exile like something putrid for such a long time, and not be able to perform the office entrusted to him at all. We grieve therefore, that his ministry, whose guidance we know to be necessary to the Church for everything and for everybody, has, for the most part, been taken away from the body of the Church. For this reason, on bended knee, we implore your clemency for him since we believe without any doubt that his sole allegiance after God belongs to you, and we desire that through our services on his behalf your clemency may increase and not diminish.

Shortly before the Lenten synod, February or March 1105.

NOTES

1. See *Ep* 325; Matilda was Marchioness and Countess of Tuscany.
2. See *Epp* 310, 331; *HN* 159 and *VA* 132.
3. For the Lenten synod of 1099, see *HN* 144; *VA* 115; *Ep* 346.

351. POPE PASCHAL TO HENRY, KING OF THE ENGLISH.

For the third time Pope Paschal admonishes King Henry not to despise the Church, to fill the long vacancy of St Augustine's, Canterbury, to receive Anselm back according to the papal decrees and to allow him to publish them, to protect the Church in her lawful liberty and to give up his evil advisors. He threatens him and his advisors with excommunication.

PASCHAL, THE BISHOP, SERVANT OF THE SERVANTS OF GOD: TO HENRY, ILLUSTRIOUS KING OF THE ENGLISH, GREETING AND APOSTOLIC BLESSING.

WE HAVE ALREADY ADMONISHED YOUR HIGHNESS in a second letter[1] to love the Church and honor the priests of the Lord as you promised on your accession to the kingdom. See now, for the third time we are forced to send you a letter of admonition and correction because we clearly perceive that, having set aside your earlier given promise, you are so despising the Church that even the monastery of St Augustine has already remained without the consolation of a master for many years due to royal violence.[2] Through the presumption of investiture[3] you are trying to show yourself as the gate to those who are to become bishops of churches, although the saying *I am the gate*[4] refers to Christ alone. In addition and besides all this, you are keeping your father, the guardian of your kingdom and salvation, the counsellor of life, distinguished for all his wisdom and sanctity, Anselm, the bishop of Canterbury, to whom, above all priests, you should have shown obedience, away from the borders of your kingdom.[5] Instead you have taken on counsellors of perdition[6] who are trying to persuade your diligence to withdraw the kingdom of the English, which you acquired with God's help by great promises[7] and miracles, from its subjection and obedience to the Apostolic see.

Wherefore, because we love you greatly, we fear for you greatly lest, while you are following the example of your royal brother, taking away from God what belongs to God,[8] you may be punished by a death like your brother's.[9] *Remember, dearest son, recall this again to your mind.*[10] Do not diminish the good beginnings of your reign by a worse usurpation lest the words spoken in Scripture about Saul appear to have been pronounced about you: *Saul was a child of one year when he began to reign, and he reigned two years over Israel.*[11] No matter how much longer he seemed to have reigned, he reigned in such a way as the Lord said through the prophet: *They reigned, but not by me; set up princes, but I knew it not.*[12] Do not pretend that you do not know, because we read that [Saul] lost the kingdom by the providence of the Lord when he presumed to usurp what pertained to Samuel.[13] Thus he doubtlessly lost the people while he tenaciously held on.

Fearing this danger for you in the investiture of churches we admonish you, and admonishing we beseech you, and by the authority of St Peter we command you to correct your errors and to desist from your domination of the churches.[14] Daily, the Church cries out to her spouse: *They have said, let us take possession of God's sanctuary; my God, make them like a wheel!*[15] Do not doubt that we shall lend you assistance in all things and shall most kindly care for the good of your kingdom if, honoring the majesty of the eternal King, you do not resist the ecclesiastical dispositions of the holy fathers.

Therefore we ask you once more and command you once more to receive with all due respect your father and shepherd, the bishop of Canterbury, in his see and permit him to act and preach freely what the Roman church has decided; and you should keep the churches in their freedom according to the law. Otherwise, we shall cut you off,[16] and your advisors, who separate you from divine obedience and have accepted investiture, even though unwillingly, by the sword of anathema.[17] If however, you consent to obey, we shall always cherish you with the heart of paternal providence.[18]

January or February 1105.

NOTES

1. See *Epp* 305, 348.
2. Wido, who had had a tumultuous rule at St Augustine's died on 9 August 1093. The vacancy lasted until 27 February 1108 when Anselm blessed Hugh de Flori as the new abbot; see *Heads*, 36.
3. See *Epp* 280, 310.
4. Jn 10:9.
5. Since Christmas 1103, see *Epp* 305, 306.
6. The Pope referred to them in *Ep* 348; he intends to excommunicate them, see *Ep* 353.
7. For the coronation charter promising liberties, see *Reg.* II 488; *EHD* II 400–402.
8. Mt 22:21.
9. King William II was killed on 2 August 1100, see *Epp* 212, 222, and *HN* 118; *VA* 123–124.
10. Is 46:8.
11. 1 K (1 Sm) 13:1 Vulg.
12. Hos 8:4.
13. See 1 K (1 Sm) 13:9,13.
14. It is noteworthy that homage of clerics to laymen is not mentioned, see *Epp* 222, 348, 389, 390, 397.
15. Ps 82:13–14.
16. For excommunication of King Henry, see *Epp* 310, 349.
17. One of them might be Roger, bishop-elect of Salisbury, the others possibly John of Bath, Robert Bloet of Lincoln and Richard of Ely, see *Epp* 280, 308, 310.
18. See also *Ep* 348.

352. PASCHAL TO MATILDA, QUEEN OF THE ENGLISH.

Pope Paschal II urges Matilda, Queen of the English, to persuade her husband, King Henry, to give up investitures and obey the will of God so that he may not lose what God has given him. He threatens the King and his evil advisors with excommunication.

PASCHAL, THE BISHOP, SERVANT OF THE SERVANTS OF GOD: TO HIS DEAREST DAUGHTER MATILDA, QUEEN OF THE ENGLISH, GREETING AND APOSTOLIC BLESSING.

WE ARE GREATLY SADDENED about your husband because although he started well at the beginning of his reign he is now trying to spoil what follows. Now, having been placed in the fullness of power, he does not fear to provoke to fury the almighty Lord who was well-disposed to him in his need. We do not believe that you are unaware of what this husband of yours promised[1] the almighty Lord in faithful devotion when he first accepted the royal crown. Now he has taken over the churches through investitures[2] and he has expelled the holy man, Bishop Anselm, from the kingdom because he opposed his wicked deeds, and has taken on counsellors of perdition.[3] Therefore we fear greatly for his salvation since we love him dearly for his previous good deeds.

Therefore, beloved daughter, we beg you to watch more carefully over his keeping and to turn his heart away from wrong counsel so that he will not continue provoking God's fury so greatly against himself. Remember what the Apostle says: *The unbelieving husband will be saved by the believing wife.*[4] *Reprove, beseech, rebuke,*[5] so that he may reinstate the aforesaid bishop in his see and permit him to act and preach as his office demands, and also return the churches to his God lest God take from him what he has given.[6] Otherwise we can no longer endure it without smiting him and his counsellors, and those who unrightfully take possession of churches through him, with perpetual anathema.⁷ But if he consents to obey he will obtain the help of almighty God and the Apostolic See against all his enemies, and by the freedom of those churches he will gain protection within his kingdom through the grace of God.

January or February 1105.

NOTES

1. For the coronation charter promising liberties, see *Reg.* II 488; *EHD* II 400–402.
2. For royal investitures after Anselm's return from his first exile in September 1100, see *Epp* 280, 310; and after Christmas 1103, the beginning of Anselm's second exile, see *Epp* 305, 306.
3. The Pope referred to them in *Epp* 348, 351; he will excommunicate them, see *Ep* 353.
4. 1 Co 7:14.
5. 2 Tm 4:2.
6. See *Ep* 351.
7. For the threat of excommunication, see *Epp* 310, 349, 351.

353. FROM POPE PASCHAL.

Pope Paschal II informs Anselm of the decisions of the Lenten synod of 1105: that Count Robert of Meulan and his associates, who had encouraged the King to continue investitures, and those who had accepted investitures from the King, had been excommunicated. The same judgement on the King has been suspended until the arrival of the royal envoys at Easter.

PASCHAL, THE BISHOP, SERVANT OF THE SERVANTS OF GOD: TO HIS VENERABLE BROTHER ANSELM, ARCHBISHOP OF CANTERBURY, GREETING AND APOSTOLIC BLESSING.

THE MEMBERS OF THE CHURCH suffer greatly at the wrong done to you since, as the Apostle says: *If one member suffers, all the other members suffer with it.*¹ For although we are separated in body yet we are united in the Head.² We bear your wrongs and rejections³ as if they were our own. We are deeply distressed that your holiness is held back from the English kingdom.[4] For *the wolf* harries *and scatters*[5] the sheep that are without a shepherd.[6] Therefore we are laboring with all the means at our disposal for your return to them.[7]

Accordingly, at the Council[8] recently held it was decided by the unanimous judgement of our brothers and fellow bishops that the King's counsellors, who incite him to the shameful practice of investiture, and those who have been invested by him, should be driven away from the thresholds of the Church because they are trying to make a maidservant out of a free woman.[9] Accordingly, by the judgement of the Holy Spirit we have promulgated that sentence against the Count of Meulan[10] and his associates[11] and, by the judgement of the same Holy Spirit we confirm the same sentence against those who have been invested by the King.[12] Sentence[13] upon the King however, has been deferred because he must send his messengers to us at the coming feast of Easter.[14]

Given at the Lateran, on March twenty sixth.

26 March 1105.

NOTES

1. 1 Co 12:26.
2. See Col 1:18; Eph 1:22–23.
3. The King despoiled Anselm in January 1104, see *Epp* 306, 310, 316, 331, 349; *HN* 159; *VA* 132.
4. At the King's request Anselm went to Rome in summer 1103 and was told not to return to England at Christmas; see *Epp* 286, 306 and Itinerary 1:341.
5. Jn 10:12.
6. See *Ep* 366.
7. Pope Paschal is referring to the negotiations which had been taking place since 1101, see *Epp* 265, 338, 339, 348 and also *Ep* 379.
8. The Lenten synod of 1105 is referred to in *Epp* 348, 349.
9. See Gal 4:22ff; *Ep* 351.
10. Robert, Count of Meulan, was the chief counsellor of King Henry I, *OV* V: 298, 314–316; VI: 18, 328. He was the son of Roger Beaumont and Adeline, daughter of Waleran, Count of Meulan, see *EHD* II: 993. He fought at Hastings and was made Earl of Leicester, *OV* IV:

206, 338; VI, 20, and, in 1081, Count of Meulan. He married Isabel, daughter of Count Hugh of Vermendois, brother of King Philip I of France, *OV* III: 128. Robert died on 5 June 1118, *OV* VI: 188. See S. Vaughn, 'Robert of Meulan and Raison d'État in the Anglo-Norman State', *Albion* 10 (1979) 352–375 and *Anselm of Bec and Robert of Meulan, The Innocence of the Dove and the Wisdom of the Serpent* (Berkeley, 1987).
11. His associates may have been Richard of Reviers and Roger Bigod, see *OV* V:290; *Ep* 430.
12. See *Epp* 280, 308, 310.
13. See *Epp* 310, 349, 351, 352.
14. The Latin here and in *Ep* 354 reads *in praeteriti Paschae tempore*, *AOO* V, 293 line 17—'at the feast of Easter now just past'. The letter was 'given at the Lateran on March twenty-sixth'. In 1105, however, Easter was on 9 April and therefore the two statements do not agree. *Praeteriti*, although confirmed by MS Lambeth 59, letter 287, is probably a scribal error and the phrase should read *in praesenti Paschae tempore*—'at the coming feast of Easter'. This reading is confirmed by a copy of this letter sent by Anselm with copies of *Epp* 222, 281 to Bishop Lambert of Arras. There they were inserted into a collection of canonical material of the bishopric of Thérouanne, published by M. Sdralek, *Wolfenbüttler Fragmente* (Münster, 1891) 55–59; see also Blumenthal, Paschal, 30–31.

354. FROM POPE PASCHAL TO GERARD, ARCHBISHOP OF YORK.

Pope Paschal reprimands Archbishop Gerard of York for not having corrected his wrongdoing nor having been a help to Anselm. He orders him to publish the sentence of excommunication passed at the Lenten synod, 1105, on Count Robert of Meulan and his associates, and on those who received investitures. The judgement on the King is suspended until the arrival of his messengers at Easter.

PASCHAL, THE BISHOP, SERVANT OF THE SERVANTS OF GOD: TO GERARD, BISHOP OF YORK.[1]

THE KINDNESS OF THE APOSTOLIC SEE knows how to tolerate offending sons for a long time so that their misdeeds may be attended to by due correction. As far as you are concerned, the roman church has done this for some time already, but as yet you have scorned to correct your aberration.[2] You yourself know that we condescended to your promotion in the hope of your becoming the assistant and co-operator of our brother Anselm, Archbishop of Canterbury, in restraining the spread of evil in the kingdom of the English.[3] But, forgetful of our clemency, you have neither troubled yourself to assist that brother nor opposed royal injustice as you should have done according to your office, but you are said rather to curry favor.[4] We however, are still supporting you with the clemency of the Apostolic See with the intention that you should correct your aberrations, amend your past life and render us satisfaction as is fitting.

You should know however, that at the synod we celebrated last Lent[5] the King's counsellors, namely the Count of Meulan and those who incite the King to the shameful practice of investiture, were driven away from the thresholds of the churches by the judgement of the Holy Spirit, and that the same judgement was affirmed against those who have received investitures. We order that this should be made known to everyone by you. Sentence in this matter upon the King however, has been deferred because he must send his messengers to us at the coming feast of Easter.[6]

End of March 1105.

NOTES

1. Note lack of a greeting indicating the tone of the letter.
2. See *Ep* 283.
3. Gerard seems to have secretly abandoned his opposition to Anselm already, see *Epp* 326, 362, 363.
4. At the King's command and in opposition to Anselm's declared wish Gerard had been prepared to consecrate William, bishop-elect of Winchester, and Roger, bishop-elect of Salisbury, at Christmas 1102, *HN* 145–146; *Epp* 261, 265.
5. Compare this passage with *Ep* 353.
6. See *Ep* 353, note 13.

355. TO FARMAN, ORDWY, AND BENJAMIN, MONKS OF CANTERBURY.

Anselm explains to Farman, Ordwy and Benjamin, monks of Christ Church Canterbury, why they cannot come to him, advises them on their problems and admonishes them to patience. He also gives his reasons for not returning to England.

ANSELM THE ARCHBISHOP: TO HIS DEAREST SONS FARMAN, ORDWY[1] AND BENJAMIN, SENDING THE GREETING AND BLESSING OF GOD, AND HIS OWN.

I KNOW, DEAREST SONS, that the abundance of your love makes you long for my presence so that, as sons to a father, you may reveal what you bear in your hearts and receive advice for your individual difficulties. But although it is good and praiseworthy to have good zeal yet, if it is not *according to knowledge*[2] it is not acceptable to God.

You wish to have permission from me to come to me,[3] but it is certainly true that this is more difficult than you think, indeed almost impossible. The way is extremely long, the people are foreign, the journey is dangerous, and the monks of that country are captured, ill-treated, and their horses and whatever else they have are taken away from them. A large amount of money would be needed, the toil severe and the irregularities numerous whereas the advantages of it are not so great as to prevent others from thinking me blameworthy if I gave my consent to it easily. If you wish to inform me about the evils being done in England, and in the Church, which you see and hear, I know them well enough and cannot change them.[4] Tell them to God, and while waiting for him to put them right, pray! If you wish to seek counsel concerning your souls you have with you our venerable brother and son Dom Prior Ernulf,[5] a spiritual man, in whom both good will and wisdom abound by the grace of God and whom

I sent you in my place as my other self. Have recourse to him as if to me, trust him as you would me, accept him as myself. I concede the same to lord Bishop Gundulf[6] if anyone should desire it.

To you, my son Farman, who ask permission to live elsewhere because, as you say, you are unable to save your soul among so many disorders, I say that it would not be proper for me to start dispersing you as long as I cannot govern you or keep you together. Therefore it is not advisable either for you to ask this or for me to grant it. Accordingly, if I permit one or two either to leave the church in order to live elsewhere, or to leave the kingdom in order to come to me, there are so many who have the same reason that it could not be done without great scandal or great disintegration. Whoever wishes this, therefore, should have the same discretion and patience that others have so that you may all alike *possess your souls in patience.*[7]

To you also, my son Benjamin, who entreat me so terribly and allege the loss of your soul, I declare as to one whose soul I ought and wish to advise that you should not have done such an unreasonable thing nor should you have placed my soul and yours in such grave danger. For since you are driving my soul, as far as you can into such danger, be certain that this is not sound advice for your soul. What you request cannot reasonably be done. It might possibly be done through unreasonable and irregular rashness. For it is not rational to follow wherever the impulse of our soul drives us without discrimination, even if with a good intention. I cannot perceive that your soul is in danger of perdition just because you are not able to speak to me. If I were anywhere in this world which you could not possibly reach, or in the next life, yet you ought not to despair of the salvation of your soul. Therefore I beseech and advise you, dearest son, to bear what God's providence has in store for your soul without offence, and according to how you see him dispose of us and what belongs to us strive, as one who is reasonable and who has trust in God, to save yourself.

As to what you, my brother and son Ordwy, allege as reasons for my not returning to England: you should know that I am not fleeing death, nor the cutting off of my limbs, nor any torments whatsoever, but sin and dishonor to God's Church and above all, to that of Canterbury. For if I returned without making it clear that the King ought not to have despoiled me and usurped the possessions of the church which were entrusted to me, as he has done,[8] I would be confirming the bad, indeed the servile and wicked custom, for myself and my successors by my own example—which God avert from me! Unless therefore, he is willing to acknowledge his sin and render satisfaction to God for the wrong he has done and continues to do against me, so that neither he nor his successor could say to me or my successors that, because of my example, he had to do this according to custom, I cannot see at all, nor can anyone of rational mind, how I can agree with him or return to him while preserving the honor of God and of our church and the salvation of my soul. If he does to me what he ought to do, I shall do what I ought to do for the honor of God.

May the peace of God, which surpasses all understanding, keep your hearts and minds.[9] Amen.

1104 or 1105 while at Lyon.

NOTES

1. See *Epp* 327, 336.
2. Rm 10:2.
3. See Itinerary, 1: 342, Anselm spent the first part of his second exile at Lyon, Christmas 1103 - end April 1105.
4. Anselm was kept informed about the troubles and the situation in England by frequent letters whose writers often cited his absence as being their cause, see *Epp* 310, 327, 330, 336, 349, 365, 366.
5. At the request of the monks of Christ Church he had entrusted the care of their souls to Prior Ernulf, see *Ep* 312.

6. Bishop Gundulf of Rochester acted as Anselm's deputy during his absence, see *Epp* 314, 316, 330, 359, 374, 381.
7. Lk 21:19.
8. The King did so in January 1104: see *HN* 159; *VA* 132; *Ep* 310.
9. Ph 4:7.

356. TO HAIMO, THE SHERIFF.

Anselm admonishes Haimo, sheriff of Kent, to return what he had unjustly taken from his land and possessions.

ANSELM THE ARCHBISHOP: TO HAIMO,[1] THE SHERIFF, HIS FRIEND, GREETING AND BLESSING.

SOME TIME AGO I WROTE AND ASKED YOU, as a faithful friend of mine and of our church, to return the market[2] which you removed from our land to the place it was when I left England, and to return to me the tax which you took from our property in Fordwich[3] because nowhere in the whole of England should the possessions of our domain submit to such taxation, and particularly not within the boundary of our archbishopric. Up to now, as I have heard, you have done neither. Moreover, on the King's order our property was to remain untouched until my return, yet your men broke into our house at Sandwich[4] and seized our fish by force; and in the city of Canterbury they broke into another of our houses, on our land, and carried off all that was in it. Therefore I ask you, as a friend whom I should be able to trust, to return to me, as I have said, what has been taken from me, and not force me to complain to anybody else.[5] For not only should no wrongs befall me and our church through you but rather, as you well know, you should repel, as far as you can, those coming from elsewhere.

summer 1105.

NOTES

1. Haimo or Hamo, son of Haimo (Hamo) was sheriff of Kent like his father who died towards the end of the reign of William II. The younger Haimo died in 1129 or 1130, see *Ep* 474. Haimo's accomplice was William Calvellus, see *Ep* 358.
2. Anselm's previous letter to Haimo is not preserved. The market in question was on the land of Holy Trinity and St Augustine's Abbey, as mentioned in Domesday book. Haimo and William Calvellus seem to have moved it to a site more convenient and lucrative for themselves, see J.F.A. Mason, 'St Anselm's relations with Laymen', *Spicilegium Beccense* 1 (Paris, 1959) 548–549.
3. Fordwich, on the north coast of Kent, where the Archbishop had seven tenements, see J.F.A. Mason, ibid., 549. Haimo granted Fordwich to St Augustine's Abbey on the Monday before Easter, 1111, see W. Urry, *Canterbury under the Angevin Kings* (London, 1967) 63.
4. The whole port of Sandwich was held by the Archbishop for the maintenance of the monks at the Cathedral. The fish seized by Haimo were doubtless some of the forty thousand herrings which Sandwich rendered for the monks' table, in addition to the annual 'farm' of 40., see J.F.A. Mason, ibid., 548.
5. Anselm is here referring to the King; thus the letter must have been written after the reconciliation between King Henry and Anselm at l'Aigle, 21 July 1105, see J.F.A. Mason, ibid., 549–550.

357. TO ERNULF, PRIOR OF CANTERBURY.

Anselm shows compassion for Prior Ernulf's troubles. He is concerned about the wicked deeds of William Calvellus and is sending copies of his letters to Canterbury. He exhorts Prior Ernulf to encourage the brothers entrusted to him to practice patience and recommends the bearer of this letter to him.

ANSELM THE ARCHBISHOP: TO HIS REVEREND BROTHER, DOM PRIOR ERNULF, WHO DESERVES TO BE LOVED WITH TRUE AFFECTION, SENDING THE GREETING AND BLESSING OF GOD, AND HIS OWN, AS FAR AS HE CAN.

I LEARN NOT ONLY ABOUT YOUR SUFFERINGS and tribulations but also about those of the whole of England in many ways by flying rumors: but whereas it is my sole duty to have compassion according to present divine disposition, it rests with God alone to succor. As for what concerns me I cannot at this moment write anything other than what I told you through Odo of London[1] and what I have instructed the bearer of this letter to tell you by word of mouth. I am certain that the evil which William[2] is carrying out with regard to Eynesford, if he did not do it himself, he would have had it done by somebody else, and perhaps even worse. I am sending you copies of the letters I have sent concerning those things which you mentioned to me in your letter.[3]

Greet our brothers, whom God has entrusted through me to your care,[4] with holy and benevolent affection as you know to be fitting and as I ought to do, and console and strengthen them according to the wisdom which God has given you. Since they are neither the first, nor the only, nor the last servants of God[5] whom the tribulation of the world oppresses, instruct them often to embrace patience, following the example of others. Give each of the youths and children the friendly expression of my love, which I used to show them and which I still have and beg them, by beseeching them kindly, to remember my admonitions.

You would be kind to the bearer of this letter, who has often worked hard on our missions, if you mitigated his poverty a little at least by giving him some old clothes, or in any other way. Farewell.[6]

summer 1105.

NOTES

1. See *Ep* 359.
2. See *Ep* 358.
3. As Prior Ernulf's letter has not been preserved we do not know which letters Anselm sent to Canterbury. There is no reason why they should only be business letters, Southern, *Anselm*, 68. Anselm was using the enforced leisure of his second exile to revise the texts

of his philosophical and theological works (see *Ep* 334) and preparing a final edition of his letters from abroad (see *Epp* 364, 379 and Introduction above, volume 1:32–39).
4. See *Epp* 312, 355.
5. See RB 7:35.
6. About the same time as *Ep* 356.

358. TO WILLIAM CALVELLUS.

Anselm admonishes William Calvellus of Canterbury to return the market belonging to the Archbishop, which he had removed to another place, to where it had been before Anselm left England or risk excommunication.

ANSELM THE ARCHBISHOP: TO WILLIAM CALVELLUS,[1] SENDING GREETING AND BLESSING.

I AM STILL GREETING YOU AS A FRIEND and son until I find out whether your friendship is pure and sincere or not. Up to now you have acted towards our church and myself so as to appear to deserve the grace of God for it and to have our friendship. But now I hear that you have transferred the market from our territory and taken it away from me and the church of Christ, your mother. Everything belongs to that church, and what belongs to the church belongs to me. Therefore I admonish you, and I beseech you as friend to friend and as bishop to his Christian son, to restore the market to our territory as it was when I left England if you do not wish to incur the wrath of God, to lose my friendship and that of the whole church which you had up to now, and to subject yourself, together with those with whose advice and help you have been doing this, to the most severe excommunication. Farewell, and I advise you to do without delay and in a friendly manner what I ordered you in a friendly manner to do.

summer 1105.

NOTES

1. William Calvellus was the accomplice of Haimo, sheriff of Kent, in their actions against the Archbishop's rights and property, see *Ep* 356. Calvellus was port reeve of Canterbury at the end of the eleventh and beginning of the twelfth century and founder of the convent of the sisters of St Sepulchre in Canterbury. His family was influential into the thirteenth century, see W. Urry, 'The Normans in Canterbury', *Annales de Normandie*, 8 (1958) 133–138, and *Canterbury under the Angevin Kings* (London, 1967) 62–64, 124–128, 140–144 and passim.

359. TO GUNDULF, BISHOP OF ROCHESTER.

Anselm apologizes to Bishop Gundulf of Rochester, who is acting as his deputy, that he cannot write any more about himself than what he has already learned from Odo of London and the bearer of this letter. He instructs him to tell William fitz Rodulf that he is giving the chrism money William is demanding for the needs of the monastery. He asks Haimo, the sheriff of Kent, not to allow the injustice of William Calvellus, about which he has written to Calvellus, to continue.

ANSELM, THE ARCHBISHOP: TO HIS TRUE FRIEND, THE REVEREND BISHOP GUNDULF,[1] GREETING.

CONCERNING MY AFFAIRS I can write nothing else to you at the moment except what I told your reverence through Odo of London, and what I have entrusted to the bearer of this letter to report by word of mouth.[2]

I hear that William, son of Rodulf, is demanding from Dom Prior Ernulf the money which priests are accustomed to give at the time when they receive the chrism[3] and which has already been spent for the work of the monastery, and which is still to be paid unless he learns that I am giving it for this purpose. Your holiness should know therefore, and tell this to William, that as far as I am able I grant this money, and if I could grant more I would do so.

I have been told that William Calvellus has transferred the market from our land, where it used to be, and has taken it away from me and our church.[4] Therefore, in a letter which you should ask him to show you, I admonished him to correct without delay what he had done wrong. For this reason I instruct you to meet the sheriff[5] and his wife, our daughter, with a greeting on our behalf, and to admonish him, asking him not to permit this injury to be done to us since we must trust in him. For although at the moment violent injustice is being done to me, yet thanks to the judgement of God my justice, which he will one day demand, is not lost. Admonish him also to listen to the letter[6] I sent to Calvellus on this matter. Farewell.

summer 1105.

NOTES

1. Gundulf acted as Anselm's deputy during his absence from England, see *Epp* 287, 299, 300, 331, 355, 374, 384.
2. See *Ep* 357.
3. The bishop blessed the chrism during the *missa chrismatis* in the cathedral on the morning of Maundy Thursday, and the priests of the diocese came to him to obtain what they needed for baptism and extreme unction throughout the year. Thus the chrism money was paid during Holy Week, see F. Barlow, *The English Church, 1000–1066* (London, 1963) 180–182.
4. See *Epp* 356, 357, 358.
5. Haimo, sheriff of Kent, see *Ep* 356.
6. See *Ep* 358.

360. TO WILLIAM, ARCHDEACON OF CANTERBURY.

Anselm reprimands William, Archdeacon of Christ Church, Canterbury, for his friendship with Peter and Salome who are living in his house, even after they had insulted Anselm and the church of Canterbury.

ANSELM, THE ARCHBISHOP: TO WILLIAM,[1] THE ARCHDEACON, SENDING GREETING AND BLESSING.

I LOVE AND PRAISE THE GOOD you are doing but if I hear that you are doing anything which is not fitting for you I ought not to refrain from telling you. I think you can recall how grave and serious was the matter which once established close friendship between me and you, and the conversation of Peter and Salome[2] which they had with you after they tried to inflict as much insult and ignominy as they could upon me and our church, the like of which we have never had to suffer from anybody. Now however, I hear that they, if as rejoicing over the effect of their design and insulting the church, live on friendly terms with you in your house, nourished by your generosity and, from your house by their presence they daily recall to mind the injury which they inflicted. How and in what manner we are to consider this, your prudence can recognize not only by yourself but also conclude from the aforesaid matter which was between me and you, and which is now written down and preserved by us. Consequently, ask your faithful wisdom what you ought to do. Farewell.

summer 1105.

NOTES

1. See *Epp* 208, 257, 374, 380, 474.
2. Peter and Salome do not appear anywhere else in Anselm's letters.

361. POPE PASCHAL TO ROBERT, COUNT OF MEULAN.

Pope Paschal II writes to Robert, Count of Meulan, that he has heard that the Count continues to persuade the King to resist the decrees forbidding lay investiture. Paschal offers remission of his sin if he is willing to obey but the wrath of God if he remains obstinate.

PASCHAL, THE BISHOP, SERVANT OF THE SERVANTS OF GOD: TO HIS BELOVED SON ROBERT,[1] COUNT OF MEULAN, SENDING GREETING AND APOSTOLIC BLESSING.

WE ACCEPTED YOU IN FRIENDSHIP and we believed you were our companion in the service of the affairs of God and Saint Peter. You actually promised that to us in your second letter.[2] However, those who know you[3] have been saying something different about you for a long time. They say that almost alone, or before everyone else, you alone are persuading the King of the English to resist the Roman Church in the matter of investitures.[4] If this is true, we are greatly disappointed in you, whose very age[5] should suggest a turning towards the Lord. Therefore, on the one hand, as one who obeys, we offer you the absolution of your sins and the grace of the Lord; on the other hand, as one who does not obey and who consents to such great evil,[6] we threaten you with the wrath of the Lord. We declare that we shall not suffer this any longer[7] without this shameful deed taking its vengeance on you.

before 26 March 1105.

NOTES

1. See *Ep* 353.
2. This letter is not preserved.
3. Possibly Anselm's messengers, such as Baldwin, Alexander and Eadmer as well as Anselm. For Eadmer's description of Count Robert, see *HN* 40, 86, 163, 170, 191–192, 207.
4. See *Epp* 353, 354.

5. As Robert took part in the Battle of Hastings in 1066 he was probably born in the mid-forties, which would make him about sixty years old when this letter was written.
6. See *Ep* 353.
7. This phrase dates the letter before 26 March 1105 when Count Robert's excommunication was pronounced, see *Epp* 353, 354, 364.

362. GERARD, ARCHBISHOP OF YORK, TO POPE PASCHAL.

Gerard, Archbishop of York, thanks Pope Paschal II for his letter of the end of March. He replies that the charge it contained was caused by a false report about him and asserts that he always favored Anselm's cause; the letters he wrote to Anselm and those he is appending will demonstrate how he supported him.

TO HIS FATHER AND LORD, PASCHAL, THE SUPREME PONTIFF: GERARD, SERVANT OF THE CHURCH OF YORK, SENDING HIS SUBJECTION, SERVICE AND OBEDIENCE.

YOUR HOLY AND LOVABLE PATERNITY did not disdain to visit the son who, although separated by the breadth of countries and seas, is close to you in affection and obedience, and the everlasting manna of life filled my soul with the sweet dew of your letter.[1] I saw, dearest father, and I rejoice to have seen your letter in which the sweetness of your charity overflows; nor was the rod of correction missing, castigating the flesh so that it would not rise up against the spirit, and strengthening the spirit so that it could dominate the subdued flesh. If there was anything bitter in the sweetness of the letter of your Holiness it was the false report[2] about me which caused this to happen. Indeed, if the desire of my soul could be satisfied so that I might be worthy of coming into the presence of your Holiness once more, you would know that my behavior in the church whose care you entrusted to me has not been unfaithful to you nor dishonorable to the Church up to now, and that, by the grace of God, it will be better instructed by your admonition and better corrected by your castigation.

I have always supported the cause of the venerable and prime Archbishop of Canterbury with prayers,[3] even in that matter where God opened the door for me.[4] As soon as I saw in your letter what I am supposed to have done to this man: on the contrary, the letters I wrote to him display without any falsity how I joined myself to him, as far as I could, in carrying the burden of the church, and I beg your Holiness to deign to look at them.[5]

May God preserve your Holiness unharmed for his Church.

c. June 1105.

NOTES

1. See *Ep* 354.
2. Gerard is referring to his part in Anselm's quarrels with Kings William II and Henry I, see *Epp* 200, 261, 265, 283; and Introduction above, volume 1:10–15, 20–23.
3. Gerard's actions were not always consistent with this statement, e.g. when he returned from Pope Paschal in August 1102 with a 'verbal message' *HN* 137–138, and when he was willing to obey Henry's command to consecrate the bishops-elect of Winchester and Salisbury at Christmas 1102, see *Epp* 261, 354; *HN* 144–146.
4. Gerard is referring to his consecration as Bishop of Hereford on 15 June 1096, when he made his profession of obedience to the Archbishop of Canterbury, see *Ep* 200; for his profession as Archbishop of York, see *Epp* 283, 354.
5. Gerard's letters to Anselm: *Epp* 255, 326, 363, 373, 386, 440, 444.

363. FROM GERARD, ARCHBISHOP OF YORK.

Archbishop Gerard of York thanks Anselm for his letter. He wishes he could speak to him personally but assures him that, since he has arrived at the truth, he and many others will be obedient to Anselm. He is sending Anselm a copy of the letter he received from the Pope as requested by his messenger.

TO THE FATHER: THE SON SENDS GREETING AND OBEDIENCE.[1]

I AM WRITING TO YOU, reverend father, for the moment passing over our names in silence, since this could bring little advantage but much disadvantage. I received your letter[2] as a sweltering man does the shade, or a thirsting man the fountain. I am happy that you wrote, though sad that you had to write. If only I were there or you were here, where we could cease writing letters and speak to one another face to face! You should really know that my soul has been clinging to you,[3] you should know that my heart truly and sincerely loves you, largely because of your kindness to me, but most of all because I know you to be the dwelling-place of the Holy Spirit.[4]

You are an exile for the sake of your loyalty to mother Church, an exile on earth, a citizen of the heavenly Jerusalem, an exile in the body. My soul is an exile with you, and I am prepared to undergo bodily exile as well if you should order it. You who are inebriated[5] by the wonderful chalice of Christ have disdained to be inebriated by the golden chalice of Babylon.[6] The charity which brought God to earth in order to redeem you has removed you for a time from the riches of this world so that you may serve God.[7] You know how to endure, for the sake of Christ, for the sake of religion—if only you would wish to fight in the same way! Nothing is more senseless than to wish to conquer by patience and kind meekness those whose strength increases through patience, is exasperated by meekness and sharpened by kindness. You have poured oil on our wounds, but the stench increases; pour wine as well, mindful that the Samaritan ordered this.[8] You have applied soothing remedies[9] and yet everywhere the rotting flesh grows rank. Apply the iron if you wish to heal, apply the fire if your heart is on fire with the fire of the Holy Spirit. Those whom you accuse of disobedience accuse you of idleness and negligence. In the church which Christ has entrusted to you he has supports covered with hay and stubble[10] as long as you act indecisively; but when it comes to the point concerning the matters which are Christ's they will openly support the Church by obeying you.

Someone who has received the power of consecrating the Body and Blood of the Lord from you through ordination[11] would be irreverent and rash if, despite your prohibition, a prohibition made for the sake of Christ,[12] he was not a consecrator but a violator and a profaner. You do not know what is in your power because you do not wish to know. But you should know one thing, namely that the church entrusted to you not only pays tribute but has become the tribute of the treasury. You can count on my obedience to the point that I may not have to answer your accusation of disobedience on the Day of Judgement. Pray for me. May the favor of divine grace so assist me that I do not promise great things before temptation and deny them in temptation at the word of the maidservant.[13]

Most beloved father, I received the letter of our venerable father,[14] and my heart rejoiced exceedingly at the blessing contained in it. Although it touched me in a way I did not deserve, yet its rebuke is sweeter to me *than honey and the honeycomb.*[15] It admonishes me about your cause, or rather ours, and I rejoice at the admonition. It imposes a rather difficult act of obedience[16] but I will carry it out as far as I can. I belong to you because you belong to God. I am sending you a copy of the letter as you instructed through your messenger, trusting in your holy faith, whatever you wish.

June or July 1105.

NOTES

1. As in *Ep* 326 Gerard has omitted the names.
2. Anselm's letter to Gerard is not preserved.
3. See Ps 62:8, and compare these lines with the assurance he gave Pope Paschal that he always favored Anselm's cause, see *Ep* 362.
4. See 1 Co 6:19.
5. See Ps 22:5.
6. See Jer 51:7.
7. Gerard is alluding to the confiscation of the revenues of the archbishopric by King Henry from January 1104 to July 1105, *HN* 159, 165–166; *Epp* 310, 331; *VA* 132; he does not mention the reconciliation between Anselm and King Henry, which took place at l'Aigle on 21–22 July 1105, see *Ep* 364; *HN* 166.
8. See Lk 10:34.
9. See RB 28:3.
10. See 1 Co 3:12.
11. Anselm ordained Gerard priest on 7 June 1096 and the following day consecrated him Bishop of Hereford; see *Epp* 200, 212.
12. At Michaelmas 1100, Anselm proclaimed the papal decrees on lay investiture and homage of clerics to laymen for the first time in England; see *HN* 119–120; *VA* 127.
13. See Mt 26:29.
14. Pope Paschal's letter to Gerard, *Ep* 354.
15. Ps 18:11.
16. Pope Paschal ordered Gerard to publish the excommunication of the King's chief counsellor, Robert of Meulan and his associates, promulgated by the Lenten synod of 1105, see *Epp* 353, 354.

364. TO PRIOR ERNULF AND THE MONKS OF CANTERBURY.

Anselm informs Prior Ernulf and the monks of Canterbury about his reconciliation with the King at l'Aigle on 21 July 1105 when the King reinvested him with the archbishopric. The King also promised to reach an agreement with the Pope by Christmas, but until this comes about Anselm will not return to England. Anselm reaffirms the canons of the synod of Westminster on celibacy. Since the Count of Meulan has promised to persuade the King to obey the Pope's command, his excommunication has been lifted, but the sentence on those who had received investiture and those who had consecrated them remains unchanged. He rejoices at Prior Ernulf's recovery from his recent illness.

ANSELM, THE ARCHBISHOP: TO HIS DEAREST BROTHERS AND SONS, DOM PRIOR ERNULF AND THE OTHERS SERVING GOD UNDER HIM AT CHRIST CHURCH, CANTERBURY, SENDING THEM THE GREETING AND BLESSING OF GOD AND HIS OWN, AS FAR AS HE CAN.

THAT I DELAYED WRITING TO YOU for so long about what was agreed between the King and myself on the eve of the feast of St Mary Magdalen[1] was not due to negligence but to a lack of opportunity which there is no need to explain. Know that the King has reinvested me with our archbishopric and he promises to return what he has received of our revenues up to now. He himself says that he does this with great joy and goodwill, and all those who are with him proclaim that they are glad about it. The King hopes for an agreement between the lord Pope and himself before the next day of the Nativity of the Lord so that I can be in agreement with them both in England without offending either. For this purpose he has arranged to send his messenger to Rome so that he can obtain certainty in the matter before the set date. But since the matter has not yet reached that certainty of peace and harmony between them, so that if I now returned to England I could without any doubt be confident of remaining there in peace, I have chosen to remain for a while out of England until the aforesaid messenger returns from Rome[2]—provided that in the meantime the possessions of the archbishopric are under my control and our people are in peace—rather than to put myself into an ambiguous situation for the moment and perhaps be forced to leave England once more on account of an insurmountable disagreement. Indeed I consider that the delay in my return will in no way harm the final agreement which we hope will come.

As regards the priests about whom the King decreed[3] that they could have both churches and wives as they had at the time of his father and Archbishop Lanfranc: since the King has repossessed me with the whole archbishopric and since at the time of his father and the archbishop such execrable unions had been forbidden by the Council,[4] I confidently enjoin, by the authority I have from the archbishopric, that not only in the archbishopric but throughout the whole of England all priests who have kept their wives shall be deprived of their churches and of every ecclesiastical benefice.

The lord Pope recently sent his greeting and blessing to the Count of Meulan on this condition, namely that he would uphold the freedom of the Church which up to now he has appeared to oppose.[5] If he does not, however, the Pope forbade him alone to enter the church just as he had previously done with regard to him and other associates of his who were advisors to the King, in a letter,[6] a copy of which I have sent to you.[7] But since the Count promised[8] me that he would try to make the King obey the Pope's commands, I permitted him to enter the church from which he has been kept away.[9] About the others, no one is named in the aforesaid letter,[10] nor can I name anyone for sure and, as I hear, everybody is relying on the agreement between the Pope and the King. The sentence has not been changed for those who received investitures and those who consecrated them.[11]

We give thanks to God that you, Dom Prior, as you have said, are recovering from your sickness and we pray to God that he may restore you to full health.

May almighty God always protect you, my dearest brothers and sons, with his grace, and make you continually grow towards better things. Amen.

July or August 1105 while at Bec.

NOTES

1. 22 July. Anselm had left Lyon at the end of April 1105 with the intention of excommunicating King Henry, see *Ep* 353; *HN* 163–164. Henry was about to conquer Normandy, see *HN* 175; *ASC* 1105 in *EHD* II 179. In order to avoid an aggravation of the conflict between the King and Anselm, Countess Adela of Blois and Chartres (see *Epp* 286, 340, 388) arranged a meeting at l'Aigle, see *HN* 164–167. Anselm did not excommunicate Henry and lifted the papal excommunication on Count Robert of Meulan (see *Epp* 353, 354). Henry reinvested Anselm with the archbishopric and promised to reach an agreement with the Pope by Christmas 1105, that he would give up investiture of bishops and abbots by conferring ring and staff, but retain the right to secure homage from the elect before consecration, see *HN* 186; *HC* 13, 14; *Ep* 181. When the King had obtained what he needed, i.e. the backing of the Church for his campaign against his brother Duke Robert, he was in no hurry to fulfill his promise, see *Epp* 367, 368, 369, 370, 371, 377, 378, and N. Cantor, *Church, Kingship and Lay Investiture in England* (Princeton, 1958) 258. For the negotiations and continuous exchange of messengers preparing this agreement, see *Epp* 338, 339, 348, 354.
2. Eadmer gives another reason for Anselm's delay in returning to England. The King had demanded that Anselm should not 'withhold his fellowship from any of those who had accepted investiture of churches from him or from those who had consecrated them', *HN* 166; see also *Epp* 280, 308, 310, 351; *HN* 148. Anselm would not consent to this demand 'as he was determined not to act in any way in breach of obedience to the Pope', *HN* 166–168. The ensuing negotiations and Anselm's illness delayed his return until early September 1106.
3. *ASC*, ed. Plummer (Oxford, 1952) 260; *Epp* 391, 392, 393, 394; W. Fröhlich, 'Ubi unus clericus et Aelfgyfa', *Liber ad Magistrum für J. Spörl* (München, 1964) 59.

4. Anselm is referring to the synod of Winchester, April 1076. Its statute forbade canons to have wives; the parish clergy who were married should not be forced to part from their wives; those not married should not take wives, and henceforth no bishop should ordain deacons who had not promised to live a celibate life, Mansi, XX, 459; W. Fröhlich, 'ubi unus', 55. Compare this with canons 4, 5, 6 of the Council of Westminster, HN 142.
5. See Ep 361.
6. See Epp 353, 354, both from Pope Paschal on this matter.
7. See Epp 357, 379.
8. Count Robert of Meulan was with the King in Normandy from the beginning of April 1105; see OV VI: 60–68. Having received the Pope's letter excommunicating him, Ep 361, dated March 1105, in May or June, he communicated with Anselm either in person or by letter. See also Ep 388.
9. Anselm seems to be transgressing papal rights by absolving Robert de Meulan from papal excommunication on his own account, see Epp 361, 388.
10. See Ep 353.
11. See Epp 308, 351.

365. ANONYMOUS TO ANSELM.

An anonymous person writes that the prolonged quarrel between King Henry and Anselm seems to him nothing but a diabolical trick and that it is causing the destruction of the whole church of the English. He complains about various abuses and attributes them to Anselm's absence.

DEAREST FATHER AND LORD,[1] ALTHOUGH YOU KNOW BEST WHAT YOU OUGHT TO DO AND WHAT YOU WISH TO DO, YET TO NEARLY EVERY WISE MAN OF SOUND UNDERSTANDING THE MATTER BEING NEGOTIATED BETWEEN YOURSELF AND THE KING WITH SUCH PROTRACTED EXPECTATION SEEMS TO BE NOTHING ELSE BUT THE ILLUSION OF DEVILISH FRAUD AND A LUDICROUS DELAY, AND—TO SPEAK YET MORE PLAINLY—THE DAILY DIMINUTION AND TOTAL DESTRUCTION OF THE WHOLE CHURCH OF THE ENGLISH AND OF CHRISTIAN LAW AND RELIGION.[2]

THE POSSESSIONS OF THE CHURCHES which have remained so long widowed of their pastors are plundered, and the practice of holy religion which has been neglected in them is being wiped out altogether. The guardians of the christian law are no longer its guardians but rather its destroyers, and following the decision of the royal will and its inclination they have become perverters of practically all justice. What can I say of the clergy who have nearly all returned to their former wickedness? What of the laity? They, but most of all the princes, take to themselves wives almost always of their own kin, get betrothed secretly, hold on to their betrothed, knowing this to be against the law of the Church, and defend themselves. What of sodomites, whom you yourself excommunicated in the great Council[3] until they do penance and make confession? And what of the long-haired men whom you, just after the Easter celebration, robed in your episcopal vestments, expelled in view of the whole people from the threshold of holy Church?[4] What are we to say when you, who should do so, give no help, and there is not a single person in the whole kingdom who would dare to reprove or try to improve these things and much else that is repugnant to God and to every servant of God in your place? If you wish to hear the truth, I confess that all these things have become much worse than could be described in writing, so much so that even the King himself now declares that never in this country has wickedness been as brazen as it is now.

All these things, without any doubt, are your concern alone and are imputed to your Holiness. Look then, and consider the burden you have taken on and to whom you have committed the duty of carrying it out in your place, while you, who have been appointed to oppose such evils, absent yourself for such a long time from the kingdom in which these evils are being practiced for no reason at all. Consider also, if it pleases you, whether your heart is so lost in God alone[5] and you yourself are already living in such quiet composure that you need not stoop to such great misery of souls and can leave the care of them to others. I know, and I know well that you know best what it is that you are doing; but that you yourself should know that it is of very little use to us. We do not yet see any good result, useful to the community, coming from your lengthy negotiation. But we do see evils, for which you alone are responsible, daily increasing everywhere in the Church of God and among the people of God.

summer 1105, most likely before 21 July.

NOTES

1. Eadmer states that the letter was sent 'by a man of no mean standing', HN 167. The *Vita Gundulfi* attributes this letter to Gundulf, supposing that he sent it to Anselm in Lyon (PL 159, 835) while Eadmer says that Anselm was at Bec when he received it. For Anselm's moves in the spring and summer of 1105, see Itinerary, volume 1:342.
2. Similar charges are made in *Epp* 310, 327, 330, 336, 355, 366.
3. Council of Westminster, Michaelmas 1102; the writer is referring to canons 4, 5, 6, 22, 24, 28, see HN 142–143.
4. Council of Westminster, canon 23; in Normandy Bishop Serlo of Séez did the same thing; see *OV* VI: 64–66.
5. This phrase recalls a sentence at the beginning of chap. 1 of the *Proslogion*: 'Attend for a while to God and rest for a time in him', AOO I: 97. This shows familiarity with Anselm's works and suggests the possibility that the anonymous author was Abbot Gilbert Crispin of Westminster. That *Ep* 366 from Gilbert deals with the same matter in poetic form strengthens this surmise.

366. FROM GILBERT, ABBOT OF WESTMINSTER.

Gilbert Crispin, Abbot of Westminster, describes the evils which have invaded the church in England because of the pastor's absence and beseeches Anselm to return to his flock.

The clear reed pipe[1]
was wont to tell your praises

in a measured melody;
now it sings
in a hoarse murmur
full of mourning.
And it says:
Why are you far from
the sheep, O shepherd?
The flock without a guide
wanders from the path;
no one leads it back.
The flock seeks pasture—
not knowing what is suitable
it feeds on harmful things—
thus the whole flock
is sick and dying.
The cunning enemy goes round;
he eyes the fold
of the abandoned sheep,
and from all sides freely
he comes in and goes,
goes out and comes;
no one drives him off.
He bares his wolfish wrath,
chasing the flock within—
no one resists him.
He overthrows everything,
everything is killed,
the weak, the fat,
the lambs and the sheep.
Indeed nothing satisfies
the gluttony of the wolves;
one wolf does not consider
a thousand thousands enough.
Realize that many wolves are within,
and see the great carnage
that comes upon the abandoned flock

from every side.
The one who entrusted them to you,
I say,
will want them back,
for everyone seeks what
he has entrusted to others.
You, I think,
will restore them—
after all, they were
entrusted to you.
No one denies that
what is due must be repaid[2]
and so you must fear.
Indeed many thousands he seeks—
entrusted to your sheepfold
they are lost.
The whole of England,
a populous people
the whole of Scotland
a long island, longer than these,
a numerous people
and they are Irish:
when were such large kingdoms
seen before?
Nobody has seen them.
Year after year passes by.
and so you must fear.

summer, 1105.

NOTES

1. This poem is similar in tone to *Epp* 310, 327, 330, 336, 355, 365, 386. Gilbert Crispin wrote his complaint in the form of a poem; see A.J. Robinson, *Gilbert Crispin, Abbot of Westminster* (Cambridge, 1911) 83; *The Works of Gilbert Crispin*, ed A.S. Abulafia, G.R. Evans (Oxford, 1986) 181-182. It was probably intended not only for Anselm but for wider circulation.

2. This line may be an oblique reference to the reasoning in Anselm's *Cur Deus Homo*, in whose argumentation Gilbert himself had been involved, see *AOO* II: 71; R.W. Southern, 'St Anselm and Gilbert Crispin', *Medieval and Renaissance Studies*, 3 (1954) 78–115; Southern, *Anselm*, 90–91.

367. FROM KING HENRY.

Henry, King of the English, apologizes for the delay in dispatching his envoy to Rome. He asks that Baldwin of Tournai accompany William de Warelwast to Rome.

TO THE MOST REVEREND AND MOST LOVING FATHER ANSELM, ARCHBISHOP OF CANTERBURY: HENRY, BY THE GRACE OF GOD, KING OF THE ENGLISH, SENDING GREETING AND HIS AFFECTION AND GOOD WILL.[1]

VENERABLE FATHER, let it not displease you that I have so long put off the journey of those whom I decided to send to Rome to carry out my business there.[2] This delay[3] will soon appear profitable to you when William de Warelwast, whom I am sending to Rome to carry out this business, as we decided, reaches you. I humbly pray and devoutly beseech you to send Baldwin of Tournai with William to Rome to handle our suit and, God willing, to bring it to a conclusion. Farewell.

August or September 1105.

NOTES

1. This letter was written in August or early September 1105, *Reg.* II, 691, and reached Anselm at Rheims, where he was staying with Archbishop Manasses; see *HN* 168–169; Itinerary, volume 1:342.
2. He is referring to the agreement of l'Aigle, 21 July 1105; see *Ep* 364.
3. This was not the only delay, see *Epp* 368, 369, 370, 371, 377, and also *Ep* 364.

368. TO HENRY, KING OF THE ENGLISH.

Anselm thanks King Henry of the English for addressing him in such an honorable way but shows concern about the delay of the royal envoy. Since God is greatly displeased that he is still separated from his office without cause, he entreats the King to set a time for his envoy to go to Rome.

TO HIS DEAREST LORD HENRY, GLORIOUS KING OF THE ENGLISH: ANSELM, ARCHBISHOP OF CANTERBURY, SENDING HIS FAITHFUL SERVICE WITH PRAYERS.

I GIVE GREAT THANKS, as I should, that your Majesty greets me so honorably and with such affection and good will in your letter.[1] Certainly, as far as I am able, I ought not to treat lightly your request, in which you so humbly ask me not to be displeased that the messenger you are sending to Rome is delayed for so long. But it is God's cause rather than mine, and for that reason, with a faithful heart and a kind spirit, I tell you what I must not keep silent about.

Surely, anything displeasing to me, except when it displeases me for God's sake, is unimportant; but anything displeasing to God must not be taken lightly on any account. Certainly it is greatly displeasing to God that a bishop should be despoiled of his possessions—a wrong which by the inspiration of God's grace you have now corrected[2]—but God judges most severely that a bishop be separated from his office and a church from its bishop without a cause which God would approve. So it is expedient for your soul that you see to it that I—whatever sort of person I may be—a bishop of a church which God entrusted to your royal power to be protected, be restored as speedily as possible to your kingdom in your peace, and that I may no longer be deprived of the opportunity of carrying out, as far as I am able, the office for which I was placed there.[3]

Moreover, I am greatly afraid that God may be displeased and the lord Pope rightly censure me because, since you and I met at the town called l'Aigle,[4] all this time I have not sent him our messenger. Through him the Pope should learn what has taken place between us in a matter of such importance and what is still to be done, and I should obtain for myself his advice and instructions. For this reason it is dangerous for me to wait so long for your messenger, whom I expected to return from Rome before next Christmas, as I understood you to have said, especially since—I do not know on whose advice or for what reason—you do not even now give me a fixed date. Since I am bound to be more concerned that I am unable to be present in the church entrusted to me than about any worldly possessions, I beseech you to give me in a letter of yours some early date when I can expect your messenger to go to Rome, because—to state the latest date—I dare not delay sending my own messenger any later than after next Christmas. Farewell.

September or October 1105 while at Rheims.

NOTES

1. See *Ep* 367.
2. See *Ep* 364.
3. For the reasons for Anselm's delay in returning to England see *Ep* 364. For Henry's delays in sending his messenger to Rome, see *Epp* 370, 371, 377.
4. The meeting took place in Aquila, the modern l'Aigle, on 21 and 22 July 1105; see *Epp* 364, 369; *HN* 164–167; *VA* 134.

369. TO ROBERT, COUNT OF MEULAN.

Anselm admonishes Count Robert of Meulan, the King's chief counsellor, to encourage the King to fulfill his promise or experience God's wrath for having kept Anselm out of England and prevented him from doing his duty.

ANSELM, THE ARCHBISHOP: TO HIS LORD AND FRIEND ROBERT,[1] COUNT OF MEULAN, GREETING.

YOU KNOW THAT WHEN THE KING AND I MET at the town of l'Aigle[2] it was said that the King would send his messenger to Rome to deal with those matters on which we could not agree without the help of the lord Pope. I understood that this would be done so that the messenger could return before next Christmas. But, as you see, my lord the King is now delaying what he then said he would do but he only tells me, who wanted to send my messenger with his, that I am not to be displeased because his messenger has been delayed so long, and does not give me any date by which he will come.[3] Consequently some people are thinking and saying that the King is not very anxious to hasten my return to England. Nor is he anxious that the Church of God, which God entrusted to him for its protection, and which has now been left desolate for nearly three years,[4] although its pastor is alive, should be comforted by his return and presence and be gladdened by the spiritual guidance of which it has so long been deprived in those who love and long for his returns.[5]

For this reason I tell you that I fear greatly that the King might provoke the wrath of God against himself and against those by whose advice he puts off fulfilling such a necessary and reasonable matter, which it is his duty to do and which he can do without losing anything of what belongs to the royal power according to the will of God. As friend and as archbishop, whatever sort of person I may be, I advise the King and those about him not to strive to satisfy their own will more than the will of God because God may one day satisfy his will against the will of those who act in this way. Give him counsel therefore and take counsel for yourselves before God shows his wrath, which up to now he has held back while waiting for you to bow to his will.

May God guide him and his advisors to his true honor and true advantage. Amen.

September or October 1105, while at Rheims.

NOTES

1. Anselm suspects Count Robert (see *Epp* 353, 361), from whom he had recently lifted the ban of excommunication (see *Ep* 364), of being the cause of the King's repeated delays in fulfilling the promises of l'Aigle, 21 July 1105, *Epp* 364, 368. Eadmer asserts that Robert was chiefly responsible for the King's delays, and states that the count of Meulan continued to be hostile to the Church, *HN* 192, 207–209.
2. 21 and 22 July 1105, see *Epp* 364, 368.
3. See *Ep* 367.
4. Anselm had left England on 27 April 1103.
5. Another twelve months would pass before Anselm could return to England, early in September 1106.

370. FROM HENRY, KING OF THE ENGLISH.

King Henry of the English informs Anselm that due to unfavorable weather conditions his messenger, William de Warelwast, did not leave for Rome at Michaelmas 1105.

HENRY, KING OF THE ENGLISH: TO ANSELM, ARCHBISHOP OF CANTERBURY, HIS MOST BELOVED FATHER, GREETING.

I AM INFORMING YOU that I would have sent William de Warelwast to you on the feast of St Michael[1] and from there to Rome on the business which I and you have discussed with each other concerning the Roman see if gales at sea, high waves and contrary winds had not detained him.

Witnessed by Waldric,[2] the chancellor, at Wycombe.

October 1105.

NOTES

1. 29 September 1105, *Reg.* II, 692.
2. Waldric became chancellor towards the end of 1102, either soon after Michaelmas or at Christmas, in succession to Roger le Poer, *Ep* 280, who was nominated to the see of Salisbury in September 1102. Waldric accompanied Henry to Normandy in 1106 and captured Duke Robert at the battle of Tinchebrai on 28 September, 1106. He became Bishop of Laon under somewhat scandalous circumstances towards the end of the year and never returned to England as chancellor, see *Reg.* II, ix, and H.W.C. Davis, 'Waldric the Chancellor of Henry I', *EHR* 26 (1911) 84–89. He was murdered on 25 April 1115 during a riot of the townsfolk of Laon, *OV* VI: 90.

371. FROM HENRY, KING OF THE ENGLISH.

Henry, King of the English, asks Anselm to send his monk, Baldwin of Tournai, to Rome with his envoy William de Warelwast.

HENRY, KING OF THE ENGLISH: TO ANSELM, ARCHBISHOP OF CANTERBURY, GREETING AND FRIENDSHIP.

I ENJOIN YOU as my dearest father to order the monk Baldwin to go with William de Warelwast to Rome on our business so that through the two of them a firm love and peace may be established between us.[1]

Witnessed by Waldric, the chancellor,[2] and Robert, Count of Meulan,[3] and Eudo,[4] the steward, at Pontefract.

October or November 1105.

NOTES

1. This is *Reg.* II, 710; compare with *Epp* 367, 368, 369, 370, 377 and also *Ep* 364.
2. See *Ep* 370 note 2.
3. See *Ep* 353 note 9.
4. Eudo or Eno, the *dapifer* or seneschal, was son of Hubert de Ria. He had served William II as steward and continued in service to Henry I until January, 1120, when he is said to have died at the castle of Préaux, see *Reg.* II, xi, 710.

372. TO GERARD, ARCHBISHOP OF YORK.

Anselm consoles Gerard, Archbishop of York, in his tribulation, and admonishes him to persevere in his praiseworthy zeal for God. He hopes the King will support the bishops but he can do nothing until he knows the Pope's decision.

ANSELM, THE ARCHBISHOP: TO THE REVEREND
ARCHBISHOP GERARD OF YORK, GREETING.

FOR THE TRIBULATIONS which your charity suffered after I left England I bear due compassion in my mind,[1] although at the moment I cannot show you any consolation by my deeds. I understand through the words of many people and from your letters[2] that your will has been enkindled by zeal for God against the evils which rage and grow exceedingly in the Church of God. Just as I suffer with you in adversity, so I rejoice with you in virtue. Therefore I beseech and admonish you that neither constancy nor the perseverance to attain to perfection may be lacking in your good intention. For to what purpose are we placed as bishops over the people[3] of God if, like *dogs unable to bark*, we remain dumb?[4]

I hope in God that our lord the King, as he himself promised me by the inspiration of God, will approach us as helper in everything good, and that if God deigns to accomplish the agreement which he has begun between him and me, the King will not retreat from our advice in those matters which pertain to our rank. Therefore I shall do nothing about our business at the moment until I learn the Apostolic decision which I am expecting shortly. Farewell.

Late 1105 or early 1106, while at Bec.

NOTES

1. See *Ep* 326.
2. See *Epp* 326, 363.
3. See Heb 5:1.
4. Is 56:10.

373. FROM GERARD, ARCHBISHOP OF YORK.

Archbishop Gerard of York admits to Anselm that he now perceives that lay investiture has the smell of heresy and he begs him to pray that he may persevere in his good intentions. He rejoices about Anselm's reconciliation with the King but grieves at his prolonged absence. He asks Anselm's advice about whom he is permitted to associate with.

TO HIS FATHER ANSELM, THE VENERABLE ARCHBISHOP: THE SON GERARD, SENDING GREETING AND OBEDIENCE.[1]

WHEN I FIRST CALLED MY SOUL BACK from that vanity in which your alien sons are straying stiff-necked against your paternity, the splendor of truth, which I first saw as if glowing amongst the clouds, but which I could not hold as it disappeared, flooded my soul with surprising clarity. Then at length I began to contemplate more attentively the dangers of that party to whose body I belonged.[2] I saw and I do see and I am afraid that I am not mistaken that a person is not far away from heresy who dissents in church matters and strives to act against the general councils held in order to bring about a prohibition in this matter,³ and against the judgement of him whose voice and person represents Peter, the prince of the apostles, on earth. If anyone, against the weight of Peter's authority, presumes to dispense the grace of the Holy Spirit through ordination, or rather a pretence of ordination,⁴ he incurs heresy. Indeed it would be an error if such a thing were not prohibited by the great authority of the Roman pontiff and of the councils called to resolve this matter. But the solemn prohibition known to everyone⁵ increases the sin the more someone sins against worthier and divine matters. While one strives to give and the other to receive God against the will of God, the fornicating soul strives to marry a celestial spouse in private adultery against the well-known defence of the legitimate bride.⁶

You beseech and admonish, father—using your own most delightful words to me⁷—you beseech that 'neither constancy nor the perseverance to attain to perfection be lacking in my good intention'. May the favor of divine grace be with me, may the help of your holy prayers be with me, so that I lack neither God nor you. My soul burns to be with you and to repay by the profit of some great labor the long period in which I grew negligent in my service of God through idleness of soul. And although I give thanks for the peace which has been initiated between you and our lord the King,⁸ I can scarcely persuade myself to acquiesce to it with tranquillity. For even though this peace is good and delightful in its hope of perfection, yet it is exceedingly bitter to me because it makes you absent from me or allows you to be absent.⁹ We indeed are sorry because we love you and desire to be nourished in the house of God by your paternity and to be taught in the law of our God by you as teacher. A man who plots against you, puffed up with empty hope of your office and hoping for your death as if it were already imminent in order to ascend a throne of such dignity, a man smeared with the blood and tears of the poor, does not feel this sorrow.¹⁰ Therefore, like an arch-flame¹¹ he already struts among his supporters, and while scarcely raising his eyes from the ground[12] I know not what opinions he mumbles under his breath since he does not yet know what the decision will be.

Concerning your bodily presence, kindest father, your presence through which you are present to me in him who is nowhere absent made me more composed, you are also present to us in the affection of charity by which souls at a distance are joined better than bodies are joined by place. This indeed would be sufficient for those whom the love of the spirit has raised more perfectly from the earth, but for me, still bound by the chains of the flesh, it will only be enough when I see you present body and soul. But behold, while the physician is absent my languor is increasing since I am forced to be in communion with those whom the judgement of the Roman pontiff and the Roman Council has either cast out completely from the communion of the faithful or has merely driven from the threshold of the church.[13] The custom of the church has two different possibilities since it sometimes prohibits entrance into the church to those whom it has not yet forbidden to be in communion with the faithful. Heal this wound, since you are my physician; make me certain where there is danger about whose inconsistency I am in doubt. Give me advice, bring help lest I incur the King's violent wrath if I am not in communion with those who abide or seem to abide in your peace in communion with him. May Christ who is *the way, the truth and the life*[14] so be for me the way to him, the truth from him and life in him as I desire with my whole heart to see you and either to obey your paternity in the peace of the Church or, if it should happen, to work with you in persecution.

late 1105 or early 1106 while Anselm was at Bec.

NOTES

1. Archbishop Gerard is replying to *Ep* 372.
2. Gerard belonged to the supporters of King Henry, see *Epp* 200, 217, 250, 261, 263, 318.

3. He is referring to lay investiture.
4. At the King's command Gerard was willing to consecrate the bishops-elect of Winchester and Salisbury, see HN 144-146; Epp 261, 265, 308, 326, 362.
5. Anselm had published these decrees on his return to England in September 1100.
6. Gerard is referring to Pope Paschal's letter to Henry, Ep 216.
7. See Ep 372.
8. See Ep 364.
9. Henry had promised to obtain an agreement with the Pope by Christmas 1105, but he delayed sending his messenger to Rome, see Epp 367, 368, 369, 370, 377.
10. Gerard may be referring to himself when he was one of the chief ecclesiastical counsellors of King Henry, see HN 145; Epp 260, 263.
11. *archflamen*, arch-flame: Schmitt believes Gerard is referring to Ranulf Flambard (see Epp 214, 223), but Liebermann's suggestion that Roger of Salisbury was the ecclesiastic intended, see *Quadripartitus*, (Halle, 1892) 158, is more probable. See N. Cantor, *Church, Kingship and Lay Investiture in England* (Princeton, 1958) 260, note 145.
12. See Ovid, *Metamorph* 2, 448.
13. The Lenten synod of 1099 in Rome passed 'sentence of excommunication on all lay persons who conferred investitures of churches, all persons accepting such investitures from their hands and all persons who consecrated to the office of any preferment so given', HN 144; see Epp 280, 281, 283, 310, 351, 353, 354, 364.
14. Jn 14:6.

374. TO GUNDULF, BISHOP OF ROCHESTER, PRIOR ERNULF AND WILLIAM, ARCHDEACON OF CANTERBURY.

Anselm solemnly confirms to Bishop Gundulf of Rochester, Prior Ernulf, and Archdeacon William of Christ Church Canterbury the excommunication which William had pronounced on those priests who had returned to their concubines and scorned his admonitions.

ANSELM, THE ARCHBISHOP: TO THE REVEREND BISHOP GUNDULF, PRIOR ERNULF AND WILLIAM, ARCHDEACON OF CANTERBURY, AND ALL THOSE IN HIS DIOCESE OBSERVING THE HOLY OBLIGATION OF THEIR ORDER FOR THE LOVE OF GOD, GREETING.

RECENTLY I WAS INFORMED of the arrogant presumption, execrable to God and hateful to all Christians, of those who call themselves priests. Our archdeacon William wrote to me that several of the priests under his charge have gone back to women forbidden to them and have sunk again into the impurity from which they had been drawn away by wholesome advice and command. When the archdeacon wanted to correct this situation, they totally scorned his admonition and the command they had received by their abominable pride. Having called together a number of holy and obedient priests, he struck the proud and disobedient ones with the sword of well-deserved excommunication. Scorning this excommunication with fierce madness, they were not afraid of desecrating their holy office as much as they could.

Therefore I, Anselm the Archbishop—although a sinner—by the authority which God the Father, the Son and the Holy Ghost have given to me through the office of archbishop, confirm that excommunication which the Archdeacon pronounced, until according to his judgement satisfaction has been rendered.[1]

late 1105 or early 1106 while at Bec.

NOTES

1. See *Epp* 257, 364; Synods of Winchester, 1 April 1078, and Westminster, Michaelmas 1102, c. 4, 5, 6, *HN* 142.

375. TO WARNER, THE NOVICE.

Anselm thanks Warner, a novice of Christ Church Canterbury, for his letter and his longing for Anselm's return, assures him that he will return as soon as reasonably possible and admonishes him to be fervent and to persevere in his monastic way of life.

ANSELM, THE ARCHBISHOP: TO WARNER,[1] HIS DEAREST BROTHER AND SON, SENDING THE GREETING AND BLESSING OF GOD, AND HIS OWN.

I GIVE YOU THANKS as my beloved brother and son for the love for me which I perceived in your letter[2] and for your desire for my return. I shall not delay my return, God granting, when, by his providence I see that I can reasonably do it.[3] I admonish you earnestly however, as one whose soul God has commended to my care, not to be negligent in learning about and keeping the Rule which you accepted, but to strive with your whole heart to progress towards what pertains to the perfection of a monk. For it is true that if a monk is tepid in his resolution as a novice he will hardly ever, or never, become fervent in his monastic way of life. Therefore, just as you wish to be found on the day of your death, so strive to show yourself daily and always prepare yourself today to give an account of your life as if you were to die tomorrow, and thus you will advance *from strength to strength*.[4] May the Lord guide and protect you.

late 1105 or early 1106 while at Bec.

NOTES

1. He is possibly the monk addressed in *Ep* 335.
2. This letter is not preserved.
3. See *Ep* 364.
4. Ps 83:7.

376. TO PRIOR ERNULF AND THE MONKS OF CANTERBURY.

Anselm informs Prior Ernulf and the monks of Christ Church, Canterbury, that the King's envoy and his are on their way to Rome. He begs them to pray that an agreement may be reached between the Pope and the King which would permit him to return to England soon.

ANSELM, THE ARCHBISHOP: TO DOM PRIOR ERNULF AND HIS MOST BELOVED BROTHERS AND SONS AT CHRIST CHURCH, CANTERBURY, GREETING AND BENEDICTION.

BECAUSE OF THE MATTER which is between our lord the King and myself,[1] the King has just sent his messengers,[2] and I mine,[3] to Rome. I instruct and beseech you to pray to God fervently that he may bring about such an agreement between the lord Pope and the King that I, with undiminished respect for his will, may be able to agree with both. If everything is well with you I rejoice, and I greatly desire that it may be so. I request you to let me know by letter, as soon as you conveniently can, how matters are with you.

May almighty God protect you and make you persevere in your holy resolution, and graciously absolve you from all your sins. Amen.

December 1105 or January 1106 while at Bec.

NOTES

1. See *Epp* 364, 367, 368, 369, 370, 371, 377.
2. William de Warelwast came to Bec.
3. Baldwin of Tournai.

377. FROM HENRY, KING OF THE ENGLISH.

Henry, King of the English, informs Anselm that he has heard that there are two popes in Rome and that the city is plunged into war. He asks Anselm to decide whether to send their envoys or not. If they are not to proceed he should retain William de Warelwast and send him Baldwin of Tournai and if they have already gone he should send him some other member of his household.

HENRY, BY THE GRACE OF GOD, KING OF THE ENGLISH: TO ANSELM, ARCHBISHOP OF CANTERBURY, HIS BELOVED FATHER, GREETING AND AFFECTION.

WE HAVE HEARD BY THE REPORT OF MANY, but most of all through Robert,[1] the clerk of my chancellor, rumors about the Pope, about which I grieve if there is any truth in what the rumor says, and since the rumor occurs more frequently with the passing of days, I fear it may be true. For they are saying in Rome that—God forbid!—there are two popes and that warlike discord prevails between them.[2]

For this reason I ask your holiness to look ahead and advise me and yourself, with whom the greater part of this matter rests, what is to be done concerning our messengers[3] in these stormy times. If it seems useful to you to retain them until a more favorable time, then retain William[4] and send me your monk Baldwin of Tournai as quickly as possible, through whom I shall inform you more intimately about our private matters, and through whom you should disclose to me what I am to hold and how I should act in this case. If it pleases you and you consider that they should go, then let them go. If they have already gone, send me immediately one of your faithful servants through whom our deliberations and business can be mutually dealt with in confidence.

Witnessed by Robert,[5] Bishop of Lincoln and Robert,[6] Count of Meulan.

January 1106.

NOTES

1. This is *Reg.* II, 716 which should be dated not 18 December 1105 but January 1106, for it took about six to eight weeks for news to reach England from Rome. Robert Pecche was clerk of the chancery from 1101–1120; in 1121 he became Bishop of Coventry where he died 22 August 1127, see *Reg.* II, xi.
2. On 18 November 1105 the archpriest Maginulf was raised by the Roman nobility, under the protection of Marquis Werner of Ancona, to the See of Rome in opposition to Pope Paschal II. He took the name of Silvester IV. Within a few days he was driven out of Rome and followed Werner to Orsino. In 1111 he joined the Emperor Henry V in his military camp before Rome and soon after this was forced to resign. Silvester IV was the last of a succession of anti-popes, Clement III (1080–1100), Theodoric (1100–1102) and Albert (1102) who contested the rightful popes Gregory VII (1073–1085), Victor III (1086–1087), Urban II (1088–1099) and Paschal II (1099–1118).
3. William de Warelwast and Baldwin of Tournai, see *Epp* 367, 376.
4. Anselm was at Bec from July 1105-May 1106, see Itinerary, Volume 1:342.
5. See *Ep* 311.
6. See *Ep* 353.

378. TO HENRY, KING OF THE ENGLISH.

Anselm tells King Henry that he is sending Gilbert, a monk of Bec, to inform him that the envoys had left for Rome before his letter reached Bec. He states that Pope Paschal was canonically elected and accepted throughout the whole Church, and predicts that the anti-pope will soon fall.

TO HENRY, HIS DEAREST LORD, BY THE GRACE OF GOD KING OF THE ENGLISH: ANSELM, ARCHBISHOP OF CANTERBURY, SENDING FAITHFUL SERVICE WITH PRAYERS.

YOUR HIGHNESS ORDERED ME in your letter[1] to send you some faithful servant of ours to whom you might safely entrust whatever you might wish to tell me. Therefore I am sending you a brother named Gilbert, a monk of Bec, a close friend of mine, to whom you can entrust as to myself anything it pleases you to tell me. He will also inform you how Dom Baldwin and William had already started out on their journey to Rome when I received your letter; and also what we have heard about Pope Paschal and about him who is said to have usurped his see by robbery.[2]

I only say this much, that Pope Paschal was elected in conformity with Church law according to the will of God and that he has already been accepted and confirmed by the whole catholic Church. The usurper, however, of whom reports speak, has no election or acknowledgement except by the sons of the devil, the enemies of the Church of God. Wherefore, we expect that what the Lord said will fall upon him if it has not already fallen: *Every plant which my heavenly Father has not planted will be uprooted.*[3] Nor should any Christian be troubled if the Church of Christ suffers persecution because he suffered the same and predicted that the Church would suffer: *In the world*, he said, *you will have oppression.* To comfort her he added, *But be confident, I have overcome the world.*[4]

May almighty God so make you reign over the English in this life that you may reign amongst the angels[5] in the life to come.

January or February 1106.

NOTES

1. See *Ep* 377.
2. Silvester IV, the anti-pope, see *Ep* 377.
3. Mt 15:13.
4. Jn 16:33.
5. Anselm is referring to the pun of Pope Gregory I: *Non Angli sed Angeli*, Bede, *EH* 2, 1.

379. TO THIDRICUS, MONK OF CANTERBURY.

Anselm assures Thidricus, a monk of Christ Church Canterbury, of his affection. He is not sending him the requested letters from King Henry to Pope Paschal, but will send him any new work in due course. He advises him on corrections.

ANSELM, THE ARCHBISHOP: TO THIDRICUS,[1] HIS DEAREST SON, SENDING THE GREETING AND BLESSING OF GOD.

THE WORDS OF YOUR LETTER[2] are delightful to me because the affection of your soul which I love is delightful to me. To prove this it is not necessary to linger on it because I am certain that you are aware of what my heart feels for you.

I am not sending you the letters from the King to the Pope[3] which you asked for because I cannot see that there is any use in preserving them.[4] If I write anything else, with God's help, it will be shown to you in due course.[5] What you are correcting in the books you have copied, make sure that, if any of them has been copied, it should also be corrected in them.

You long for my presence; may God show you his presence and in the meantime may it dwell in you through his grace. Amen.

c. 1105 or 1106 while at Bec.

NOTES

1. See *Ep* 334 and Introduction, volume 1:45–46.
2. The letter of Thidricus is not preserved.
3. On Thidricus' edition of Anselm's correspondence see Introduction, volume 1:32–39. None of these letters of King Henry to Pope Paschal is preserved, only two from the Pope to the King, *Epp* 348, 351; although the tone of these letters is conciliatory, they nevertheless firmly insist on the prohibition of lay investiture without mentioning homage. Neither of these letters was included in MS L which Thidricus

was working on when this letter reached him. They are part of a small, complete collection of twenty-three letters from Christ Church Canterbury, now in Brit. Lib. MS Add 32091: *Epp* 206, 210, 214, *213*, 216, 219, 220, 222, 223, 224, *226*, 284, 227, 280, 281, *305*, *348*, *351*, *352*, *354*, *397*, *422*, *423*. Those italicized are not in L. For a description of the MS see W. Holtzmann, *Papsturkunden in England*, Part 1 (1930), 166–167. For the discussion about the genesis of Anselm's collection of letters see AOO 226*–239*; N. Cantor, *Church, Kingship and Lay Investiture in England* (Princeton, 1958) 169–170; Southern, *Anselm*, 67–68, 174, 238; AOO 239*; W. Fröhlich, 'Die Enstehung der Briefsammlung Anselms von Canterbury,' *Historisches Jahrbuch* 100 (1980) 457–466.
4. During his second exile Anselm sent other letters to Canterbury, see *Epp* 357, 364.
5. This is to enable Thidricus to add it to the final edition of Anselm's philosophical and theological works in Oxford Bodleian MS Bodley 271, see *Ep* 334.

380. TO PRIOR ERNULF AND WILLIAM, ARCHDEACON OF CANTERBURY.

Anselm asks Prior Ernulf and Archdeacon William of Canterbury to provide for Robert, a convert from Judaism, from the revenues of the archdiaconate in such a way that he may not regret his conversion.

ANSELM, THE ARCHBISHOP: TO DOM PRIOR
ERNULF AND ARCHDEACON WILLIAM, SENDING
THE GREETING AND BLESSING OF GOD.

WITH THE DEEPEST AFFECTION OF MY HEART I instruct you and beseech your piety to take care of Robert with that cheerful sense of duty and that dutiful cheerfulness with which all Christians should welcome and assist anyone fleeing from Judaism[1] to Christianity, lest by any need or chance which we can avert he be forced to regret that, for the sake of Christ, he gave up his parents and their law. It is indeed a great disgrace for Christians, and above all for religious, that through their negligence and insensibility, they permit this to take place in their very presence. Therefore you, Dom Prior, should allot something to him from the alms, not through servants who *seek their own interests* rather than those of God,[2] but through the monk-almoner; and you, Dom William, should allot something from the revenues of the archdiaconate which you should keep for me. Then this man with his little family may not suffer harsh poverty but may rejoice in having passed from falsehood to the true faith and experience through our loving-kindness that our faith is nearer to God than Judaism. If necessary I would prefer to spend everything due to me from the revenues of the archdiaconate, and even much more, rather than to let this man, who has fled to us as to servants of God and true Christians from the hands of the devil, live in misery among us. Once more I beseech and implore you to show in this that you have a Christian sense of duty and the love of Christianity. His want, either of food or of clothing greatly wounds my heart. Therefore, act so that my heart may cease burning from this wound, if you do not like it. Farewell.

1105 or 1106 while at Bec.

NOTES

1. On Anselm's contact with Jews and the origin of his *Cur Deus Homo* see R.W. Southern, 'St Anselm and Gilbert Crispin, Abbot of Westminster', *MARS* 3 (1954) 78–115; J. Gauss, 'Anselm von Canterbury, Zur Begegnung und Auseinandersetzung der Religionen', *Saeculum* 17 (1966) 277–363. On the conversion of Jews at Rouen, see *HN* 99–101; N. Golb, 'Les juifs de Normandie à l'époque d'Anselme', *Spicilegium Beccense* 2 (Paris, 1984) 149–160.
2. See Ph 2:21.

381. TO GUNDULF, BISHOP OF ROCHESTER.

Anselm informs Bishop Gundulf of Rochester that he had asked Prior Ernulf and Archdeacon William of Christ Church Canterbury to take care of the Jewish convert, Robert, and asks Gundulf to provide for this man if they should fail to do so.

ANSELM, THE ARCHBISHOP: TO THE
REVEREND BISHOP GUNDULF, GREETING.

I HAVE ASKED DOM PRIOR and our archdeacon, with as much affection as possible, to take care of this Robert, who has been converted from falsehood to the mercy and holiness of the true faith, so that he may suffer no harsh want of food or clothing. Therefore I ask you to read the letter[1] I sent them, and if at any time they should neglect to do what I told them—which I do not expect—you should supply with dutiful cheerfulness whatever is lacking out of our possessions.

1105 or 1106 while at Bec.

NOTES

1. See *Ep* 380.

382. TO PRIOR ALFER AND THE MONKS OF ST EDMUNDS.

Anselm praises the constancy of Prior Alfer and the monks of Bury St Edmunds in their tribulations and admonishes them to persevere. He absolves all those who have or who will confess their sins.

ANSELM, THE ARCHBISHOP: TO HIS BELOVED SONS AND BROTHERS, DOM PRIOR ALFER AND THE OTHER SERVANTS OF GOD LIVING UNDER HIM IN THE MONASTERY OF ST EDMUNDS,[1] SENDING THE GREETING AND BLESSING OF GOD, AND HIS OWN, FOR WHAT IT IS WORTH.

I GIVE THANKS TO GOD and to you for the constancy and patience which you are showing *in tribulations*,[2] and I exhort and beseech you as my dearest sons not *to lose heart*[3] but with forbearance, as you have begun, to await the consolation of God. May no adversity hold you back from the service of God, may nothing turn you away from carrying out his will. Remember that *all who wish to live a godly life in Christ*[4] must suffer tribulations. Therefore, the more tribulations rise against you, the more each one of you should occupy himself in the exercise of holy monastic life and bind himself more firmly in the protection of his order. If you do this you should know that you will obtain the consolation of God, perhaps sooner than you think.

None of you should love his sins or wish to hide them, but with a pure and simple heart should confess them to Dom Prior or to whoever he has appointed, and amend himself according to his judgement; furthermore he should strive to guard himself in every way. As to those who have confessed or will confess their sins in this way and with this intention: I absolve them as far as I can by the authority which God gave me by the representative of St Peter, prince of the apostles, and I humbly pray that almighty God may forgive them.[5] Farewell and pray for me.

1105 or 1106 while at Bec.

NOTES

1. See *Epp* 252, 267.
2. See *Epp* 251, 252, 266, 271, 280.
3. See Eph 3:13.
4. 2 Tim 3:12.
5. Since there was no rightful abbot at Bury, Anselm assumed abbatial functions from a distance, see *Ep* 397. In 1102 the Council of Westminster deposed Robert, illegitimate son of Earl Hugh of Chester and the new abbot, Prior Robert of Westminster, who was appointed in autumn 1102, was not blessed until 15 August 1107, see *Heads*, 32.

383. TO WIDO, THE MONK.

Anselm praises Wido for living quietly among his fellow monks and admonishes him not to let his soul incline towards the world.

THE ARCHBISHOP: TO HIS BELOVED SON WIDO, SENDING GREETING AND THE BLESSING OF GOD.

I HEAR THAT YOU ARE LIVING IN PEACE and quiet in the cloister and that you are zealous for the service of God and the salvation of your soul, and for this reason I rejoice greatly. Therefore I admonish you, although it may not be necessary, dearest son, to cast the world and everything which belongs to it far from your soul,[1] and not to bow down to the love of it in any way. Love God and serve him zealously because through his grace you have never had a better opportunity of serving him than you have now. You asked for my absolution, which I am sending you.

between 1104 and 1106.

NOTES

1. See 1 Jn 2:15.

384. FROM MATILDA, QUEEN OF THE ENGLISH.

Queen Matilda of the English expresses her great joy about a letter from Anselm. She informs him that she has given Dom Aedulf the temporalities of the Abbey of Malmesbury but has left the bestowal of the spiritual care to him. She longs for his return.

TO HER LORD AND FATHER ANSELM, ARCHBISHOP OF CANTERBURY, EQUALLY TO BE REVERED AND HONORED: FROM MATILDA, THE QUEEN, DEVOUT HANDMAID OF HIS HOLINESS, SENDING GREETING WITH CHRIST.

AS OFTEN AS YOU GRANT ME the protection of your Holiness, through the kindness of a letter, you brighten the nebulous gloom of my soul through the light of renewed happiness. Holding your letter and the pleasing, oft-repeated reading of it, is, as it were, like seeing you again, although you are absent. Indeed, my lord, what is there more wonderfully adorned in style and more replete with meaning than your writings? They do not lack the seriousness of Fronto,[1] the fluency of Cicero[2] or the wit of Quintilian;[3] the doctrine of Paul,[4] the precision of Jerome,[5] the learning of Gregory[6] and the interpretation of Augustine[7] are indeed overflowing in them. And what is even greater than all this: from them pours the sweetness of evangelical eloquence. Through this grace pouring over me from your lips[8] *my heart, and my flesh thrill with joy*[9] at the affection of your love and the effect of your paternal admonition. Indeed, by the most frequent repetition of your exhortation and of your most kind entreaty memory causes the portal of my heart to resound and decide in favor of compliant obedience.

Relying on the favor of your Holiness I have committed the Abbey of Malmesbury,[10] in those things which are under my jurisdiction, to Dom Aedulf,[11] a monk and once sacristan of Winchester, who I believe is known to you. You retain completely whatever pertains to that monastery for your own donation and disposition, so that the bestowal of the crozier and pastoral care is delivered wholly to the judgement of your discretion. May the worthy gift of the grace of your good will, which never grows cold towards me, recompense him like the reward of heavenly grace. Moreover, may Christ, who blesses you on earth, redeem your dignity, and may he soon give me reason to rejoice over your return. Amen.

summer 1106.

NOTES

1. Marcus Cornelius Fronto, c. AD 100–170, was regarded as the greatest Roman orator after Cicero.
2. Marcus Tullius Cicero, c. 106–43 BC, was the greatest writer of Latin prose and created its classic form.
3. Marcus Fabius Quintilian, c. AD 35–100, was a celebrated teacher of rhetoric and the educator of the princes at Domitian's court.
4. Paul the Apostle.
5. Jerome, c. 347–420, doctor of the Church. At the request of Pope Damasus he translated the Bible into Latin between 380 and 406. The Vulgate Bible, which became the standard text of the Latin Church, was largely his work.
6. Gregory I, c. 540–604, doctor of the Church, was pope 590–604.
7. Augustine, 354–430, bishop of Hippo in North Africa and doctor of the Church.
8. See Ps 44:3.
9. Ps 83:3.
10. Matilda gave only the temporal goods of the abbey to Aedulf and left the spiritual gift—the pastoral staff—to Anselm, who praises her for acting thus, *Ep* 385. She seems to have done this in the spirit of the compromise suggested by King Henry at l'Aigle, 21–22 July 1105 (*Ep* 364) accepted by the Pope, 23 March 1106 (*Ep* 397) and ratified by the curia regis, 1 August 1107 (*HN* 186). This suggests a date between the return of William de Warelwast and Baldwin of Tournai from the Pope at Benevento, *Ep* 387, and Anselm's return to England in early September 1106.
11. Aedulf or Eadwulf, abbot of Malmesbury 1106–1118, see *Heads*, 55.

385. TO MATILDA, QUEEN OF THE ENGLISH.

Anselm replies to Queen Matilda that he cannot confirm Aedulf as the new abbot of Malmesbury since he had sent him a goblet, which Anselm regarded as a sin of simony.

TO HIS DEAREST LADY AND DAUGHTER MATILDA, THE GLORIOUS QUEEN OF THE ENGLISH: ANSELM, ARCHBISHOP OF CANTERBURY, SENDING FAITHFUL SERVICE WITH PRAYERS.

MOST BELOVED LADY, your excellency should know that concerning the Abbey of Malmesbury, and the brother about whom you wrote to me,[1] I would gladly confirm your will if I could. For, in what pertains to you, you have acted well and according to the will of God, in what you did there; but he himself did something very foolish in this matter which he should not have done. For, by the same messengers who brought me the letters from you and from others about this case, he sent me a goblet. This goblet I did not wish to keep under any circumstances, but I was very sorry because I do not see how he can be excused from guilt in this matter.[2]

May almighty God guide all your actions in his good pleasure and defend you from all evil. Amen.

summer 1106.

NOTES

1. See *Ep* 384.
2. Anselm perceived an attempt at simony in Aedulf's foolish action.

386. FROM SEVERAL ENGLISH BISHOPS.

Archbishop Gerard of York and the bishops Robert of Chester, Herbert de Losinga of Norwich, Ralph Luffa of Chichester, Samson of Worcester, and William, the bishop-elect of Winchester, beseech Anselm to return to England and promise him their assistance. They offer to come to him if he wishes it.

TO OUR MOST BELOVED FATHER ANSELM, ARCHBISHOP OF CANTERBURY:[1] GERARD, ARCHBISHOP OF YORK,[2] AND BISHOPS ROBERT OF CHESTER,[3] HERBERT OF NORWICH,[4] RALPH OF CHICHESTER,[5] SAMSON OF WORCESTER,[6] AND WILLIAM, BISHOP-ELECT OF WINCHESTER,[7] SENDING GREETINGS.

WE LOOKED FOR PEACE and it was withdrawn further from us; we sought good and disorder prevailed.[8] *The roads to Zion mourn*[9] because the uncircumcised trample them.[10] The temple laments because laymen have broken into the Holy of Holies and gone up to the very altar. Arise, as the aged Mattathias once did.[11] In your sons you have the strength of Juda, the vigor of Jonathan, the prudence of Simon.[12] They will fight with you the battle of the Lord. And if you should be gathered to your fathers[13] before us, we will receive the inheritance of your labor from your hands.

But now you must not delay. Why are you wandering abroad while your sheep perish without a shepherd?[14] No excuse is left you now before God! For we are prepared not only to follow you but even to go ahead of you, if you so command. Therefore, come to us, come quickly; or command us, or some of us, to come to you, lest, while we are separated from you, the counsels of those who seek their own ends[15] lead you into a treacherous way. In this matter we are not seeking our own ends but God's.[16]

February or March 1106.

NOTES

1. Anselm was at Bec until May 1106, see Itinerary, volume 1:342.

2. Gerard of York, Robert of Chester and Herbert of Norwich had been royal envoys to Rome in 1102, see HN 137–141; Epp 217, 250, 261, 397; W. Fröhlich, 'Anselm and the Bishops of the Province of Canterbury', Spicilegium Beccense 2 (Paris, 1984) 125–145.
3. Robert de Limési of Lichfield-Chester-Coventry, see L.C. Loyd, The Origins of Some Anglo-Norman Families (London, 1951) 54.
4. Herbert de Losinga of Norwich, see B. Dodwell, 'The Foundation of Norwich Cathedral', T.R.H.S., 5th series, 7 (1957) 1–18; Ep 254.
5. Ralph Luffa of Chichester, see Fröhlich, Bischöfliche Kollegen, AA 1 (1969) 254–255; Barlow, English Church, 68 and passim; H. Mayr-Harting, 'The Bishops of Chichester, 1075–1207: Biographical Notes and Problems', The Chichester Papers, No. 40 (Chichester City Council, 1963).
6. Samson of Worcester, see Fröhlich, Bischöfliche Kollegen, AA 2 (1970) 119–122; F. Barlow, William Rufus (London, 1983) 147, 179, 206, 209 and passim; Epp 464, 465.
7. William Giffard, bishop-elect of Winchester, see Epp 212, 229, 236, 265, 273, 274, 275, 276, 322, 344, 404.
8. See Jer 14:19 and Ps 121:9.
9. Lam 1:4.
10. See Is 52:1.
11. See 1 M 2:1.
12. See 1 M 2:2–5.
13. See 1 M 2:69.
14. Compare Epp 310, 327, 330, 336, 355, 365, 366.
15. See Ph 2:21.
16. See Ph 2:21.

387. TO SEVERAL ENGLISH BISHOPS.

Anselm replies to his fellow bishops that he cannot help them until he knows what message the envoys he is expecting from Rome are bringing from the Pope. He congratulates the bishops for their good judgement and intentions.

ANSELM, ARCHBISHOP OF CANTERBURY: TO HIS FRIENDS AND FELLOW BISHOPS WHOSE LETTER[1] HE HAS RECEIVED THROUGH THE BEARER OF THIS LETTER, SENDING GREETING.

I GRIEVE AND SUFFER in mind with you at the tribulations which you and the church[2] of England are bearing;

but at present I cannot come to your aid, according to my will and yours, because I am not yet sure on what I can firmly rely or how far I can safely go until I learn from our messengers, whom I am shortly expecting to return from Rome,[3] what they have achieved in speaking with the lord Pope.[4]

Yet it is good and makes me glad that you have finally realized where your patience—to put it more kindly—has led you, and that you are promising me your help, not in my cause but in God's, and urging me not to delay in coming to you. Although I cannot do this at present, because the King does not yet wish me to be in England unless I disagree with the Pope's command and agree to his will, and since, as I have said, I am not yet sure myself what I can do, nevertheless I rejoice about your good intention as bishops as well as the loyalty you promise and the exhortation you address to me.

As to your request that I should make some of you come to me lest, while we are separated from one another persons seeking their own ends[5] should pervert my advice, I do not think it opportune at the moment. For I trust in God that no one will succeed in turning my heart away from the truth, as far as I perceive it, and that God will soon show me what I can do and I will then notify you as quickly as I can. Your prudence knows well enough what you ought to do in the meantime. For myself I can only say that, so far as trusting in God I know my own conscience, to save my life I would not give my consent nor make myself the minister or executor of that evil which I hear has recently been proclaimed against the churches of England.[6] Farewell.

c. March 1106.

NOTES

1. *Ep* 386.
2. Eadmer uses the plural when quoting Anselm's letter, *HN* 174.

3. According to *Ep* 378 the envoys had left for Rome in December 1105. Anselm expected them back in April or early May.
4. See *Ep* 397.
5. See Ph 2:21.
6. King Henry had extorted money to equip his large army to win Normandy, see *HN* 171-173, and *Epp* 364, 391, 392, 393, 394.

388. TO POPE PASCHAL.

Anselm briefly informs the Pope about his meeting with King Henry at l'Aigle. There he was reinvested with his archbishopric, and he and the King are sending envoys to the Pope about the matters on which they still disagree. He has lifted the excommunication from Count Robert and requests the Pope's advice concerning the others. He intercedes for the suspended Archbishop William of Rouen.

TO HIS LORD AND FATHER PASCHAL, THE SUPREME PONTIFF, TO BE LOVED WITH REVERENCE: ANSELM, SERVANT OF THE CHURCH OF CANTERBURY, SENDING DUE SUBJECTION WITH FAITHFUL SERVICE AND PRAYERS.

I AM WRITING BRIEFLY to your Highness about the matter between the King of England and myself[1] which was recently dealt with because I leave it to his messenger and ours[2] to explain it more fully.

After your authority had forbidden entrance to the church[3] to the Count of Meulan and the others who prevent the King from obeying your command, I approached Normandy, and through the Countess of Chartres,[4] the King's sister, a most faithful servant of the Church of God and obedient to your commands, we, the King and I, met for a talk with some hope of a good outcome. There the King reinvested me with the archbishopric[5] of which he had despoiled me[6] and, regarding the matters about which we did not agree, namely the investiture of churches and the homage of prelates—I had heard identical prohibitions at the Roman Council[7] about both issues at the same time—he decided that he would appeal to the Apostolic See through his messenger before the coming feast of the Lord's Nativity.[8] I did not consider that I ought either to prohibit his legation or refuse my reinvestiture. What he either concedes or demands in the aforesaid matters your Holiness may learn through that messenger. But since the outcome of the whole matter depends on your decision I have sent our messenger at the same time so that I may learn how you and the King agree, and what your command requires of me.[9]

On the authority of the letter[10] you sent to the Count of Meulan, in which I read that if he obeys you he will obtain your grace, I permitted him entrance to the church[11] because he promised that he would try to make the King obey your commands concerning the freedom of the Church. Concerning the others[12] about whom I am asking your authority through the messengers, I urgently beg for your reply through them if it pleases you.

On behalf of my reverend father, the Archbishop of Rouen,[13] I humbly throw myself at your feet in spirit and beg that, according to what you shall learn from his messengers, you may grant him the kindness of Apostolic mercy because of his supplication and humility and the need of his church.

May almighty God long preserve your safety in all prosperity for his Church. Amen.

December 1105 while at Bec.

NOTES

1. For the meeting at l'Aigle, 21 and 22 July 1105, see *Ep* 364.
2. William de Warelwast and Baldwin of Tournai, see *Epp* 367, 378.
3. See *Epp* 353, 354.
4. A serious illness of Adela, Countess of Blois and Chartres (*Epp* 286, 287, 340) made Anselm change his mind and hasten to Blois. By the time he arrived she had recovered, *HN* 164–165.
5. See *HN* 165–166; *Ep* 364.

6. *HN* 159; *VA* 132; *Epp* 319, 330, 338.
7. The Lenten synod of 1099, see *HN* 114; *Ep* 213.
8. See *Epp* 304, 367, 368, 369, 370, 371, 377, 378.
9. The memory of the scandal caused by the conflicting reports of Gerard of York, Robert of Chester and Herbert of Norwich about their meeting with the Pope in 1102 still haunts Anselm, *Ep* 250.
10. See *Ep* 361.
11. See *Ep* 364.
12. See *Epp* 308, 351, 353, 364.
13. William Bona Anima, Archbishop of Rouen, 1079–1110, *Ep* 18, 'had been suspended from his episcopal office', *HN* 177; *OV* V: 322, perhaps because he had consecrated the brother and sons of Ranulf Flambard who had been appointed to the see of Lisieux by Duke Robert, *OV* V: 320–322; *Epp* 398, 404; G. H. Williams, *The Norman Anonymous of 1100* AD, (Cambridge, Ma., 1951) 118–119.

389. TO HUGH, ARCHBISHOP OF LYON.

Anselm asks Archbishop Hugh of Lyon to give his prudent advice to him, and also to his messengers, the bearers of this letter, who are on their way to Rome. He believes that the King has accepted the papal decree on investitures but is appealing to the Pope on the homage of prelates.

TO HIS LORD AND FATHER HUGH, THE REVEREND ARCHBISHOP OF LYON, SINCERELY TO BE LOVED BY MOTHER CHURCH: ANSELM, SERVANT OF THE CHURCH OF CANTERBURY, WISHING HIM WHAT HE CAN UNDERSTAND MORE PROFOUNDLY AND BETTER.

WHAT I HAVE DONE SINCE I LEFT the amiable presence of your paternity[1] and how matters stand between the King of England and myself does not require a long explanation by letter because the bearers[2] of this letter can inform you more fully and better by word of mouth. Since, if it were possible, I would wish in all my actions to make use of your counsel more than that of any other man I know, particularly in this business[3] for which I am sending these messengers to Rome, I humbly beg that they may be instructed and strengthened by your prudence. I even dare to ask you, if it appears fitting to your holiness, to suggest something to the lord Pope, as you perceive expedient in this matter.[4] You know that when the disposition of any matter depends on the counsel of many, and as not everyone has the same opinion so they do not always give the same assent. Since therefore I am sure that your mind is steadfast in truth I would like your opinion to be made known wherever the freedom and the true good of the Church of God are being dealt with.

The whole difficulty of the case between the King and myself now seems above all to come to this:[5] the King, although he allows himself to be convinced, as I believe, by the papal decrees on the investitures of churches, nevertheless does not yet wish, he says, to lose the homage of prelates.[6] On this he is appealing through his legation to the Apostolic See to obtain freedom to carry out his own will in this matter. If he should achieve this I am uncertain what I ought to do if some religious man who has been elected should refuse to become the King's man in return for a bishopric or an abbacy. It would seem harsh for me to command him to do this through obedience; and if I do not do so I shall appear, to irreligious men wishing to do it, to condone the boldness of those who are advancing unworthily to high office. Concerning those who have already accepted forbidden investitures and those who have consecrated them, I think the King will demand that they should remain in the office which they have illegally assumed.[7] Wherefore I ask for your wisdom on these and other matters through our messengers, and beg that your decision be made known to me.[8]

May almighty God keep your holiness unharmed with all prosperity. Amen.

December 1105 while at Bec.

NOTES

1. Anselm had left Lyon at the end of April 1105. For his move north see Itinerary, volume 1:342 and *Ep* 364; *HN* 163–175.
2. William de Warelwast and Baldwin of Tournai were the envoys who had left Bec for Rome, December 1105, see *Epp* 364, 367, 368, 369, 370, 371, 376, 377, 378.
3. See *Ep* 364.
4. Anselm frequently asked the advice of Archbishop Hugh, see *Epp* 100, 109, 176, 208, 210, 260, 261, 322, 390, and *HN* 91, 118, 164.
5. See *Ep* 364.
6. See *Epp* 222, 348, 351, 390, 397.
7. See *Epp* 280, 305, 306, 310, 352.
8. See *Ep* 390.

390. FROM HUGH, ARCHBISHOP OF LYON.

Archbishop Hugh of Lyon feels that Anselm has achieved the greater part of what he intended and advises him to obey the papal command; he expresses his sorrow that he may not see Anselm any more.

TO THE FATHER AND LORD HE LONGS FOR AND LOVES WITH HIS WHOLE HEART, ANSELM, VENERABLE BISHOP OF THE ENGLISH: HUGH, SERVANT OF THE CHURCH OF LYON, WISHING HIM THE CONTINUAL CONSOLATION OF DIVINE PROTECTION.

YOUR HOLINESS REMEMBERS, reverend father, that we have always desired and advised you, if it could be done according to the will of God, to take on again the care of the English church which was entrusted to you, and not to refuse to bend your neck in obedience to the yoke of such a heavy burden for the sake of the common salvation of the flock entrusted to you. I have just learned from the report of Dom Baldwin that the matter for which you have worked so hard up to now to achieve, and for which you exposed not only your possessions but even yourself, you have finally, for the most part, achieved by the grace of God, so that you can now be encouraged to hope for what still remains.[1] We pray your holiness with advice, and advise you with prayers, not to neglect to obey the papal command lest by making more of your judgement than of papal authority you be considered to be resisting not only the world and royal authority but even the Church and the priesthood. For it is possible that in the field of the English church some seed falls on a rock, some by the wayside and some among thorns; but good earth is also to be found in that field, and having received the seed of your preaching it will bring forth fruit in patience.[2]

But woe is me, because I myself am the author and instigator of my desolation, I who am trying to remove my only solace and joy, and after God, the life of my soul, from the sight of these eyes of mine which already seem to wander uselessly while what they freely used to enjoy, namely the presence of my most gentle father, is no longer left for them to see, nor even the hope of ever seeing him again. But far be it from me to begrudge for my own temporal comfort the general salvation of so many and such important people; I must indeed seek what belongs to Jesus Christ rather than what is mine.[3] Therefore hold me, most holy father, in the bosom of your memory, even though it may not be granted to me to enjoy the sight of your presence. We wish you always to enjoy good health and to take care of your salvation.

January or February 1106.

NOTES

1. Hugh is referring to the King's offer to compromise on investitures (*Epp* 389, 364) and his reluctance to change his attitude to homage, see F. Liebermann, *Anselm von Canterbury und Hugo von Lyon, Festschrift für G. Waitz* (Hannover, 1886) 197–199. Compare Hugh's advice with Pope Paschal's decision, *Ep* 397.
2. Lk 8:5–15.
3. See Ph 2:21.

391. TO HENRY, KING OF THE ENGLISH.

Anselm rebukes King Henry for exacting money from priests who had broken the canons of the Westminster synod of 1102, since the right to do this belongs to the bishops or the primate, and not to the King. He reminds him that he had restored the archbishopric to him in Normandy.

TO HENRY, HIS DEAREST LORD, BY THE GRACE OF GOD KING OF THE ENGLISH: ANSELM, ARCHBISHOP OF CANTERBURY, SENDING FAITHFUL PRAYERS WITH FAITHFUL SERVICE.

IT IS MY DUTY, if I hear that you are doing anything which is not for the good of your soul, not to be silent about it to you, lest—which God forbid!—God may be angry with you for doing what is not pleasing to him and with me for keeping silent.

Now I hear that your excellency is inflicting punishment upon priests in England and exacting fines[1] from them for not having kept the decree of the Council[2] which I, with other bishops and religious persons, held in London with your approval. Up to now this has been unheard of and unprecedented in the Church of God on the part of any king or any prince. By the law of God it is not for anyone except each bishop in his own diocese to punish an offence of this kind or, if the bishops themselves are negligent in this, then for the archbishop and primate. Therefore I beseech you as my dearest lord, whose soul I love more than the present life of my body, and I advise you as a true friend of your body and soul, not to cast yourself into such a grave sin contrary to ecclesiastical custom and, if you have already begun to do so, to give it up completely. I tell you that you ought to fear greatly that money received in such a way—not to mention how harmful it is for your soul—will not help your earthly business as much when it is spent as it will inflict harm later on.[3] Moreover, you know that in Normandy you received me into your peace and repossessed me of my archbishopric,[4] and that the care and punishment of such an offence pertains above all to the archbishopric, since I am more a bishop for spiritual care than for earthly possessions.

May almighty God so direct your heart according to his will in this and your other deeds that after this life he may lead you to his glory. Amen.

March or April 1106 while at Bec.

NOTES

1. See *Ep* 364, and also *Epp* 65, 223, 254, 257, 374, 392; *HN* 172, 175.
2. Synod of Westminster, Michaelmas 1102, c. 4, 5, 6, *HN* 144.
3. Henry was collecting money from wherever he could get it in order to equip his army for a war he was planning against his brother Robert, see *ASC* 1104, 1105, 1106, *EHD* II: 175–180; *Ep* 364; *HN* 171–175.
4. See *Ep* 364.

392. FROM HENRY, KING OF THE ENGLISH.

King Henry of the English informs Anselm that he is surprised by his letter and that after a court meeting on Ascension Day he will send him a satisfactory reply.

HENRY, BY THE GRACE OF GOD KING OF THE ENGLISH: TO ANSELM, ARCHBISHOP OF CANTERBURY, GREETING.

ON ST GEORGE'S DAY[1] a letter fastened with your seal[2] was delivered to me at Tonbridge. In that letter you told me certain things about which I was greatly surprised because I believe that what I have done I did through you. On Ascension day[3] I shall have all my barons assembled with me, and following their advice I shall give such a satisfactory answer that, when I speak to you I believe you will not blame me for it. Whatever may be done at another time you should know that, throughout all your territories your men, whatever they have done, have been left in peace.

Witnessed by Wanderic[4] the chancellor, at Tonbridge.

during the last week of April 1106, at Tonbridge.

NOTES

1. 23 April 1106.
2. See *Ep* 391.
3. 3 May 1106; the King was at Salisbury for Whitsun, 13 May 1106, ASC 1106, *EHD* II: 180.
4. Wanderic is a misspelling of Waldric, see *Reg.* I: 750.

393. TO HENRY, KING OF THE ENGLISH.

Anselm thanks King Henry for having promised him a satisfactory reply to his letter on the exaction of money from non-celibate priests. He emphasizes that the King cannot claim to have done this at his instigation.

TO HIS DEAREST LORD, HENRY, BY THE GRACE OF GOD KING OF THE ENGLISH: ANSELM, ARCHBISHOP OF CANTERBURY, SENDING HIS FAITHFUL SERVICE AND FAITHFUL PRAYERS.

I GIVE THANKS TO GOD and to your Majesty for promising in your letter[1] to give me a satisfactory reply to the request I made to you in my letter regarding priests in England, and I pray the Lord, whose counsel remains forever,[2] that he himself will counsel you to reply and to do what is pleasing to him, and thus the friends who truly love your soul may rejoice. Regarding what I read in your letter, that you believe that you are doing what you are doing through me, know for sure, my lord, that it is not through me since I would be acting against God if it were through me. Wherefore, I beseech you again with deep and faithful affection not to persist in doing what you have begun on the advice of anybody.

May almighty God defend and guard your body and soul from all evil, bodily and spiritual. Amen.

May 1106 while at Bec.

NOTES

1. See *Ep* 392.
2. See *Ps* 32:11.

394. FROM HENRY, KING OF THE ENGLISH.

King Henry assures Anselm that he had acted in good faith. He will soon be crossing to Normandy and will correct any wrongs he may have committed.

HENRY, KING OF THE ENGLISH: TO ANSELM, ARCHBISHOP OF CANTERBURY, SENDING GREETING AND FRIENDSHIP.

CONCERNING WHAT YOU WROTE TO ME about the priests,[1] you should know that I have acted as properly, I think, as I should have done. Nor should you be left uninformed that I shall be crossing the sea fairly soon.[2] And after I have spoken to you, if I have committed anything wrong in these matters, I shall correct it with the guidance of almighty God and you.[3]

Witnessed by Waldric, the chancellor, at Marlborough.

shortly after Whitsun, May or June, 1106.

NOTES

1. See *Epp* 391, 393.
2. The King held court at Salisbury at Whitsun, 13 May 1106, and the decision was taken there for the final conquest of Normandy: 'Before August the King went overseas into Normandy', *ASC* 1106, *EHD* II: 180.
3. The problem in question was settled during the meeting between Henry and Anselm at Bec on 15 August 1106, *HN* 183.

395. FROM MATILDA, QUEEN OF THE ENGLISH.

Queen Matilda of the English assures Anselm that the more certain she is about his imminent return the more ardently she longs for it.

TO HER MOST BELOVED LORD AND FATHER, ANSELM, ARCHBISHOP OF CANTERBURY: MATILDA, QUEEN OF THE ENGLISH, SENDING INCESSANT GREETINGS WITH LOVE AND FAITHFUL SERVICE.

THE CONSOLING LOVE of your holiness may not be unaware, dearly beloved father, that my soul will be seriously disturbed by your very long and wearisome absence.[1] Indeed, the sooner and the closer the date of your desired return is promised to me by many people,[2] the more it is desired by me, since I long to enjoy your presence and conversation. My soul, most reverend father, will therefore not be delighted by any perfect joy or brightened by any true affection until I am able to rejoice at seeing again your presence for which I long with all the strength of my soul. In the meantime, separated from you, I implore the mellifluous sweetness of your kindness to deign to console and gladden me by the charm of your correction and the charm of your letter.

May the almighty and holy Lord protect you everywhere and make me happy by your return into my presence. Amen.

May or June 1106.

NOTES

1. Anselm had left England on 27 April 1103.
2. The news of Pope Paschal's assent to King Henry's suggested compromise at l'Aigle may have already reached England, see *HN* 181–183; *Epp* 387, 397.

396. FROM HENRY, KING OF THE ENGLISH.

King Henry informs Anselm of a recent visit by Duke Robert of Normandy and also about his intention to cross to Normandy. If William de Warelwast and the other messengers return from Rome Anselm should keep them at Bec until the King arrives, or send them on, as he thinks fit.

HENRY, KING OF THE ENGLISH: TO HIS BELOVED FATHER ANSELM, ARCHBISHOP OF CANTERBURY, SENDING THE GREETING AND LOVE OF A SON.

THE WISDOM OF YOUR HOLINESS, reverend father, should know that my brother, Duke Robert, came to me in England, and departed in a friendly manner.[1] You should also know that I am prepared to cross the sea on the day of the Lord's Ascension.[2] When I have crossed over I shall do everything which has to be done through you and your advice.[3] If William de Warelwast and our other messengers should return from Rome[4] in the meantime, however, it will depend on the decision of your will whether they cross to me in England before I cross over or whether they stay with you[5] until they can speak to me together with you.

Witnessed by Walderic the chancellor, at Northampton.[6]

between 1 and 7 February 1106.

NOTES

1. The *ASC* 1106 (*EHD* II: 179–180) conveys a different impression of this meeting: 'Before spring the king was at Northampton, and Count Robert of Normandy, his brother, came there to him, and because the king would not give up to him what he had won from him in Normandy, they separated without coming to an agreement and the count went back overseas again forthwith'. For Henry's campaigns to wrest the Duchy out of his brother's hands, see *Ep* 364; F. Barlow, *Feudal Kingdom of England* (London, 1955) 177–179; A.L. Poole, *From Domesday Book to Magna Carta 1087–1216* (Oxford, 1958) 119–121.
2. Ascension Day was 3 May 1106.
3. See *Epp* 391, 392, 393, 394.

4. See *Epp* 378, 387. Pope Paschal's letter to Anselm (*Ep* 397) is dated 23 March 1106, his letter to King Henry is not preserved, see *Ep* 379.
5. Anselm was at Bec until May 1106.
6. Henry was at Northampton from 1–7 February 1106, see *Reg.* I, xxix, 737.

397. FROM POPE PASCHAL.

Pope Paschal II rejoices to inform Anselm that King Henry of the English has consented to obey the Apostolic See and that he has exercised clemency in this matter. He absolves Anselm from obedience to the decrees of the Lenten synod of 1099 and grants him power to absolve all those who received investiture from laymen, all who consecrated or blessed the invested or who did homage to laymen in return for their preferment. He should not deprive any so invested of their consecration. Only Richard, abbot of Ely, remains excommunicated. Anselm may also have communion with those bishops whose false reports had deceived the souls of many. He is to absolve the King and Queen and those who favored the King's cause. Finally, he places the decision about Archbishop William of Rouen into Anselm's hands.

PASCHAL, THE BISHOP, SERVANT OF THE SERVANTS OF GOD: TO HIS VENERABLE BROTHER ANSELM, BISHOP OF CANTERBURY, GREETING AND APOSTOLIC BLESSING.

THAT THE MAJESTY OF ALMIGHTY GOD has inclined the heart of the English king to obey the Apostolic See, for this we give thanks to the Lord of mercies in whose hand the hearts of kings are held.[1] We believe that this was surely brought about by the grace of your charity and the perseverance of your prayers so that, in this respect, divine mercy is mindful of that people over whom your solicitude presides. You will understand that we are making such concession to the King[2] and to those who appear to deserve punishment because of our affection and compassion so that we may be able to raise up those who have fallen. Whoever, while himself standing, stretches out his hand to one who has fallen in order to raise him up, will never raise the fallen one unless he stoops himself. Although bending seems very close to falling, yet he does not lose his position of uprightness.

We now absolve[3] you, our venerable and dearest brother in Christ, from that prohibition, or as you consider it, from that excommunication, which you know was pronounced by our predecessor, Pope Urban of sacred memory, against investitures and acts of homage. Accordingly, with the help of the Lord, you should receive those who have accepted investiture or have consecrated those so invested or have done homage,[4] when they render that satisfaction about which we are informing you through William and Baldwin, those loyal and truthful men, your joint messengers.[5] As deputy of our authority you should absolve those men and then either bless them yourself[6] or have them blessed by whoever you order, unless perhaps you find something else in them for which they ought to be barred from sacred honors. Moreover, you are to withdraw the fellowship of communion with you from the abbot of Ely as long as he presumes to retain the abbacy, which in contempt of the prohibition which we ourselves pronounced in his presence and hearing he has presumed to usurp by renewed investiture.[7] From now on, if anyone should accept preferment apart from investitures of churches, even if they have done homage to the King, they are not on any account to be banned because of that from the gift of the blessing until, by the grace of almighty God, the heart of the King is softened by the showers of your preaching to give up this practice.[8]

Furthermore, as to the bishops[9] who, as you know, brought a false report from us, our heart is exceedingly oppressed because they have not only wronged us but have deceived the souls of many simple people and have turned the King against the charity of the Apostolic See. Hence, with the help of the Lord, we shall not allow their crime to go unpunished. Nevertheless, since the perseverance of our son, the King, intercedes with us urgently on their behalf, you may not refuse the fellowship of your communion even to them until they receive a command to appear before us.

According to our solemn promise you should discreetly absolve the King and his consort from their penances and sins and also those nobles who, on our instruction, have exerted themselves at the King's court in this matter and will continue doing so, and whose names you will learn through the private information of the said William.[10]

Since the almighty Lord has granted you to progress so far in this reform in the kingdom of England for the sake of his glory and that of his Church, your fraternity should, from now on, prevail upon the King and the barons with such gentleness, tact, wisdom and foresight that those things which have not yet been corrected may, through the zeal of your solicitude, be corrected with the help of our Lord God.[11] You should be aware that in this matter our support is with your love so that we loose whatever you loose and we bind whatever you bind.[12]

We have committed to your consideration the case of the bishop of Rouen and the prohibition which, when justice so required, was pronounced against him.[13] Whatever you grant him, we grant.

May the divine majesty preserve your fraternity unharmed for a long time to come. Given on March twenty-third.

23 March 1106 at Benevento.

NOTES

1. See Pr 21: 1.
2. Compare Pope Paschal's assent to Henry's offer of compromise with Archbishop Hugh's recommendations, *Ep* 390; also *Ep* 364 and Eadmer's report of Henry's reaction, *HN* 181–182.
3. The Pope frees Anselm from implementing the decrees of the Lenten synod of 1099, see *Ep* 373; *HN* 114.
4. See *Epp* 280, 305, 306, 310, 352, 390; Blumenthal, *Pascal*, 19, 97.

5. For the messengers of the King and Anselm, see *Epp* 367, 378.
6. King Henry was in Normandy from August 1106 to April 1107 fighting his brother Robert and implementing his rule. After his return to England the compromise was ratified by the *curia regis*, 1–3 August 1107. Then, Anselm consecrated on 11 August at Canterbury the bishops-elect William of Winchester, Roger of Salisbury, Reinelm of Hereford, William de Warelwast of Exeter and Urban of Glamorgan. He was assisted by Archbishop Gerard and Bishops Robert of Lincoln, John of Bath (*Epp* 308, 351), Herbert of Norwich, Robert of Chester, Ralph Luffa of Chichester and Ranulf of Durham, *HN* 187. On the same day he restored the pastoral staff to Ealdwin of Ramsey. On 15 August he blessed Robert of Westminster as Abbot of Bury St Edmunds, *Ep* 382. The blessing of Hugh de Flori as Abbot of St Augustine, Canterbury, was delayed because of his lack of orders, *HN* 188–191. From August 1107 changes took place at the following monasteries:

Battle: Prior Ralph of Rochester elected Abbot;
Canterbury: Prior Ernulf resigned, became Abbot of Peterborough;
Chertsey: Hugh of Winchester elected Abbot;
Evesham: Robert or Maurice succeeded Abbot Walter;
Eynsham: possibly Nigel succeeded Columbanus;
Gloucester: Prior Peter elected to succeed Abbot Serlo;
Malmesbury: Eadwulf gained Anselm's pardon and blessing, *Ep* 384;
Milton and *Muchelney* received new abbots;
St Benet of Hulme: Richer, appointed in 1101, now blessed;
Tavistock: Osbern administered the abbey from 1102, now formally blessed;
Tewkesbury: Gerald of Avranches, appointed 1102, now blessed;
Winchester: Geoffrey became Prior of the cathedral, see Heads, and *Epp* 280, 310.

7. For Abbot Richard see *Epp* 280, 310, 422.
8. For the compromise which solved the investiture controversy, see *HC* 13–14; *Ep* 181.
9. Gerard of York, Robert of Chester and Herbert of Norwich, see *HN* 137–141 and *Epp* 217, 218, 219, 220, 225, 247, 250, 280, 281, 283, 354, 388.
10. See *Epp* 348, 351, 352, 353.
11. See Hugh's advice in *Ep* 390.
12. See Mt 16:19.
13. See *Epp* 388, 398, 404.

398. POPE PASCHAL TO ARCHBISHOP WILLIAM OF ROUEN.

Pope Paschal informs Archbishop William of Rouen that, moved by the intercession of Archbishop Anselm and William de Warelwast, he has referred his case to Anselm. He admonishes him to get rid of his evil counsellors.

PASCHAL, THE BISHOP, SERVANT OF THE SERVANTS OF GOD: TO HIS VENERABLE BROTHER WILLIAM, BISHOP OF ROUEN, GREETING AND APOSTOLIC BLESSING.

ALTHOUGH THE NATURE OF YOUR CASE[1] has greatly tried our patience, yet out of respect for our brother, the bishop of Canterbury, and because of our love for our son William,[2] the bearer of this letter, who have both interceded with us very earnestly on your behalf, we are moved with paternal kindness towards you. Accordingly we have entrusted your case to our said brother, the bishop of Canterbury, so that whatever he grants you we grant, but with this consideration and on condition that you banish from your company those evil counsellors at whose instigation you have committed many irregularities.[3]

Given at Benevento, 28 March.

28 March 1106 at Benevento.

NOTES

1. See *Epp* 388, 397.
2. William de Warelwast.
3. Having received the papal mandate, Anselm left Bec for Rouen to call a synod, see *HN* 177, 179–181.

399. FROM HENRY, KING OF THE ENGLISH.

King Henry is greatly concerned about Anselm's illness. He says he would have been in Normandy already if he had not been expecting him in England. He begs him to take care of his health and to treat his Norman possessions as his own. He is about to come to Normandy.

HENRY, BY THE GRACE OF GOD, KING OF THE ENGLISH: TO ANSELM, ARCHBISHOP OF CANTERBURY, HIS DEAREST FATHER, SENDING GREETING AND FRIENDSHIP.

YOUR KIND PATERNITY SHOULD KNOW that I am grieved and greatly saddened within because of the pain and weakness of your body.[1] Know too that I would have already been in Normandy if I had not been expecting you here.[2] I would have been glad if I had been able to receive you before leaving my realm. Now however, I beseech you as a son his father to be more indulgent to the natural disposition of your body for a little while and not to afflict your body so much. Moreover, I wish and command that everywhere in my possessions in Normandy you should act as if you were in your own domain, and my heart will be full of joy if you will do this. But now indeed await me in Normandy,[3] for I am about to cross over again.

Witnessed by Walderic, at Windsor.[4]

June 1106 at Windsor.

NOTES

1. Having received the Pope's reply from William de Warelwast, King Henry immediately recalled Anselm to England in May 1106. His letter to Anselm is not preserved, see *Ep* 379; Eadmer reports on it, *HN* 181–182. On his way to England Anselm fell ill at Jumièges and informed the King about the delay, *HN* 182.
2. Anselm would not have left Bec if the King had not called him back to England, *HN* 182–183.
3. After about a month at Jumièges Anselm returned to Bec 'thinking that it would be more convenient and more proper to await the King's

coming there than anywhere else', *HN* 182. The King crossed about 1 August and met Anselm, who had just recovered from another serious attack of his illness, on 15 August 1106 at Bec, *HN* 182.
4. See *Reg.* II: 757.

400. FROM MATILDA, QUEEN OF THE ENGLISH.

Queen Matilda of the English grieves bitterly about Anselm's sickness, which is prolonging their separation and begs him for information about himself.

TO HER DEAREST LORD AND FATHER, ARCHBISHOP ANSELM: MATILDA, QUEEN OF THE ENGLISH, WISHING HIM THE STRENGTH OF GOOD HEALTH.

THE SWEETNESS OF EXPECTED JOY recently promised me the arrival of your holiness. As great as was the joy and consolation you were about to grant me, so much greater was the disappointment of lonely sadness brought to me when that arrival was prevented by sickness.[1] Knowing the affection of your paternity for me, I come with pitiable weeping, begging that if your care for me has not completely melted away, you should put an end to the anxiety of my concern about your health by some messenger as soon as possible. I shall immediately rejoice either over your health and mine, or—which God in His mercy forbid!—I shall suffer the blow of our mutual fate with indifference. May the most holy omnipotence of God make you healthy.[2] Amen.

June 1106.

NOTES

1. See *HN* 181–182; *Ep* 398.
2. Anselm overcame the illness which had been so serious in July that everybody expected him to die. On 15 August King Henry came to Bec; he restored everything to Anselm 'and further promised that

so long as he lived he would not take anything from the churches during any period that they were without a pastor', *HN* 183. Having thus ended their quarrel, the King was free to bring his campaign in Normandy to a successful end, *Epp* 364, 401.

401. FROM HENRY, KING OF THE ENGLISH.

King Henry of the English informs Anselm of his victory over Duke Robert of Normandy at Tinchebrai. He is aware that the victory was given him by God and wishes this to be the beginning of greater devotion to God and peace for the Church.

HENRY, KING OF THE ENGLISH: TO ANSELM, ARCHBISHOP OF CANTERBURY, SENDING GREETING AND FRIENDSHIP.

WE INFORM YOUR PATERNITY AND HOLINESS that on an appointed and fixed day[1] Robert, Duke of Normandy, with all the forces of knights and foot soldiers which by begging or buying he was able to bring together, fought with me furiously outside Tinchebrai,[2] and in the end, by the mercy of God, we were victorious without any great slaughter of our own men. Why should I say more? Divine mercy delivered into our hands the Duke of Normandy,[3] the count of Mortain,[4] William Crispin,[5] William of Ferrers,[6] the aged Robert of Stuteville[7] and others to the number of four hundred knights and ten thousand foot soldiers, and Normandy itself. Of those slain by the sword there is no reckoning.

I attribute this victory not to my own excellence and pride nor to my own strength but to the gift of divine providence.[8] Therefore, venerable father, humbly and devoutly prostrate at the knees of your holiness, I beseech you to beseech the heavenly judge, by whose decision and will this victory, so glorious and so advantageous, has come to me, that it may not turn out to my loss or detriment but may lead to the initiation of good works and the service of God and to the preserving and strengthening of the position of God's holy Church in tranquillity and peace so that henceforth it may live at liberty and not be shaken by any storms of war.

Witnessed by Waldric, the chancellor, at Elbeuf.[9]

c. 1 October 1106.

NOTES

1. 28 September 1106, ASC in EHD II: 180. There is some uncertainty about the exact date of the battle, see OV VI: 89.
2. The castle of Tinchebrai, belonging to William of Mortain, was some fifty-two kilometers east of Avranches. For the battle and its consequences see F. Barlow, *Feudal Kingdom of England* (London, 1955) 178-179; A.L. Poole, *From Domesday Book to Magna Carta 1086-1216* (Oxford, 1958) 120-123.
3. Duke Robert was sent to Cardiff Castle where he lived in honorable captivity until his death in 1134.
4. Count William of Mortain, son and heir of Robert, Count of Mortain, half-brother of the Conqueror (EHD II: 983) was sent to England to live in captivity, ASC 1106; OV VI: 94.
5. William Crispin, brother of Gilbert Crispin, Abbot of Westminster, 1085-1117, was later pardoned by King Henry, OV VI: 180.
6. William was the son of Henry of Ferrers (Ferrières-Sainte-Hilaire), castellan of Tutbury, OV VI: 84, II: 264, IV: 232.
7. Robert of Stuteville was sent to England to live in captivity, ASC 1106; OV V: 94.
8. Eadmer commented that: 'not unnaturally it was the declared opinion of many that it was in consequence of his having made peace with Anselm that the King gained his victory', HN 184.
9. Elbeuf, eighteen kilometers south of Rouen on the left bank of the Seine. Immediately after Tinchebrai, Henry proceeded by way of Falaise to Rouen, OV VI: 92; Reg. II, xxix, 788.

402. TO HENRY, KING OF THE ENGLISH AND DUKE OF THE NORMANS.

Anselm congratulates King Henry on his victory and encourages him to persevere in those things he so piously proposed: the peace and freedom of the Church.

TO HENRY, BY THE GRACE OF GOD, GLORIOUS KING OF THE ENGLISH AND DUKE OF THE NORMANS:[1] ANSELM, THE ARCHBISHOP, SENDING HIM FAITHFUL SERVICE WITH FAITHFUL PRAYERS AND WISHING THAT HE MAY ALWAYS INCREASE TOWARDS GREATER AND BETTER THINGS AND NEVER DECREASE.

I REJOICE AND GIVE THANKS with as much affection as I can to God *from whom all good things come*[2] for your prosperity and your successes. I also rejoice and give thanks from the bottom of my heart because he has so enlightened your heart with his grace, while bestowing earthly prosperity on you, that you impute nothing in his generosity and your progress to yourself or to human strength but everything to his mercy, and also because you promise peace and liberty to his Church, as far as you can.[3]

Wherefore, I earnestly beseech you and advise you as your faithful servant to persevere in this because in it lies the strength of your highness. I therefore pray to almighty God with heart and lips, as much as my spirit is capable of, both myself and through others, that in the mercy of his grace which he has begun to expend on you,[4] he may unceasingly continue to lead you from earthly exaltation after this life to the heavenly kingdom and eternal glory. Amen.

October 1106 from Canterbury.

NOTES

1. Henry became Duke of Normandy through the defeat of his brother Robert at Tinchebrai, see *Ep* 401.

2. Collect of the Mass of the 5th Sunday after Easter.
3. Anselm echoes Henry's letter, *Ep* 401.
4. Anselm is referring to the solution of the investiture controversy, see *Epp* 364, 397.

403. TO EULALIA, ABBESS OF SHAFTESBURY, AND HER NUNS.

Anselm thanks Abbess Eulalia of Shaftesbury and her nuns for their prayers during his exile and asks them to pray that his return may be prosperous. He admonishes the nuns to be obedient to their mother superior, not to regard any sin as small and to keep peace among themselves.

ANSELM, THE ARCHBISHOP: TO THE REVEREND ABBESS EULALIA AND HER DAUGHTERS,[1] GREETING.

I GIVE THANKS TO YOUR DEVOUT LOVE because you prayed for me, longing for my return, while I was in exile out of England. Now I ask you even more earnestly to pray that my return[2] may be prosperous. I wish you to know that my love for you has existed as long as I have known you, still lives and continues, and that as long as I live, God granting, will continue. Wherefore, while this love still endures I wish to write you something, although you do not need it, in order that you may know that I love you and have care for you.

You, beloved sisters and daughters of mine, I exhort and admonish to be subject and obedient to your mother, not merely before human eyes but also before the eyes of God, to whom nothing is hidden. True obedience is when the will of the subordinate so obeys the will of the superior that, wherever the subordinate may be, she wishes what she knows the superior wishes, as long as it is not against the will of God. Your community ought to be a temple of God and the *temple of God is holy*.[3] If therefore, you live in a holy manner, as I hope you do, then you are the temple of God. You live in a holy manner if you diligently keep your rule and your intention. You do this diligently if you do not scorn the smallest things. Your intention should always be to strive for progress and to dread regress with all your heart. For it is written *that one who despises little things fails little by little.*[4] One who fails makes no progress. Therefore, if you wish to progress and dread regress do not despise the little things. As it is true that *one who despises little things fails little by little* so it is true that one who does not despise little things progresses little by little.

Do not think that any sin is small, although one may be greater than another. Nothing done by disobedience—and that alone drove man out of paradise—should be called small. What sin will be small if Truth bears witness that *one who is angry with his brother will answer for it before the court of justice; one who says 'Raca' must answer for it before the council; and one who says 'You fool' must answer for it in hell fire?*[5] I ask you therefore, my dearest daughters, not to neglect anything but to strive to keep your works and your hearts always as if they were in God's sight.

Keep peace among yourselves because *in peace God makes his abode;*[6] and *great peace have they who love* God's *law and nothing shall offend them.*[7] I pray with heart and lips that God's blessing and absolution may come upon you and, as far as I am able, I give and send you my own, if it is worth anything. Farewell.

autumn 1106.

NOTES

1. See *Epp* 183, 208, 337.
2. Anselm returned to England in early September 1106; he had been absent since 27 April 1103.
3. 1 Co 3:17.
4. Si 19:1 (Ecclesiasticus 19:1)
5. Mt 5:22.
6. Ps 75:3.
7. Ps 118:165.

404. TO HENRY, KING OF THE ENGLISH AND DUKE OF THE NORMANS.

Anselm advises Henry, King of the English and Duke of the Normans, that it would be difficult to translate Bishop Hervey canonically from Bangor to Lisieux.

TO HENRY, HIS DEAREST LORD, BY THE GRACE OF GOD BOTH KING OF THE ENGLISH AND DUKE OF THE NORMANS: ANSELM, THE ARCHBISHOP, SENDING FAITHFUL SERVICE WITH PRAYERS.

YOUR HIGHNESS INFORMED ME through the bishop-elect of Winchester[1] that I should write to you whether lord Hervey,[2] bishop of Bangor, could be made bishop of the church of Lisieux.[3]

I do not see how this can be done easily. For just as no bishop ought to be consecrated for any church without the assent and advice of the archbishop and the other bishops of the whole province, so he who has been consecrated bishop cannot canonically be made a bishop in any other province without the advice and assent of the archbishop and the bishops of that province with papal authority, nor without release by the archbishop and the bishops of the province in which he was consecrated. This release cannot be given without an extensive and joint enquiry and the advice of those people, without whom, as I have said, he could not be consecrated, even if his bishopric appears to be so completely destroyed that he cannot stay there.[4]

May almighty God guide you in this and in all your other actions.[5] Amen.

late 1106.

NOTES

1. William Giffard, see *Epp* 212, 397.
2. In the wake of the expansion of Norman rule into Wales under Earl Hugh of Chester, Hervey, a Breton, was made Bishop of Bangor in 1092. His stay there was short-lived because the Normans were

pushed back, and in 1100 he had to return to England. In 1109 he was made bishop of the newly-created see of Ely, which he ruled until his death on 30 August 1131, see M. Brett, *The English Church under Henry I* (Oxford, 1975) 29, 57–58 and passim.

3. Gilbert Maminot, Bishop of Lisieux from 1077, died in August 1101. During the ensuing vacancy Ranulf Flambard tried to establish his family at Lisieux. He had his brother Fulcher consecrated bishop of Lisieux by Archbishop William of Rouen in June 1102, but Fulcher died in January 1103, *OV* V: 320–322. Then Flambard procured the bishopric for his sons, aged about twelve, on the condition that if the elder died the other should succeed him, *OV* V: 322–323. Thomas ruled for three years, not as bishop but as guardian. To replace Flambard's sons Archdeacom William of Evreux was canonically elected but was unable to attain consecration because Archbishop William was suspended, *Epp* 388, 397. Ranulf tried to secure the see by intruding his clerk William of Pacy, *OV* V: 322, who was rejected because of simony. After the battle of Tinchebrai Henry vainly tried to end the scandalous situation at Lisieux by translating Hervey from Bangor. In 1107 Archdeacon John of Séez became Bishop of Lisieux, see *OV* V: 320–322.

4. For the situation of the church of Bangor and Welsh dioceses, see Southern, *Anselm*, 132–133.

5. King Henry was at Lisieux about 15 October 1106 and again in March 1107, from whence he returned to England, *Reg.* II, xxix. At the later date, after the agreement with Pope Paschal on lay investitures (*HN* 181, *Ep* 397), Henry may have received the homage of John, Archdeacon of Séez, before his consecration as Bishop of Lisieux. Thus Henry's enquiry and Anselm's reply should probably be connected with Henry's earlier stay at Lisieux.

405. TO MABILIA, A NUN.

Anselm admonishes the nun Mabilia not to wish to live both a worldly and a monastic life and discourages her from visiting her relatives.

ANSELM, THE ARCHBISHOP: TO HIS DEAREST
DAUGHTER, THE NUN MABILIA, SENDING THE
GREETING AND BLESSING OF GOD, AND HIS OWN.

I LOVE YOU and in the way I love my own soul I love yours as well. I love my own soul so that it may merit to enjoy God in this life and enjoy him in the life to come.

This I love and desire for you. Wherefore I exhort and admonish you as my dearest daughter not to delight in worldly things because no one can love the goods of the world and those of eternity at the same time. I do not wish you to love the secular but the monastic way of life. There should be nothing between you and this world if you wish to be a nun and a spouse of God. Say with St Paul the Apostle: *The world has been crucified to me, and I to the world.*[1] With the same Apostle regard all the transitory things of this world as dung.[2]

My daughter, what need is there for you to visit any of your relatives since they do not need your advice or help in any way, nor can you receive any advice or help from them regarding your intention and profession which you could not find in your cloister. The intention of your life is different from their way of life.[3] They will not become monks because of you nor will you return to secular life because of them. What have you in common with them, my beloved daughter in God, if you are of no use to them in the life they are leading nor they to you in what you ought to love most of all? If they want to see you or need your advice or help in any way, let them come to you, for they are free to wander and run around wherever they like. Do not go to them because you are not allowed to leave the monastery except for a necessity which God may make known. Do not, my daughter, do not love the world because *a friend of this world is an enemy of God.*[4] Do not love the friendship of those in the world because the more you are friendly with them of your own accord the less you will be friendly with God and his friends, the angels. Do not be anxious to be known in the world, for so much the more will God say to you, *I do not know you.*[5] Desire to please God alone;[6] long to know God alone and those things which help you towards this. Commend yourself to him daily; I commend you, as much as I can, to him. May he rule, guide and guard you always. Amen.[7]

c. autumn or winter 1106–1107.

NOTES

1. Gal 6:14.
2. See Ph 3:8.
3. Compare Anselm's advice with that he gave Prior Henry of Christ Church Canterbury in *Ep* 17.
4. Jm 4:4.
5. See Mt 25:12.
6. See Pope Gregory I, *Dialogues* 2 (the life of Benedict) Preface.
7. *Ep* 405 is letter 332 in MS L, where it is in sequence with *Epp* 404 and 406. This indicates that it was written after Anselm's return to England in early September 1106.

406. TO MATILDA, QUEEN OF THE ENGLISH.

Anselm explains to Queen Matilda of the English that he cannot give testimony to the bearer of her letter, as he does not know him.

TO MATILDA, HIS DEAREST LADY AND DAUGHTER, BY THE GRACE OF GOD GLORIOUS QUEEN OF THE ENGLISH: ANSELM, THE ARCHBISHOP, SENDING FAITHFUL PRAYERS WITH FAITHFUL SERVICE AND WISHING HER ALWAYS TO REJOICE IN THE GRACE OF GOD IN THIS LIFE AND IN THE LIFE TO COME.

THE BEARER OF THIS LETTER brought me your seal with a letter[1] from you. This indicated to me that you wish his disgrace to be driven from him by the testimony of my letter because of a certain act of expiation he had made, and that through my intercession he might regain from my lord the King what he had lost on the King's order.

I ought not, nor do I wish to disregard your will, but I am certain about the benevolence of your Highness, that you do not wish me to act otherwise than is fitting for me. Your prudence knows that it is not for me to give testimony about matters I have neither seen nor heard, but that it is for those who have seen. Nor is it for me to intercede for someone whose life and character I know nothing about, so that he may recover what he had lost by royal command. Therefore I pray that the benevolence of your Highness may not be displeased that I hesitate to do anything which I perceive not mine to do.[2]

May almighty God always protect and guide you with his blessing. Amen.[3]

possibly winter 1106–1107.

NOTES

1. Matilda's letter is not preserved.
2. This is the last letter from Anselm to Queen Matilda that has been preserved. On their relationship and correspondance see Southern, *Anselm*, 182–193.
3. This letter can be dated by its position in MS L.

407. TO HELGOT, ABBOT OF ST OUEN.

Anselm informs Abbot Helgot of St Ouen, his friend, about how he was received in England. The King has entrusted the kingdom and all his possessions to his care but he feels that nothing important should be begun before the King's return. All is well with him, except for his bodily weakness, which grows daily.

ANSELM, THE ARCHBISHOP, SERVANT OF THE CHURCH OF CANTERBURY: TO HIS DEARLY BELOVED FRIEND, THE VENERABLE ABBOT HELGOT[1] OF THE MONASTERY OF ST OUEN, WISHING HIM WHATEVER CAN BEST BE DESIRED FOR A FRIEND.

A TRUE FRIEND IS ALWAYS ANXIOUS about a true friend as if about his other self so that he may be aware of what concerns him and be able either to rejoice or suffer with him according to the circumstances. Since no one loves pain I am somewhat amazed that if there is any reason for sharing pain a true friend would rather know about it so that he could share it than be ignorant of it so that he feels no pain. Your love, so beloved and delightful to me, desires to know my state and everything about me so that just as my heart knows how I am, so your heart may also know how I am.

By the providence of God's grace and with the help of your prayers and those of other servants of God, our friends, I have recently returned to England[2] where I was received with as much joy and honor as people could show, by great and small, by nobles and subjects. You heard that my lord the King commended his kingdom and all his possessions to me, and that my will is to be done in everything belonging to him—this is true. In this he demonstrated the generosity of his will and his great love for me. But because it is written: *All things are permitted to me but not all things are advantageous,*[3] and elsewhere: *All things are permitted to me, but not all things edify,*[4] I do not think it wise to try by myself to begin anything important at the moment.[5] But when God, in his grace, brings back the King to us[6] with that good disposition which I perceive,[7] I hope that God in his grace will do many things among us to his own honor, through the King, so that we may rejoice. According to what the changes in this world[8] permit, everything concerning me physically and otherwise is prospering by the gift of God, except for the weakness of my body which I feel increasing daily.[9]

May all the blessings which you invoke on me in your letter[10] also come upon your own head. I greet our brothers, your dearly-beloved sons, and beg them to remember me.

winter or spring 1106–1107.

NOTES

1. See *Epp* 25, 29, 48. Helgot, prior of Caen from 1075, outstanding for his learning and virtuous life, was elected abbot in place of venerable Nicholas who died in 1092; he ruled the Abbey of St Ouen, near Rouen, for about twenty years, see *OV* IV: 308.
2. Early in September 1106.

3. 1 Co 6:12.
4. 1 Co 10:23.
5. Anselm seems to be planning another synod for church reform. It took place at Whitsun, 24 May 1108, at Westminster, *HN* 193–195; *CS* 694–704.
6. King Henry was in Normandy from August 1106-April 1107. He spent Easter (14 April 1107) at Windsor.
7. Anselm is referring to the agreement of l'Aigle on 21 July 1105, the subsequent assent to it by Pope Paschal II, *HN* 181; *Ep* 397; and the meeting with King Henry at Bec 15 August 1106, *HN* 182–183; *Epp* 394, 399.
8. See the collect for the Fourth Sunday after Easter.
9. Anselm was seriously ill in June and July 1106, *HN* 181–182, in May and June 1107, *HN* 185, and July 1108, *HN* 197; *Epp* 399, 400.
10. Helgot's letter is not preserved.

408. TO PRIOR ELFER AND THE MONKS OF BURY ST EDMUNDS.

Anselm explains to Prior Elfer and the monks of Bury St Edmunds that he had withdrawn his communion from Robert, the abbot-elect, at the Pope's command. Now, however, also at the Pope's command, he accepts him, and for this reason they are to obey their abbot in all things.

ANSELM, THE ARCHBISHOP: TO HIS BELOVED SONS AND BROTHERS, DOM PRIOR ELFER[1] AND THE OTHERS SERVING GOD IN THE MONASTERY OF ST EDMUNDS, SENDING THE GREETING AND BLESSING OF GOD, AND HIS OWN.

UP TO NOW I HAVE HELD BACK from communion with Dom Robert.[2] This I have done according to the command and in obedience to the lord Pope. Now however, at the order of the same lord Pope, for the reason that he has commanded me,[3] I have accepted Dom Robert in peace and communion and I instruct and command you to be obedient to him in all things from now on, and to make your confession to him and do all the other things which monks owe to their abbot, and not to desist from doing them unless I command you otherwise in future. I ask you, and exhort and admonish you in every way I can, to be zealous in the observance of your rule so that nothing may ever be heard about you save what is fitting to be heard about good monks and true servants of God. Amen.

c. winter 1106–1107.

NOTES

1. Elfer or Aelfer, see *Ep* 382.
2. Prior Robert of Westminster, elected abbot of Bury in autumn 1102, was not blessed until 15 August 1107; see *Epp* 280, 382; *Heads* 32.
3. See *Ep* 397; *VA* 139.

409. FROM HUGH, ABBOT OF CLUNY.

Abbot Hugh of Cluny informs Anselm about the death of Archbishop Hugh of Lyon on 7 October 1106.

TO HIS MOST REVEREND FATHER AND MOST GENTLE FRIEND, DOM ANSELM, ARCHBISHOP OF CANTERBURY, AND ALL HIS MONKS: BROTHER HUGH, A SINNER, ABBOT OF CLUNY, SENDING HIM GREETING AND JOY WITHOUT END.

BECAUSE WE KNEW what a great friendship, by the grace of God, existed between you and lord Hugh, Archbishop of Lyon, we thought it fitting to inform you of his death, which is for us and all good men an event of great and unalterable sorrow, so that you and your people may try, now that he is dead, to repay him the true love which he showed during his life. He died in peace at Susa[1] on October seventh on his way to a meeting called by the Pope[2] and was worthily buried there in the Abbey of St Just. We desire to know more about your agreement[3] and to be more abundantly gladdened by news of your prosperity when time and place make it possible. May Jesus Christ, the supreme pontiff, work with you in all things.

c. November 1106.

NOTES

1. Hugh, Archbishop of Lyon, died on 7 October 1106 at Susa, situated at the eastern foot of the Mt Cenis pass, some forty kilometers west of Turin.
2. On 22 October 1106 Pope Paschal celebrated the Council of Guastalla, between Verona and Mantua in Lombardy, with the intention of solving the problems resulting from the schism (see Ep 377), advancing the reform movement, and defining the relationsip between Church and Empire anew, see Mansi XX, 1209–1216; Blumenthal, *Paschal*, 32–73; C. Servatius, *Paschalis II 1099–1118* (Stuttgart, 1979) 200–205.
3. Hugh seems to be referring to the agreement of l'Aigle, see HN 165–167; Epp 364, 397.

410. TO P., A MONK OF ST MARTIN OF SÉEZ.

Anselm disapproves of the wish of a monk of St Martin of Séez to go to Jerusalem because it is against his vow of stability, against the papal command and against his abbot's wish.

ANSELM, SERVANT OF THE CHURCH OF CANTERBURY: TO HIS DEAR BROTHER P., MONK OF THE MONASTERY OF ST MARTIN OF SÉEZ, SENDING GREETING AND WISHING HIM ALWAYS TO BE GUIDED AND CONSOLED BY THE GRACE OF GOD.

I HEAR, MY DEAREST FRIEND, that you long to go to Jerusalem.[1] Wherefore, first of all I tell you that this desire of yours does not come from a good quarter, nor is it good for the salvation of your soul. It is against your profession at which, before God, you promised stability[2] in the monastery in which you took on the habit of a monk. It is also against the obedience due to the Pope[3] who commanded by his great authority that monks should not presume to take on such a journey except for some religious persons who might usefully be employed in ruling the Church of God and in teaching the people, and even this only on the advice of and in obedience to their superior. I was in fact present when the Pope promulgated this decree.[4] It is also against the obedience you owe to your abbot who hates this wish and curses it as a danger for your soul.[5]

possibly winter 1106–1107.

NOTES

1. See *Ep* 195 for Anselm's advice in a similar case.
2. RB 58:17–18.
3. At the Council of Clermont Pope Urban II called for the first crusade on 27 November 1095. He urged able-bodied laymen to take the cross; clerics and monks were not to take the cross without the permission of their bishop or abbot, see Mansi XX, 815–820; C. Hefele, *Conciliengeschichte* (Freiburg, 1886) V, 231; S. Runciman, *History of the Crusades* (London, 1965) 1:109.
4. Anselm was present at the synod of Bari, October 1098, *HN* 104–110, and at the synod in Rome, 24 April 1099, *HN* 112–114. However, no canons from these synods mentioning this prohibition for monks and clerics have been preserved, see Mansi XX, 950, 961. Hefele, ibid., 254, 258, states that the crusades were a matter of discussion.
5. Since this letter is in sequence with letters 409 and 411 in MS L, the date appears to be winter 1106–1107.

411. FROM HUGH, ABBOT OF CLUNY.

Abbot Hugh of Cluny writes that he has not had any word from Anselm since his departure from Cluny in May 1105. He commends to him his monks who are going to England on business and asks for his decision regarding the monk Theardus.

TO HIS MOST BELOVED AND GLORIOUS FATHER, DOM ANSELM, THE VENERABLE ARCHBISHOP OF CANTERBURY: FROM BROTHER HUGH, A SINNER, ABBOT OF CLUNY, WISHING HIM HEALTH OF MIND AND BODY[1] IN CHRIST AND JOY WITHOUT END.

AFTER YOU LEFT US,[2] man beloved by God, we were not able to find out what was happening to your holiness. However, we hope that by the mercy of God, wherever your holiness may be, divine help may be with you. How could anyone, having experienced the sweetness of your discourse ever be so uncivil as not to receive and venerate you *like an angel of God*?[3] Therefore we, although completely unworthy, implore divine clemency that he who has granted you such grace on earth may deign to bestow on you eternal glory in heaven.

And now, father, we have sent our sons, your true servants and faithful friends, to that country for the general business of our monastery.[4] As we recommend them to your holiness we wish that they may be accompanied by your advice and strengthened by your help as they are going about their business in those regions.

Concerning the case of our son, Dom Theardus, we particularly ask you, since the lord Pope placed the entire decision about his ministry into your judgement, and you conceded him the competence of his whole ministry as long as he remained in clerical habit as we learned from him, that now, since you have been restored to primatial dignity[5] by the mercy of God, you do not disdain to communicate to us by letter[6] what we should tell him. May your holiness rejoice for a long time and remember us.

winter 1106–1107.

NOTES

1. Compare this part of the address with the collect *concede nos* of Feasts of the Blessed Virgin Mary in the *Commune Sanctorum* of the Roman Missal.
2. Anselm left Cluny in May 1105, HN 164.
3. Esth. 15:16.
4. There were Cluniac houses at Bermondsey (Surrey), Castle Acre (Norfolk), Lewes (Sussex), Montacute (Somerset), and Thetford (Norfolk); see *Heads*, 114–125.
5. At l'Aigle King Henry received Anselm back into his friendship and reinvested him with the archbishopric on 21 July 1105, *Ep* 364; he recalled him to England in May or June 1106, after receiving Pope Paschal's assent, *Ep* 397. The meeting at Bec on 15 August 1106 marked the final reconciliation between them, *Epp* 394, 399, 400. Anselm left Bec for England in early September 1106.
6. If there was a reply it has not been preserved.

412. TO EARL HUGH.

Anselm informs Hugh, Earl of Chester, that the bearer of this letter, a monk of Cluny, has complained that the Earl has imprisoned one monk of Cluny and buried another monk in an improper grave. He asks him to make amends for these things.

ANSELM, THE ARCHBISHOP: TO HIS LORD AND DEAREST FRIEND EARL HUGH,[1] SENDING THE GREETING AND BLESSING OF GOD, AND HIS OWN.

THE BEARER OF THIS LETTER, a monk of Cluny, complains that you have taken captive and are holding in captivity a certain monk of Cluny, and that another man, recently made a monk and now dead, has been carried off by your men and buried where it pleased them.

If these things are so I am very grieved about you on this account, because they have acted in a way quite out of keeping with what is fitting for you. Therefore I instruct, beseech and advise you as my friend, do not delay to release the monk you are holding; and since you took him captive you should offer to make him reparation for what you did. Indeed your honor demands that you do this. Afterwards, if you have anything against this monk, make your claim and you will be compensated according to what justice requires. About the dead man, I advise you to offer to make amends in like manner, and that he be where he rightfully should be. I speak to you openly, as to a man whose honor and service I greatly love, because if you do not do as I say you will be reproached; and as for me, if I fail to do what ecclesiastical discipline demands to be done in such a case, I will be reproached by many. I greet your wife, my dearest daughter.

before 27 July 1101.

NOTES

1. Hugh, Earl of Chester died at St Werburgh on 27 July 1101, see *Ep* 189; *OV* V: 314; *Epp* 251, 252, 266; *HN* 27–28; *VA* 63, and J.F.A. Mason, 'St Anselm's relations with laymen', *Spicilegium Beccense 1* (Paris, 1958) 550–553, 560; E.A. Freeman, *The Reign of William Rufus* (Oxford, 1882) 2:580.

413. TO ALEXANDER, KING OF THE SCOTS.

Anselm congratulates Alexander, King of the Scots, on his ascension to the throne after the death of his brother Edgar, for whom he promises to pray. He exhorts the King to combine royal courage with constancy of virtue and commends to him the monks he has sent to Scotland at the request of his brother.

TO ALEXANDER, BY THE GRACE OF GOD KING OF THE SCOTS: ANSELM, SERVANT OF THE CHURCH OF CANTERBURY, SENDING GREETING AND FAITHFUL PRAYERS, AND THE BLESSING OF GOD AND HIS OWN, FOR WHAT IT IS WORTH.

WE GIVE THANKS TO GOD, both I and the whole community of Christ Church Canterbury, and rejoice that God has raised you by right of inheritance to the kingdom of your father after your brother, and has adorned you with a character worthy of your royal dignity.[1] For your brother who, by his holy life deserved to pass from this life by a good end, by the mercy of God, we pray and will continue to pray, according to your request,[2] as for a beloved friend of ours. May God grant his soul the eternal joy of his glory among his elect and accord him everlasting happiness.

I know that your Highness loves and desires my advice. First of all I pray to God that he himself may so guide you by the grace of his Holy Spirit and grant you his advice in all your deeds that he may lead you after this life to his heavenly kingdom. Our advice is that you should strive to retain the fear of God and those good and pious habits which you began to have from your childhood and in your youth, with the help of him from whom you received them. For kings reign well when they live according to the will of God and serve him in fear,[3] and when they reign over themselves and do not succumb to vices but overcome their persistence by constant fortitude. For constancy in virtues and royal fortitude are not incompatible in a king. Certain kings, like David, lived a holy life and ruled the people entrusted to them with the severity of justice and the gentleness of loving-kindness, as the matter demanded. Show yourself in such a way that the wicked fear you and the good love you. In order that your life may always be pleasing to God, your mind should always remember the punishment of the wicked and the reward of the good after this life. May almighty God entrust you and all your actions to nothing else but his own holy providence.

As to our brothers[4] whom we sent to Scotland according to the will of your brother who has passed from the labors of this life to his rest, as we trust, we do not think it necessary to request your kindness for them, because we are well aware of your good will.

February or March 1107.

NOTES

1. 'In the course of this year also died King Edgar of Scotland on January 13' (other authorities say 8 January). 'Alexander, his brother, succeeded to the throne with King Henry's consent', *ASC* 1107 in *EHD* II: 180. King Edgar (1098–1107) and King Alexander (1107–1124) were brothers of Queen Matilda, wife of Henry I of England. Their parents were King Malcolm III Canmore (1058–1093) and his second wife Margaret (1068–1093), sister of Edgar Atheling. Malcolm III had been succeeded by his brother Donald Bane (1094–1098). For a genealogical table of the Kings of Scotland, see *EHD* II: 997.
2. King Alexander's letter is not preserved.
3. See Ps 2:11.
4. Probably monks from Canterbury. Both Edgar and Alexander furthered the introduction of religious institutions from England to Scotland. Edgar refounded Coldingham for Durham monks in 1098 or 1099, see E.A. Freeman, *The Reign of William Rufus* (Oxford, 1882) 2:120–126. At a later date Alexander and David I brought Canterbury monks to Dunfermline, see Barlow, *English Church*, 187.

414. TO ROBERT AND HIS NUNS.

Anselm praises the devout lives of Robert, his nuns and their chaplain William. He explains the causes of good and evil deeds and advises them how to ward off evil thoughts. He thanks Robert for his care for these Anglo-Saxon ladies.

ANSELM, THE ARCHBISHOP: TO HIS DEAREST FRIEND AND SON ROBERT[1] AND TO HIS MOST BELOVED SISTERS AND DAUGHTERS SEIT, EDIT, THYDIT, LWERUN, DIRGIT AND GODIT, SENDING THE GREETING AND BLESSING OF GOD, AND HIS OWN, IF IT IS WORTH ANYTHING.

I REJOICE AND GIVE THANKS TO GOD for the holy intention and holy way of life you are leading together in the love of God and in holiness of life, as I have learned through our brother and son William. Your love, dear to me, dearest daughters, requests that I should send you some admonition to teach and inflame you towards leading a good life, although you have with you our beloved son Robert, whom God has inspired to take care of you according to the will of God, and to teach you daily by word and example how you ought to live. Yet since I ought to support your holy petition if I can, I shall try to write you a few words to satisfy your desire.

My dearest daughters, every action, whether praiseworthy or blameworthy, earns praise or blame according to the intention behind it. For the root and principle of all actions that are in our own power lie in the will, and even if we cannot do what we wish, yet each of us is judged before God according to his will. Do not therefore consider only what you do but what you intend to do; not so much what your deeds may be but what you intention is. For every action which is done rightly, that is to say with a just intention, is right, and whatever is done without a right intention is not right. The man with a just intention is called just, one with an unjust intention is called unjust.

Therefore, if you wish to live a good life, continually keep watch over your will in both great and small things, in those things subject to your power and in those over which you have no control, so that your will may not deviate from righteousness in any way.

If you wish to know whether your intention is right: what is subject to the will of God is certainly right. Whenever you plan or think of doing anything great or small, speak thus in your hearts: 'Does God want me to want this or not?' If your conscience answers: 'Yes, God does want me to want this and such an intention pleases him', then whether you are able to do what you want or not, cherish that intention. If, however, your conscience tells you that God does not want you to have that intention, then turn your heart away from it with all your might. If you want to drive it completely away from you, exclude the memory and thought of it from your heart as far as you can.

Consider and observe the modest advice I give you about how to exclude a bad intention or a bad thought from yourselves. Do not struggle with wicked thoughts or with a wicked intention, but when they molest you do your utmost to occupy your mind with some useful thought and intention until they disappear. For no thought or intention is ever driven out of your heart except by some other thought or intention which does not agree with it. Therefore, be so disposed towards useless thoughts and intentions that by attending with all your might to profitable ones your mind may refuse to remember them or to take any notice of them. When you wish to pray or to engage in any good meditation, if thoughts which you ought not to entertain irritate you, never wish to give up the good you have started because of their irritation lest their instigator, the devil, may rejoice because he made you give up the good beginning, but overcome them by despising them in the way I have described. Do not grieve or be sad because they molest you, as long as by despising them, as I said, you do not submit to them, lest in a moment of sadness they return to your memory and renew their irritation. For it is customary with the human mind that whatever delights or saddens it returns to memory more frequently than whatever it feels or thinks ought to be ignored.

A person zealous in the pursuit of a holy intention should behave in the same way in the face of any unbecoming emotion of the body or the soul, such as the *sting in the flesh*[2] of anger or envy or vainglory. For such feelings are most easily quenched when we refuse to indulge in them or to think about them or to carry out anything at their suggestion. Do not fear that such emotions or thoughts will be imputed to you as sin as long as your intention does not associate itself with them on any account, because there is *no condemnation for those who are in Christ Jesus, who do not walk according to the flesh.*[3] For to walk according to the flesh is to give in to the will of the flesh. The Apostle, however, calls every vicious emotion in soul or body 'flesh' when he says: *The flesh lusts against the spirit and the spirit against the flesh.*[4] We easily quench such suggestions if, according to the advice given above, we crush them when they first start. But it is difficult to do so once we have admitted their heads into our minds.[5]

I give you as much thanks as I can, dearest friend and son Robert, for the care and love you bestow on these handmaidens of God for God's sake, and I beseech you with my whole heart to persevere in this holy and pious intention. You can be certain that a great reward from God awaits you for this holy zeal.

May almighty God always be the guardian of your whole lives. Amen. May the almighty and merciful Lord grant you absolution and remission of all your sins,[6] make you always progress towards the better in humility and never fail.[7]

1106–1109.

NOTES

1. See *Ep* 230, where Anselm calls Rodbert [sic], Seit and Edit 'his dear children'.
2. 2 Co 12:7.
3. Rm 8:1.
4. Gal 5:17.
5. In his letter to this small community Anselm displays the warmth he used to show to larger communities like Bec and Canterbury in his earlier years, see Southern, *Anselm*, 254. Anselm here emphasizes the importance of will and intention in leading a holy life, a concept later developed by Abelard.
6. Formula of sacramental absolution in e.g. *Collectio Rituum* (Collegeville, 1964) 184–185.
7. Possibly written after Anselm's return to England in early September 1106.

415. TO WALRAM, BISHOP OF NAUMBURG.

Anselm replies to the first question of Walram, Bishop of Naumburg, who had asked about the difference between Greeks and Latins by sending him his sermon De processione Spiritus Sancti *against the Greeks. He treats Walram's second question concerning the use of leavened or unleavened bread in the Eucharist at greater length and briefly answers Walram's third question concerning the difference of marital impediments between the Greeks and the Latins.*

before December 1105.

416. FROM WALRAM, BISHOP OF NAUMBURG.

Walram, Bishop of Naumburg, humbly begs to be instructed by Anselm, the pinnacle of knowledge, on four differences between Greeks and Latins:
- on their different ways of administering sacraments;
- on the use of different kinds of bread in the Eucharist;
- on the different kinds of blessing of bread and wine;
- on whether the chalice ought to be covered during Mass.

before August 1106.

417. TO WALRAM, BISHOP OF NAUMBURG.

Anselm congratulates Walram, Bishop of Naumburg, for having left the party siding with the Emperor and for supporting the papal decrees on lay investiture. He briefly deals with Walram's questions on the sacraments.

c. 1107.

NOTES

The preceding three letters of c. 1105–1107 are printed among the theological tracts of Saint Anselm in *AOO* II:221–242; ET in *Anselm of Canterbury*, edited and translated by J. Hopkins and H. Richardson (Toronto, 1976) 3:231–249. Walrum was bishop of Naumburg in Thuringia, 1091–1111. On his life and his correspondence with Anselm, see Fröhlich, 'Bischof Walram von Naumburg', *AA* V (1976) 261–282.

418. TO TUROLD, MONK OF BEC.

Anselm congratulates Turold for having resigned the bishopric of Bayeux and entered the monastery of Bec. He exhorts him not to look back but to persevere in his monastic intention.

ANSELM, SERVANT OF THE CHURCH OF CANTERBURY: TO HIS DEAREST BROTHER AND FRIEND TUROLD,[1] BY THE GRACE OF GOD MONK OF BEC, SENDING GREETING AND WISHING THAT HE MAY PERSEVERE IN HIS GOOD INTENTION UNTIL THE END.[2]

BLESSED BE GOD IN HIS GIFTS and *holy in all his works*,[3] who has turned your heart from vanity to truth. All those follow vanity who desire the dignities and honors and riches of this world,[4] for these things can in no way satisfy the mind as they promise to do, but the more abundant they are, the more they cause the soul to hunger, and they do not lead to any good end. They indeed hold the truth who despise earthly and transitory things with their whole hearts and rise to true humility with all their strength. To spiritual eyes those who humble themselves do not at all appear to be descending but rather to be climbing the loftiest mountain from which they ascend to the kingdom of heaven.[5]

Divine clemency has led you on to the road to paradise, or rather it has introduced you to a sort of paradise in this life when it introduced you to the enclosed way of life of your monastic intention. Therefore, let your prudence take care that your heart does not look back.[6] For a monk looks back when he often recalls what he has left behind. If he does this frequently heavenly love grows cool within him, and love of the world and dislike and weariness with his intention come to life again. Therefore, just as your body is separated from the secular way of life, so may your heart be separated from worldly thoughts and may it always be occupied with some useful, spiritual meditation.[7]

May the Holy Spirit always dwell in your heart[8] and make you ever rejoice and give thanks to God for your good beginning. Amen.

c. 1107.

NOTES

1. See *Ep* 298; Turold entered Bec under Abbot William in 1107. He is four hundred forty-sixth in the Bec profession-roll. He died in 1147, *OV* V: 210.
2. See Mt 10:22; 24:13.
3. Table blessing *post coenam* in the *Breviarum Monasticum* (Bruges, 1941) 1:261*; the second phrase comes from Ps 144:13, 17, also listed in *Epp* 121, 231, 235, 335.
4. See 1 Jn 3:17.
5. See RB 7:5–7. Anselm informed Eadmer that he himself had had a vision of this kind, *VA* 4–5.
6. See Lk 9:62.
7. See *Ep* 414.
8. See 2 Tim 1:14.

419. TO WILLIAM, ARCHBISHOP OF ROUEN.

Anselm protests to Archbishop William of Rouen that he had never said to William, the chamberlain, and his wife that they could ratify their illegal marriage by almsgiving.

TO HIS LORD AND FATHER, THE REVEREND ARCHBISHOP
WILLIAM OF ROUEN: ANSELM, SERVANT OF THE
CHURCH OF CANTERBURY, SENDING GREETING
AND HIS FAITHFUL PRAYERS WITH SERVICE.

YOU TOLD ME IN YOUR LETTER that William, the chamberlain, and his wife say that I told them that they could free themselves by almsgiving from their sin, namely that William keeps as his wife the woman who had previously been the wife of his relative. Your holiness should know that I never said such a thing to them, but on the contrary I say that neither of them, if they should die in this sin, will see the kingdom of God.[1] Farewell.[2]

c. 1107.

NOTES

1. See Jn 3:3.
2. Archbishop William no longer seems to be suspended, see *Epp* 388, 397, 398, 404.

420. TO BASILIA.

Anselm teaches Basilia, widow of Hugh of Gournay, then living at Bec, that the present life is a path ascending through good deeds or descending through evil ones.

ANSELM, THE ARCHBISHOP: TO BASILIA,[1] HIS DEAREST FRIEND AND DAUGHTER IN THE LORD, SENDING THE GREETING AND BLESSING OF GOD, AND HIS OWN, IF IT IS WORTH ANYTHING.

I LEARNED FROM YOUR MESSENGER that you eagerly long for a letter from us. In this I perceive your goodwill and Christian intention, for I do not see any reason why you should desire it except that you wish to receive from it some sound advice for your soul. Therefore, although the whole of Holy Scripture, if you have it explained to you, teaches you how you ought to live, yet I ought not to be miserly and inexorable to your holy petition.

Let me tell you something, dearest daughter, which, if you frequently consider it with the complete attention of your mind, will enable you to inflame your heart greatly to the fear of God and the love of a good life. Let there always be before the eyes of your mind the fact that this life has an end and that no one knows when the last day, which he is constantly approaching day and night, will come. This life is a journey.[2] For as long as man lives, he is always moving. He is always either ascending or descending. Either he is ascending towards heaven or descending to hell. Whenever he does any good deed he makes one step up, and when he sins in any way he makes one step down. This ascent or descent is perceived by each soul when it leaves the body. Whoever strives diligently while living here to climb by good conduct and good deeds will be placed in heaven with the holy angels; and whoever descends through bad conduct and bad deeds will be buried in hell with the fallen angels. You should be aware that it is much quicker and easier to descend than to ascend. For this reason a Christian man and a Christian woman should consider carefully in each of their desires or actions whether they are ascending or descending; and they should embrace with their whole heart those things in which they see themselves ascending. Those things, however, in which they perceive descent they should flee and abhor just as they would hell. Therefore I admonish and advise you, most beloved daughter and friend in God, that as far as possible with the help of God you should draw back from every sin, great or small, and engage in holy deeds.

I pray almighty God to protect, direct and preserve you always and everywhere. Amen.[3]

c. 1107.

NOTES

1. The widow of Hugh de Gournay, living at Bec, see *Epp* 68, 147.
2. See *Ep* 183.
3. Possibly sent together with *Ep* 419 to Bec.

421. TO LAMBERT, ABBOT OF ST BERTIN.

Anselm advises Abbot Lambert of St Bertin, who has been offered the archbishopric of Rheims, not to do anything to obtain the office but to obey the Abbot of Cluny in this matter.

ANSELM, SERVANT OF THE CHURCH OF CANTERBURY:
TO HIS DEAREST FRIEND LAMBERT,[1] THE REVEREND
ABBOT OF THE MONASTERY OF ST BERTIN,
GREETING AND AFFECTION WITH PRAYERS.

SINCE THE CHURCH OF RHEIMS[2] desires and asks your reverence, as you have written to me, to take on the government of the archbishopric, your prudence asks the advice of my lowliness about what you should do in such an important, burdensome and perilous case.

First of all, I pray to God that he may allow nothing to be done in your case unless it pleases him and is advantageous for you. Since you ask for my advice, as far as I can understand it appears to me more beneficial that your will, as far as it lies with you, should offer no consent. Do not say or do anything which could lead to your being dragged[3] for any reason to the burden to which you are being called. No necessity forces you except unconditional obedience alone. You should not acknowledge any command under obedience to accept this office except from the lord Abbot of Cluny, to whom you subjected yourself.[4]

But as to what you say, that you would rather incur the guilt of disobedience than take on such a burdensome labor and laborious burden, that is not my advice. For disobedience which is not followed by repentance is more dangerous than obedience which undertakes, in the hope of God's mercy, even what seems impossible.[5] When obedience alone leads a man into danger, the virtue and the merit of obedience either protect him from sin or, if by chance he does sin, it is less serious if always accompanied by repentance. Indeed, whoever lives in disobedience cannot perform any good deed without blemish.

winter 1106–1107.

NOTES

1. Lambert was Abbot of St Bertin at St Omer from 1095–1125, see *Ep* 197.
2. Archbishop Manasses II of Rheims died on 17 September 1106. He was succeeded by Radulf or Ralph le Vert almost immediately although the election was disputed. Peace returned in 1108 and Radulf governed the archdiocese until his death in 1124, *OV* IV: 263; *GC* IX, 80–82.
3. This recalls the circumstances of Anselm's own investiture, *HN* 35.
4. See *Ep* 197. For Anselm's advice not to accept any office willingly, see also *Ep* 52.
5. RB 68:1, 5.

422. FROM POPE PASCHAL.

Pope Paschal II permits Anselm to admit the sons of priests whom he judges suitable to holy orders, to receive back into his communion Richard, abbot of Ely and to confirm him as abbot. He entrusts all matters to be dealt with in the Church in England to Anselm's care.

PASCHAL, THE BISHOP, SERVANT OF THE SERVANTS OF GOD: TO HIS VENERABLE BROTHER ANSELM, BISHOP OF CANTERBURY, GREETING AND APOSTOLIC BLESSING.

CONCERNING THE SONS OF PRIESTS, we do not believe that your fraternity is ignorant of what has been decreed in the Roman Church.[1] Since there is such a large number of these cases in the kingdom of the English, so that almost the greater and better part of the clergy is subject to censure in this respect,[2] we commit the right of dispensation in this matter to your solicitude. We allow those whose knowledge and life recommends them to you to be promoted to the sacred offices for the need of the times and the good of the Church, but in such a way that no precedent is established for ecclesiastical policy in the future.[3]

Concerning the person of Richard, Abbot of Ely,[4] at the request of our sons, King Henry and William de Warelwast, we give you permission to receive him back to communion with you when he has made reparation; and if he is seen to be beneficial for the rule of the monastery, we entrust it to your disposition.

May the solicitude of your wisdom and holiness also dispense all other matters which must be dispensed in that kingdom for the need of the times and according to the uncivilized state of the race and the true interests of the Church.[5]

Given on thirtieth of May.[6]

30 May 1107, at Troyes.

NOTES

1. For Pope Paschal's position on admitting the sons of priests to the priesthood, see *Epp* 223, 282. The Council of Westminster excluded them, see canon 7, *HN* 142.
2. As a rule the higher as well as the lower clergy in the Anglo-Norman kingdom were married. The situation is amply displayed in Anselm's letters referring to married priests, see *Epp* 217, 218, 219, 220, 223, 225, 247, 250, 254, 255, 256, 307, 331, 364, 365, 391, 392, 393, 394 and *HN* 182–184; see the two Councils of Westminster: *1102*: canons 4, 5, 6; *HN* 142–144; *CS* 668–688; *1108*: canons 1–10, *HN* 193–195; *CS* 694–704. See also C.N.L. Brooke, 'The Gregorian Reform in Action: Clerical Marriage in England', *Cambridge Historical Journal* 12 (1956) 1–21, and 187–188; W. Fröhlich, 'Ubi unus clericus et Aelfgyfa...', *Liber ad Magistrum für J. Spörl* (München, 1964) 53–61; G. Denzler, *Papsttum und Amtszölibat* (Stuttgart, 1973).
3. Anselm took up Pope Paschal's suggestion of dispensation for suitable sons of priests. The Council of Westminster in 1108, solely concerned with the enforcement of celibacy, dropped the decree on priests' sons but rigorously tightened the decrees on clerical marriage, *HN* 193–195; *CS* 694–704.
4. Abbot Richard of Ely may not have learnt about the Pope's pardon since he died on 16 June 1107; see *Epp* 280, 397.

5. See *Ep* 223.
6. Paschal celebrated a general synod at Troyes on Ascension Day, 23 May 1107, Mansi XX, 1217–1224. For the issues dealt with, see Blumental, *Paschal*, 74–101; C. Servatius, *Paschalis II 1099–1118* (Stuttgart, 1979) 209–214; they included the reinforcement of celibacy of deacons and sanctions for a breach of celibacy, see Monumenta Germaniae Historica, *Constitutiones* I, 566; Denzler note 2, p. 78; also *HN* 184–185. Pope Paschal had demanded the attendance of the royal and the archiepiscopal envoys, William de Warelwast and Baldwin of Tournai, at Troyes, *HN* 185.

423. FROM POPE PASCHAL.

Pope Paschal II instructs Anselm to investigate whether the imprisoned Robert of Mowbray, Earl of Northumbria, has broken the law of consanguinity in his marriage.

PASCHAL, SERVANT OF THE SERVANTS OF GOD: TO HIS VENERABLE BROTHER ANSELM, ARCHBISHOP OF CANTERBURY, GREETING AND APOSTOLIC BLESSING.

WE GIVE THANKS TO ALMIGHTY GOD that through your many labors the darkness has been driven away and its former light has been rekindled in the Engiish church.[1] Nevertheless you must be vigilant lest an enemy spread weeds[2] among the good seed in the field of the Lord and an evil root bring forth a bad plant. Furthermore, we have heard that a certain count Robert[3] who is held in captivity by the english king, has taken a wife whose relatives gave her to the aforesaid count despite the impediment of consanguinity. Therefore we instruct your love to meet this count, and if you find this to be true you should summon fitting witnesses and act so wisely that, when they have both been freed from their sins, they will be able to serve God freely.[4] May your love pray for us.

c. 30 May 1107 at Troyes.

NOTES

1. Pope Paschal is here referring to the solution of the investiture controversy, see *Epp* 364, 388, 389, 390, 397.
2. See Mt 13:24–25.
3. This was Robert of Mowbray, Earl of Northumbria. He was captured while in rebellion against King William II in late summer 1095, *ASC*, *EHD* II: 171–172; he lived for about thirty years in captivity, *OV* IV: 280. He was married to Matilda, daughter of Richer of l'Aigle.
4. Anselm seems to have investigated the case, for 'with the permission of Pope Paschal, to whom the affair was made known by men of the court, Nigel of Aubigny took her as his wife', *OV* IV: 282. Nigel divorced Matilda about ten years later, *OV* IV: 284.

424. TO HENRY, KING OF THE ENGLISH.

Anselm replies to Henry, King of the English, that his daughter cannot lawfully be married to William of Warenne, Earl of Surrey, because of their close relationship.

TO HIS DEAREST LORD HENRY, BY THE GRACE OF GOD KING OF THE ENGLISH: ANSELM, THE ARCHBISHOP, SENDING FAITHFUL SERVICE WITH PRAYERS.

I GIVE THANKS TO GOD *for the good will*[1] which he gave you, and to you who are striving to retain it. Your Highness asks for advice about what is to be done regarding the agreement to give your daughter[2] to William de Warenne,[3] as he and your daughter are related on one side in the fourth degree and on the other side in the sixth degree.

You should know without doubt that no agreement which is against the law of Christianity should be kept. If they are so related they can on no account be legitimately joined without the condemnation of their souls and without grave sin for those who arrange for this to take place. Therefore, in place of God I beseech and advise you as my dearest lord not to involve yourself in this sin in any way nor to give your daughter to this William against the law and will of God.

May almighty God guide you and all your actions in his benevolence.

c. 1107.

NOTES

1. See Ph 2:13.
2. Matilda, born in January or February *(Reg.* II: 550) or summer *(OV* V: 200) 1102, was the only legitimate daughter of King Henry I and Queen Matilda, see *Epp* 305, 320, 321. (For the children of William II and Henry I, see *EHD* II: 985.) In 1109, as a child of seven, Matilda was betrothed to Emperor Henry V and sent to Germany in 1110, *ASC, EHD* II: 181. Their marriage was celebrated on 7 January 1114. After Henry's death in 1125 Matilda returned to England. In 1133 her father gave her in marriage to Geoffrey, Count of Anjou, *OV* V: 200.
3. William de Warenne, son of William, Earl of Surrey, and his wife Gundreda, 'was distinguished for his integrity and might under both William II and Henry I', *OV* IV: 180–182. He had been a suitor of Queen Matilda before she was married to King Henry, *OV* IV: 272.

425. TO ERNULF, ABBOT OF TROARN.

Anselm consoles Ernulf, Abbot of Troarn, in his sickness and advises him that just as he took office through obedience so he should not give it up except in obedience.

ANSELM, SERVANT OF THE CHURCH OF CANTERBURY: TO HIS BELOVED FRIEND ERNULF,[1] REVEREND ABBOT OF TROARN, SENDING GREETING AND WISHING HIM THE CONTINUAL PROTECTION AND CONSOLATION OF THE GRACE OF GOD.

THE LETTER WHICH YOU SENT ME by Dom Abbot Rodulf[2] concerning your illness and your distress has deeply moved our heart with charitable compassion. In it your holiness requests advice from my lowliness about the administration of your church since, because of the gravity of your illness, you have little hope of ever being able to govern and administer it as you have done up to now and as you ought.

Regarding your illness, your mind should take great consolation because God *chastises every son whom he receives*.[3] The examples of holy men who suffered many and very serious illnesses should comfort you greatly, like holy Job and, as you can read[4] about a certain holy man who was stricken by paralysis of his whole body and handed over to women by his brothers because they were unable to treat him. Nowhere do we read that the illnesses of saints caused them harm but we always read that they progressed towards the better through their tribulations. For although good works are sometimes hindered by feebleness, yet the grace of God is not diminished but increased if good will does not decrease in tribulation. Nor does God demand of his servants more than they are capable of doing.

Now, regarding the advice which you request about the administration of your church, we pray God that he himself may counsel you and always protect and rule you and your church together with your sons. Yet it appears to me, as far as I can understand, that I ought not to be silent. The care of the church, which you undertook not through your own will but in obedience and charity for those to whom this was due you must not cast off, solely of your own will but continue to preserve obedience until death.[5] But if, with the assent and advice of your archbishop[6]—for you have no bishop[7]—and of your brothers and those who understand the necessity of the situation, such a person were elected who could worthily take on the burden which you have borne up to now, then indeed, if you have no hope of returning to good health, you may lawfully put aside what you took on in obedience.

I exhort and advise your sons, seeing that they are not able at present to make use of your help and counsel to take all the more care not to neglect their religious observance, which flourished among them when you were healthy and to exhort each other in charity and keep their holy intention inviolable.

Since you requested me to send you a blessed cowl I have blessed our[8] own, which I have used for a long time, and I am sending it to you with the absolution which I have read. Farewell.

c. 1107.

NOTES

1. Ernulf or Arnulf, Abbot of Troarn, 1088–1112, see *OV* II: 22; IV: 164, 296; V: 264; and *Ep* 123.
2. Rodulf or Ralph d'Escures, Abbot of Séez, appears to be the only contemporary Norman abbot of this name. He succeeded Gundulf as bishop of Rochester on 9 August 1108, and became Archbishop of Canterbury after a five-year vacancy in 1114. He died on 20 October 1122, *OV* IV: 168–170; Fröhlich, 'Bischöfliche Kollegen', *AA* II (1970) 157–158; Barlow, *English Church*, 81 and passim.
3. Heb 12:6.
4. See Cassian, *Collatio* VII: 26 in PL 49: 703ff; CSEL, ed. M. Petschenig, (Vienna, 1886) 205–206.
5. See Ph 2:8.
6. William Bona Anima, Archbishop of Rouen, see *Epp* 18, 388, 397, 398, 404, 419.
7. Troarn is in the diocese of Bayeux. Bishop Turold resigned in 1106 and entered Bec as a monk in 1107, see *Epp* 298, 418.
8. Until very recently it was common for religious to speak of clothes and such personal possessions as 'our cowl, our shoes' indicating that they did not own them—an expression of evangelical poverty.

426. FROM MUIRCHERTACH, KING OF IRELAND.

King Muirchertach of Ireland thanks Anselm for having helped his son-in-law, Ernulf of Montgomery.

MUIRCHERTACH,[1] KING OF IRELAND: TO ANSELM, ARCHBISHOP OF THE ENGLISH, GREETING AND FAITHFUL SERVICE.

WHAT GREAT THANKS I ought to give you, my lord, because, as I am told, you hold the memory of me, a sinner, in your ceaseless prayers; but even more so because you helped my son-in-law Ernulf[2] through your assistance and intervention as far as your dignity allowed. You should also know that I will be your servant in whatever you command. Farewell.

1106 or 1107.

NOTES

1. See *Ep* 201.
2. Ernulf or Arnulf of Montgomery, Earl of Pembroke and Holderness, was in possession of large estates in Yorkshire and South Wales. He had joined his brother, Robert of Bellême, in his rebellion against Henry I, and in 1102 they were both dispossessed and exiled. He was married to the daughter of King Muirchertach, Ua Briain. Due to Anselm's intervention Ernulf was allowed to return to England. For his devotion to Anselm, see *VA* 146–147 and J.F.A. Mason, 'St Anselm's relations with Laymen', *Spicilegium Beccense* 1 (Paris, 1959) 560.

427. TO MUIRCHERTACH, KING OF IRELAND.

Anselm praises Muirchertach, King of Ireland, for keeping peace in his kingdom. He exhorts him to correct evils in his realm: marriages should not be so easily dissolved, relatives should not intermarry and bishops should not be consecrated by one bishop alone or in unsuitable places.

TO MUIRCHERTACH, BY THE GRACE OF GOD GLORIOUS KING OF IRELAND: ANSELM, SERVANT OF THE CHURCH OF CANTERBURY, SENDING GREETING WITH PRAYERS AND WISHING HIM ALWAYS TO BE RULED AND PROTECTED BY THE MERCY OF GOD.

I GIVE THANKS TO GOD for the many good things which I hear about your Highness. Among these is the fact that you let the people of your kingdom live in such peace that all good men who hear this give thanks to God and desire a long life for you. For where there is peace it is possible for all men of good will[1] to accomplish what they choose without being disturbed by evil men. Therefore, your Highness, through whom God does this, can most certainly look forward to a great reward from him.

Upon this foundation of peace it is easy to build the other things which the religion of the Church demands. For this reason I beseech the constancy of your good will to consider whether there are any things in your kingdom which have to be corrected for the sake of eternal life and you should earnestly strive, with God's help, to amend them so that the grace of God may increase more and more within you. For nothing which can be corrected should be neglected. God exacts from everyone not only what they do wrong but also the wrongs they fail to correct which they can correct. And the more power they have to correct, the more strictly God demands of them that in proportion to the power mercifully granted to them they should will and do what is right. This seems above all to apply to kings since they are known to possess greater power and to suffer less opposition among men. If however, you cannot do everything at once, you should not for that reason give up trying to progress from better things to even better ones; for God usually perfects good intentions and good efforts with kindness and repays them with abundance.

We have heard that in your kingdom marriages are being dissolved and altered without any grounds; that those related to each other do not fear to live together openly without reproof despite canonical prohibition, either under the name of marriage or in some other way.[2] Moreover, bishops who ought to be a pattern and example of canonical religious practice to others are being irregularly consecrated as we hear, either by one bishop alone, or in places where they ought not to be ordained. I beseech, implore and advise you, as one whom I greatly love and whose progress in everything I desire, to strive to correct these and other things which the prudence of your magnificence perceives to be needing correction in Ireland according to the advice of good and wise men of your kingdom, and I pray to God that you may cross over from the earthly kingdom to the heavenly one. Amen.[3]

1106 or 1107.

NOTES

1. See Lk 2:14.
2. In a letter to Archbishop Lanfranc in 1073, Pope Gregory VII banned these same unlawful practices and Lanfranc repeated these instructions to Guthric, King of Dublin, and to Toirrdelbach Ua Briain, King of Munster, in 1073 or 1074, see *The Letters of Lanfranc, Archbishop of Canterbury*, ed. and trans. H. Clover and M. Gibson (Oxford, 1979) 64–73; A. Gwynn, 'Lanfranc and the Irish Church', *Irish Ecclesiastical Records* 57 (1941) 481–500, 58 (1941) 1–15.
3. A. Gwynn, 'Anselm and the Irish Church', *Irish Ecclesiastical Records* 59 (1942) 1–14.

428. FROM GILBERT, BISHOP OF LIMERICK.

Gilbert, Bishop of Limerick, congratulates Anselm that the Normans are now subject to the decrees of the fathers and that abbots and bishops can be canonically elected and consecrated. He sends Anselm twenty-five pearls.

TO ANSELM, BY THE GRACE OF GOD, ARCHBISHOP OF THE ENGLISH: FROM GILBERT,[1] ALSO BY THE MERCY OF GOD, BISHOP OF LIMERICK, SENDING FAITHFUL SERVICE AND PRAYERS.

I HEAR, FATHER, of the labor of your struggle and the victory of your labor,[2] namely that the unrestrained minds of the Normans have been subjected to the canonical decrees of the holy fathers[3] so that the election and consecration of abbots and bishops is done according to law. I give abundant thanks to divine clemency and I pour out as many prayers as I can to God that he may bestow on you perseverance and the reward of such a great labor.

As a small present of my poverty and devotion I am sending you twenty-five small pearls, some of the best and some of less value, and I ask you not to be unmindful of me in your prayers in which, after divine generosity, I have confidence. Farewell.

c. 1107.

NOTES

1. Gilbert, a monk of Bangor, was bishop of Limerick from 1107–1139; for his career, see M. Brett, *The English Church under Henry I* (Oxford, 1975) 32.
2. Gilbert is referring to Anselm's exile and the solution of the investiture controversy, see *Epp* 364, 368, 389, 390, 397.
3. The term 'holy fathers' may refer either to the popes or the bishops and spiritual superiors assembled in councils or synods.

429. TO GILBERT, BISHOP OF LIMERICK.

Anselm thanks his friend, Bishop Gilbert of Limerick, for his congratulatory letter and exhorts him, since he has recently been elected bishop in Ireland, to correct the morals of the people with pastoral care and to encourage the king and the bishops to do likewise.

ANSELM, SERVANT OF THE CHURCH OF CANTERBURY: TO GILBERT, BISHOP OF LIMERICK, GREETING.

I GIVE THANKS to your reverence for showing joy in your letter[1] because God has deigned to cause some progress in religious observance to take place in his Church through me.[2] Since we got to know each other at Rouen some time ago and are united by love, and I now learn that you have been raised to episcopal dignity by the grace of God,[3] I confidently dare to beseech you and, according to what I perceive to be necessary, to advise you.

God has raised your prudence to such high dignity in Ireland and has set you up to strive for the vigor of religious observance and the benefit of souls. Therefore strive diligently—as it is written, *he who rules* [should do so] *with diligence*[4]—to correct and uproot vices in that people, and to plant and sow good morals as far as you can. Moreover, as far as you can, attract your king and the other bishops and anyone you can to this end by persuasion and by showing the joys which are prepared for the good and the evils which await the bad, so that you may merit to receive from God the reward for your good deeds and the good deeds of others.

I render thanks to you for the gift which you kindly sent me. Pray for me.

c. 1107.

NOTES

1. See *Ep* 428.
2. Anselm is referring to the solution of the investiture controversy in England.
3. Gilbert became Bishop of Limerick in 1107.
4. Rm 12:8.

430. TO POPE PASCHAL.

Anselm informs Pope Paschal II that King Henry, despite much opposition, has given up the investiture of churches on the advice of Robert of Meulan and Richard of Reviers; in the election of prelates he listens to the judgement of good men. He thanks the Pope for his concern and affection for him.

TO PASCHAL, HIS REVEREND LORD AND FATHER, THE SUPREME PONTIFF: ANSELM, SERVANT OF THE CHURCH OF CANTERBURY, SENDING DUE SUBMISSION WITH CONSTANT PRAYERS.

I MUST NOT FAIL to inform your Excellency of what, by the grace of God, is being accomplished through you in England and Normandy. The King, who rules the English and the Normans, has obediently accepted your command and in the face of much opposition has entirely given up the investiture of churches.[1] Robert, Count of Meulan,[2] and Richard of Reviers,[3] as faithful subjects of yours and sons of the Church, prompted by your warnings, have been zealous in urging him to do this. When choosing persons for preferment the King does not follow his own will at all but entrusts himself completely to the advice of religious men.[4]

As for myself, I cannot sufficiently express in writing the many thanks I owe your paternal kindness but they are written in the book of my heart where I constantly read them. For when you command me, as your servants and our beloved brothers, William and Baldwin[5] told me, with such kindly solicitude to take care of my fleeting life lest it soon fail, you demonstrate that your greatness has not slight feeling of holy affection for my lowliness.

May almighty God long preserve your life for us in all prosperity. Amen.

1107 or 1108.

NOTES

1. Anselm seems to be referring to the stormy meeting of the *curia regis*, 1–3 August 1107, at the end of which the agreement of l'Aigle was ratified, see *HN* 186; *Epp* 364, 388–390, 397.
2. See *Epp* 353, 354, 361, 364, 369, 467.
3. Richard of Reviers held an honor (a fief) with its *caput* at Nehon in the Contentin. He was one of Henry's most loyal followers and was rewarded with the honor of Plympton, Devon, see *OV* IV: 220, 250; V, 298, 314. He was most likely one of Count Robert's associates in supporting King Henry when he defied the decrees against investiture and was excommunicated with him, see *Epp* 348, 351, 352, 353, 397.
4. Anselm seems to be referring to the elections, investitures and consecrations after 1 August 1107; see *Ep* 397.
5. Together they had attended the general synod of Troyes at the Pope's command, see *Ep* 422.

431. TO ADRIAN, AN APOSTATE MONK OF CANTERBURY.

Anselm beseeches Adrian and Airard, monks who left the monastery of Christ Church Canterbury to return in obedience.

ANSELM, BY THE GRACE OF GOD, ARCHBISHOP OF CANTERBURY: TO ADRIAN, WHO WAS A MONK AT CHRIST CHURCH CANTERBURY AND WHO, BY THE PERSUASION OF THE DEVIL,[1] RELINQUISHED HIS HABIT. IF HE WISHES TO RETURN TO HIS MONASTERY AND TO HIS MONASTIC INTENTION, GREETING AND TRUE AFFECTION.

I OUGHT NOT CALL YOU 'brother' or 'son' until I know that you are doing penance for your sin and error, and this I would learn through your return. If I were to see that this has happened through the inspiration of God and by his grace according to my desire, you can be sure that with God's assent you would find in me paternal *lovingkindness* and sincere fraternal *charity*.[2] Therefore I advise you, and advising beseech you as a man for the salvation of whose soul I long with the affection of my heart, and I command by the authority given to me by God and the Church of God over everyone living in the aforesaid monastery who has professed obedience and stability, and I adjure you through that profession and the stability which you promised before God[3] to observe in that place, and through both comings of our Lord Jesus Christ:[4] as you wish the first coming to be for your salvation and the second not for your damnation[5] you should come to your senses and return to that church in which you were a monk with regard to the habit and ought to be according to truth, and to me and to the brothers who long for you for the sake of the salvation of your soul, if you do not want to die in excommunication and anathema. For no living man in this life can absolve you from these bonds of excommunication and anathema unless you do what I beseech and advise you to do in true love.

By this letter of mine I command you, if any spark of obedience is still alive in you, to show it, if you have the opportunity, to Airard, who left Christ Church with you; and whatever I write to you I tell him with the same charity and authority. Although you do not yet deserve that I pray for you, nevertheless, I pray almighty God that he may turn you to himself,[6] and to the salvation of your souls, and that he may gladden me with your longed-for return. Amen.[7]

probably between 1106 and 1109.

NOTES

1. See RB 58:28.
2. 2 Co 6:6.

3. See RB 58:17-18.
4. The birth of Christ at Bethlehem and his final coming on the day of the Last Judgement.
5. See the third prayer before communion in the Roman Missal.
6. See Lam 5:21.
7. In MS L this letter is number 361—suggesting a date between 1106 and 1109.

432. TO JOTSERANN, ARCHBISHOP OF LYON.

Anselm thanks Josserand, Archbishop of Lyon, for rejoicing at his return to England and grieves about his affliction.

TO HIS LORD JOTSERANN,[1] ARCHBISHOP OF LYON, TO BE REVERED WITH LOVE AND LOVED WITH REVERENCE: ANSELM, SERVANT OF THE CHURCH OF CANTERBURY, SENDING GREETING WITH PRAYERS AND SERVICE.

WE GIVE THANKS that your true charity rejoices with us that God *who does not forsake those who put their trust in him*[2] has gladdened us with his consolation *for the days on which he humbled us;*[3] and as we feel that you join in our joy we rejoice even more.[4]

Indeed, we suffer and grieve with your reverence that you are afflicted by many great tribulations from those from whom you expected help and consolation in your need.[5] But this consoles us since we trust in God that your constancy will not be shaken by any onslaught of rivers or winds,[6] and that God who *opposes the proud but gives grace to the humble*[7] will break the pride of evildoers and lay them beneath the feet of your authority; and when your virtue has been tested you *will receive the* promised *crown of life.*[8]

As to my present situation, about which your benevolence desires to be informed, you can learn more through your messenger than through a letter.

between 1107 and 1109.

NOTES

1. Josserand or Jotserann succeeded Hugh as Archbishop of Lyon, 1107–1118, see *GC* IV: 109–113; C. Servatius, *Paschalis II* (Stuttgart, 1979) 290f, 295, 297, 314.
2. Jdt 13:17.
3. See Ps 89:15.
4. Anselm is referring to the solution of the investiture controversy, see *Epp* 364, 388, 389, 390, 397, 430.
5. He may be referring to resentment against Archbishop Hugh's successor at the beginning of Josserand's rule, *GC* IV, 110.
6. See Mt 7:25.
7. 1 P 5:5.
8. Jm 1:12.

433. FROM THE MONK WALTER.

Walter rejoices at Anselm's return to England but as he cannot visit the archbishop he begs for a letter of consolation.

TO HIS LONGED-FOR LORD ANSELM, WHO IS TO BE GATHERED INTO THE DEPTHS OF THE HEART OF HIS MOTHER, THE CATHOLIC CHURCH: BROTHER WALTER,[1] ONE OF HIS OWN, THE LEAST OF HIS DEVOTED FOLLOWERS, WISHING HIM A FULFILLING DRAUGHT OF THE DESIRED FULLNESS OF INNERMOST SWEETNESS.

MY TONGUE CLEAVES to my mouth, my mind is stupefied, my hand shakes while I read the sweetness of the greeting[2] with which your highness deigned to bend down to such a worthless manikin. See, my bones have been fortified by your voice, my heart filled with delight because now indeed I know that I have not loved your glory in vain since you have not scorned to take notice of my humility. And indeed, the less readiness and vigor I see in myself, the more I cherish your attentiveness towards my weakness.

All your friends, together with me, offer *a sacrifice of praise*[3] to almighty God who, through the happy return of your holiness, has given joy to this age of ours which had been deprived of the light of your presence. For he expelled, as he wished, everything that resisted the gentle tranquillity of your will and in a moment of time, which seemed very long to us, he most speedily accomplished it with the fullest effect for us. Your return[4] took place peacefully both for us and for you since you also remained calm until you had put an end to the protracted quarrel[5] by a canonical meeting of the churches. And so all your friends give thanks for your tranquillity and the common good; and since they cannot be joined to you in body[6] they do not cease from visiting you with the footsteps of yearning. I speak especially about your monks whom you have more closely bound to yourself by the gift of greater friendship and by assistance rendered in our most dangerous need.[7] But since I have started to talk about my affairs I must return to myself.

What I would desire most of all, if it were possible, would be to enjoy the sight of you before my death and to open my heart to you about my calamities. For my time is running out and I do not know whether I have collected any fruit during the course of my long life. But since the weakness of old age resists my will, behold here where I am, I sigh and display to you the wretchedness and langour of soul from which I suffer. Most of all I beseech you, as you have become *all things to all men*,[8] to deign to inform me in writing in that meek manner of yours with which you would console me if I had managed to come into your presence. For this will be the great protection in my need and a gracious monument to your sweetness. To this end, this prayer of mine longs that as I cannot enjoy you totally because of my vow you concede to me at least a little portion of yourself, not to enjoy in place of you, but one at the sight of which I may live in your consolation;

not because my sickness lacks the sufficient nourishment of the Scriptures, but because it is always better for a sick person to be given what he desires. Often the single touch of one person brings the comfort which the medicines of many do not contain.

May almighty God long preserve your mind and tongue for the consolation of his little ones, and may he subject the efforts of your adversaries to your gentle will with the right hand of his power. Amen.

winter 1106 to 1107.

NOTES

1. Walter may have been a member of the community of Bury St Edmunds.
2. Anselm's letter is not preserved.
3. Ps 115:17.
4. Anselm returned to England in early September 1106.
5. See *Epp* 364, 397; *HN* 182–184.
6. Anselm went to Bury St Edmunds after the Easter court meeting at Windsor; Easter Sunday was on 14 April 1107. He fell seriously ill and stayed there until Whitsun; Whit Sunday was on 2 June 1107, *HN* 185.
7. Anselm seems to have favored Bury St Edmunds, as Eadmer mentions, see *HN* 185; *VA* 139–140, 168–170.
8. 1 Co 9:22.

434. TO THE MONK WALTER.

Anselm answers the affectionate letter from the monk Walter with words of friendship.

ANSELM, THE ARCHBISHOP: TO HIS BROTHER AND BELOVED FRIEND WALTER, SENDING THE GREETING AND BLESSING OF GOD, AND HIS OWN, FOR WHAT IT IS WORTH.

I RECEIVED THE LETTER[1] of your holy kindness as a rich honeycomb, overflowing and dripping thick, sweet drops of inexplicable love for me. In that letter your soul, filled to the brim with a holy fervor, and beloved and worthy of being loved by mine, indicates that it is burning with a great desire for conversation between us. Since you despair that this can take place, you desire at least our greetings and an edifying exhortation in writing. My soul wonders whence your soul conceived such a great feeling of love for me—unless it is that *the Spirit blows where it will, and you hear its sound but you do not know from where it comes or where it is going.*[2] Indeed my merits are unable to bring this about with the Lord and with men, to make me so loved by any man, but the Holy Spirit, through whom charity is poured into the hearts of the servants of God[3] has made your soul fruitful with so much and such great affection. It is the Spirit's voice I hear in your letter but I do not know the source of this inspiration because I find nothing in myself which could bring it about. I beg him never to depart from you but always to remain in you and to cause your whole spirit to burn unceasingly with love of God and of your neighbor.

I give thanks to God for granting me to be so loved by you; but he has bestowed a much greater gift on you when he filled your heart with such love for your neighbor. It is far more pleasing to God to love one's neighbor than to be loved by one's neighbor. We should always strive more to love than to be loved,[4] and to rejoice more, realizing that we gain more when we love than when we are loved. Moreover we should grieve more deeply and believe it a greater loss when we lose the love with which we love than when we lose the one by whom we are loved. For the reward is due to the one who loves, not the one who is loved.

I pray to God that he, for whose love you love me, may himself love you, that he may teach you how to live a good life, as you asked of me, and that he may absolve you from all your sins and lead you to life everlasting. Amen.

winter 1106–1107.

NOTES

1. See *Ep* 433.
2. Jn 3:8.
3. See Rm 5:5.
4. See RB 64:15.

435. TO MUIRCHERTACH, KING OF IRELAND.

Anselm praises Muirchertach, King of Ireland, for the good things he has done and exhorts him to correct other abuses, namely illicit marriages and the uncanonical consecration of bishops. Anselm cannot send him Dom Cornelius, due to his father's poor health.

TO MUIRCHERTACH,[1] GLORIOUS KING OF IRELAND: ANSELM, THE ARCHBISHOP, SERVANT OF THE CHURCH OF CANTERBURY, SENDING FAITHFUL ALLEGIANCE WITH PRAYERS AND WISHING THAT HE MAY MERIT THE CELESTIAL KINGDOM THROUGH THE EARTHLY ONE.

SINCE MANY THINGS ARE TOLD about your excellency which befit royal dignity, we rejoice greatly and give devout thanks for them to God, from whom all good comes.[2] We trust that he who gave you his grace for doing the good which you do may also give you the strength to bring to completion those things which you perceive he wants you to do over and above what you are doing now. Wherefore, glorious and dearest son in God, I beseech you to correct with all speed and care those things in your kingdom which you perceive to need amendment according to the Christian religion.[3] For this purpose indeed God has put you in a place of royal sublimity so that you may govern your subject people with *the sceptre of equity*[4] and with that sceptre strike and remove whatever is against righteousness in them.

Indeed it is said that in that people which you have undertaken to govern, something is being done which desperately needs correction because it is totally against Christian religion. It is said that husbands freely and publicly exchange their wives for the wives of others, as if they were exchanging one horse for another or anything whatever for something from someone else, or they abandon them at their pleasure and without reason. How evil this is, anybody who knows Christian law understands. If your excellency is not able to read the passages of the divine Scriptures which forbid this infamous business yourself, order the bishops and religious clerics who are in your kingdom to read them to you; so that when you understand them you may understand with what zeal you should take care that this evil may be corrected.

It is also said that in your country bishops are elected at random and appointed without any definite place for their bishopric, and ordained bishop by one bishop only, just like any priest. This is of course totally against the holy canons which order that those who have been appointed or ordained in this way, as well as those who ordained them, are to be deposed from their episcopal office. For indeed a bishop, unless he has a particular diocese and a people whom he watches over, cannot be appointed according to the will of God, for even in secular affairs he who has no flock to feed can have neither the name nor the office of pastor. Episcopal dignity suffers not a little whenever someone is raised to a bishopric without knowing where, as an ordained bishop, he is to reside nor knowing for sure over whom he is to preside through his episcopal ministry. Also, no bishop should be ordained by fewer than three bishops for many other sensible reasons which the shortness of a letter does not permit me to elaborate, but above all so that the faith, the way of life and the good intentions of the one who is to watch over them be confirmed by suitable and legal witnesses.

I therefore beseech, exhort and admonish your excellency to take pains to have these evils in your kingdom corrected so that the rewards which you are seeking from God for other good deeds may be increased for you by these. Finally, if you should find in yourself or in those whom you have undertaken to govern anything contrary to the will of God, strive diligently to amend it so that when you pass from the earthly kingdom you may come to the heavenly one. Amen.

With regard to our brother Cornelius whom your Highness asked me to send you, I tell you that he is so occupied in taking care of his father that he cannot be separated from him without risking his father's life, nor can he bring him with him under any circumstances since he is already very old.

possibly 1106–1107.

NOTES

1. See *Ep* 201.
2. See *Jm* 1:17.
3. This letter reiterates *Ep* 427, of which it might be another version.
4. Heb 1:8.

436. TO ODO, MONK AND CELLARER.

Anselm encourages Odo, monk and cellarer, who wishes to abandon his obedience because of infirmity and old age, to persevere to the end in his charge unless freed from it by his abbot.

ANSELM, THE ARCHBISHOP: TO HIS DEAREST
BROTHER ODO, MONK AND CELLARER, SENDING THE
GREETING AND BLESSING OF GOD, AND HIS OWN.

IT IS SAID that because of old age and sickness you feel your end approaching and therefore you wish to forsake the obedience in which, up to now, you have served God and the community of the church in which you live.

However, I wish it to be known to your love that this intention does not come from a good motive. We ought to do penance for our evil deeds and give them up before death lest the last day finds us in them, but we should persevere in good deeds until the end so that our soul may be taken from this life in them, for of those who persevere in doing good it is said: *One who perseveres to the end will be saved*,[1] not of those who, before the end, abandon their good deeds. Therefore it is for the good of your soul, my dearest brother and son, that you should persevere in the obedience which, as far as we can perceive, you have preserved as well as you could to God's good pleasure and to the good pleasure of your abbot and your brothers, and you should continue doing this as long as you have life in you and your abbot commands you to do it, with a good and happy spirit[2] and without any rancor or grumbling,[3] so that you may give up your spirit[4] while speaking and settling something out of obedience. Then what is promised to those who persevere to the end[5] will come to pass for you.

Do not fear that because of the weakness of your body you will not be able to work and care for the things which have to be done in that obedience as effectively as you once could in good health and youth. God does not demand from you more than you can do. Do not let any adversities, from wherever they may come, with which the enemy of your soul wants to vex and tire you, disturb you so that you give up before the end and lose the reward of perseverance.

Therefore I exhort and beseech you to resolve and establish this in your heart so that you never forsake, as long as you live, the good work which, up to now, you have faithfully carried out with God's help, unless your abbot and your brothers order you to do so not because of your importunity but of their own free will. Be certain that the greater the difficulties in fulfilling the obedience laid upon you because of your weakness or of any other adversities the greater will be the reward you receive from God.

I pray to almighty God that he himself may guide your heart; and as far as I am able I send you, dearest brother, God's blessing and absolution.

1100–1109.

NOTES

1. Mt 10:22, 24:13.
2. See RB 5:16.
3. See RB 5:14.
4. See Mt 27:54.
5. See Mt 10:22; 24:13.

437. TO LAMBERT, BISHOP OF ARRAS.

Anselm asks Bishop Lambert of Arras for safe conduct for a papal clerk through his diocese.

ANSELM, ARCHBISHOP OF CANTERBURY: TO HIS FRIEND, THE REVEREND BISHOP LAMBERT OF ARRAS,[1] GREETING.

I BESEECH YOUR HOLINESS, for the love you bear the lord Pope and us, to have this cleric of his[2] guided through your bishopric, insofar as it pleases you. Farewell.

1100–1109.

NOTES

1. Lambert was Bishop of Arras, 1093–1115, *GC* III, 322–324; see also *Ep* 285. As a token of Anselm's friendship Lambert received Anselm's private copy of his philosophical and theological works after his death, see *AOO* 91*–93*, 213*, as well as copies of three letters Anselm had received from Pope Paschal II: *Epp* 222, 281, 353. See also Introduction, Volume 1:46–47.
2. For the scanty evidence about papal envoys in 1106, see *CS*, 689.

438. FROM LAMBERT, BISHOP OF ARRAS.

Bishop Lambert of Arras enquires about Anselm's health and begs him to greet Dom Baldwin on his behalf.

TO THE HONORABLE LORD, AND IN TRUTH BELOVED ANSELM, BY THE ORDINATION OF GOD ARCHBISHOP OF CANTERBURY: LAMBERT, UNPROFITABLE SERVANT[1] OF THE HOLY CHURCH OF ARRAS, WISHING HIM *WHAT NO EYE HAS SEEN, NOR EAR HEARD, NOR HUMAN HEART CONCEIVED.*[2]

WITH GREAT DESIRE I have desired[3] to know about your situation and your state of health.[4] I write to your paternity, most delightful to me, that you may deign to assure us about these things in a letter of yours. With a contrite heart and in a spirit of humility.[5] I desire your holiness, moved by my entreaty, to remember me, a sinner, at the Lord's table and in your holy prayers, and to obtain for me from God the remission of my sins.

May your holy and pious way of life in the Lord prosper long and forever, best of fathers, and we ask you fervently to greet on our behalf Dom Baldwin, our friend of Tournai,[6] the son of your holiness.

c. 1108–1109.

NOTES

1. See Lk 17:10.
2. 1 Co 2:9.
3. Lk 22:15.
4. For Anselm's growing feebleness see *Epp* 399, 400, 407. He was worn down by ill-health, *HN* 203, and in the winter and spring of 1108–1109 the serious illness from which he was suffering worsened from day to day, *HN* 205.
5. See Ps 50:19, and the prayer at the offertory of the Roman Mass.
6. See *Epp* 124, 151.

439. TO LAMBERT, BISHOP OF ARRAS.

Anselm answers Bishop Lambert of Arras that he is healthy in body but suffers from growing weakness.

TO LAMBERT, THE VENERABLE BISHOP OF ARRAS, HIS DEARLY BELOVED FRIEND: ANSELM, SERVANT OF THE CHURCH OF CANTERBURY, SENDING GREETING AND FAITHFUL PRAYERS.

I GIVE THANKS to your reverend love for the solicitude which you show for me in wishing[1] to know so much about our health. I therefore tell you that by the grace of God I am healthy in body but suffer from continual weakness. Since you ask me to remember you in our prayers, you should know with certainty that, although my prayers are worthless, I nevertheless remember you daily in them and, God granting, I shall continue to do so.

May almighty God always protect you from all evils by his grace and may he kindly grant you his consolation.

c. 1108 or 1109.

NOTES

1. See *Ep* 438.

440. FROM GERARD, ARCHBISHOP OF YORK.

Gerard, Archbishop of York, asks Anselm to grant help on the recommendation of the Pope to a certain cleric against the injustice of Engelram, a cleric of Lincoln.

TO HIS LORD AND FATHER ANSELM, THE VENERABLE ARCHBISHOP OF CANTERBURY: GERARD,[1] HIS SON, AND ARCHBISHOP OF THE CHURCH OF YORK, GREETING AND SERVICE.

YOUR CHARITY SHOULD KNOW that a certain cleric[2] threw himself at the feet of the lord Pope to beg for justice from Engelram, a cleric of the bishop of Lincoln, who usurped his church by simony and clings to it by force. Therefore I advise your honor and ask you to do justice to this cleric, as the Pope himself writes to you.[3] Farewell.

spring 1108.

NOTES

1. Gerard, Archbishop of York, died at Southwell on 21 May 1108 (*HC* 14) while on his way to the Westminster synod at Whitsun, 24 May 1108, see *Ep* 299.
2. For this unnamed cleric's appeal to Pope Paschal, see M. Brett, *The English Church under Henry I* (Oxford, 1975) 51, 94, 237.
3. Pope Paschal's letter is not preserved.

441. TO POPE PASCHAL.

Anselm requests Pope Paschal's confirmation for the decision of the Council of Westminster, Whitsun 1108, to divide the diocese of Lincoln and create the new bishopric of Ely. The see is to be established at the abbey of Ely and the monks to assist the bishop as cathedral chapter.

TO HIS REVEREND LORD AND FATHER PASCHAL,
THE SUPREME PONTIFF: ANSELM, SERVANT OF THE
CHURCH OF CANTERBURY, SENDING DUE OBEDIENCE
WITH FAITHFUL ALLEGIANCE AND PRAYERS.

SINCE THE POWER of decisions which are profitably made in the Church of God depends upon the authority of your prudence, they should all be brought to your knowledge and judgement when they are made, so that when they have been confirmed by Apostolic consent, the decisions which have been soundly established cannot be violated by any ensuing presumption but remain valid for ever.

There is a certain bishopric in England, namely that of Lincoln, whose diocese is so extensive that one bishop cannot fully accomplish those things which can only be done by a person of episcopal rank. When the King, the bishops and the barons, and other men of understanding and religion in the kingdom of the English, considered this matter they decided, for the benefit of the Church, to divide the aforesaid bishopric into two parts in such a way that the new episcopal seat should be established in a certain abbey, situated on an island called Ely[1] and in the aforesaid diocese; the monks should remain there, as there are many bishoprics which have monks in the mother church and not canons. The bishop of Lincoln, Robert by name,[2] willingly consents to this, since in place of those parts which are taken away from his church to establish the new bishopric in Ely, so much is given in compensation to the church of Lincoln that he considers it to be sufficient and agreeable to him.

Considering both the need mentioned above and the great number of persons also named above who are in favor of this plan, it seemed right to me, saving your authority, to give my consent in this matter. Therefore my lowliness humbly beseeches that what has been thus decided for the good of the Church be approved by your authority for ever, so that what has been well founded may not be violated by any ensuing presumption.[3]

We pray that almighty God may guard you for his Church in prosperity for many years to come.

shortly after Whitsun 1108.

NOTES

1. The creation of the new bishopric of Ely was decided upon by the Council of Westminster at Whitsun, 24 May 1108. For the events preceding this decision, see M. Brett, *The English Church under Henry I* (Oxford, 1975) 57–58, 79–80. Bishop Hervey of Bangor, driven from his diocese in about 1100, became the first Bishop of Ely, see *Ep* 404.
2. Robert Bloet, Bishop of Lincoln, see *Ep* 311.
3. For the Pope's confirmation, see *Epp* 457, 458, 459, 460.

442. TO RANULF, BISHOP OF DURHAM.

Anselm answers Bishop Ranulf Flambard of Durham that until the consecration of Thomas II, the archbishop elect of York, Turgot, the bishop-elect of St Andrews in Scotland, cannot be consecrated by anybody but himself.

ANSELM, ARCHBISHOP OF CANTERBURY: TO RANULF,[1] BISHOP OF DURHAM GREETING.

YOU INFORMED ME through a certain knight, Scolland by name, that you wished the bishop-elect of the church of St Andrew of Scotland[2] to be consecrated before the archbishop-elect of York has been consecrated[3] and that you wished this to be done with my counsel and permission. But this ought not and cannot be done canonically by the archbishop-elect, nor by anyone authorized by him, before he himself has become archbishop by canonical consecration. Accordingly I do not advise or permit this, nay rather I forbid this to be done before the consecration of the archbishop-elect, unless it is done by me if perchance necessity should demand it.[4] Farewell.

July or August 1108.

NOTES

1. See *Epp* 214, 223, 225, 373, 418. According to *OV* V: 320–322, the bishop of Durham did not return to England until after the battle of Tinchebrai, 28 September 1106, see Fröhlich, 'Bischöfliche Kollegen', *AA* II (1970) 138–140.
2. Turgot or Thurgod, monk and prior of Durham, had been chosen by King Alexander of Scotland (see *Ep* 413) and the clergy and people to be bishop of St Andrews (*HN* 198) in 1106 or 1107. He was consecrated by Thomas II, Archbishop of York, on 1 August 1109 and died on 31 August 1115, see *Heads*, 43.
3. Gerard, Archbishop of York, died on 21 May 1108 (*Ep* 440) and was succeeded six days later (27 May) by Thomas, the King's chaplain, provost of St John's, Beverley. Thomas was the son of Bishop Samson of Worcester, brother of Bishop Richard of Bayeux, nephew of

Archbishop Thomas I and probably a disappointed candidate for the archbishopric of York at his uncle's death eight years earlier, HC 15. For Thomas II, see Fröhlich, Ibid., 158–162; Barlow, *English Church*, 82 and passim. The archbishop-elect of York delayed his consecration, see *Ep* 443.
4. Written between 27 May and 6 September 1108; see *Ep* 443.

443. TO THOMAS, ARCHBISHOP-ELECT OF YORK.

Anselm reprimands Thomas, the archbishop-elect of York, for delaying his consecration beyond the canonical time limit and orders him to come to Canterbury on 6 September 1108 to make his profession of obedience to the Archbishop of Canterbury and to be consecrated. He forbids Thomas to consecrate Turgot before his own consecration.

ANSELM, ARCHBISHOP OF CANTERBURY: TO HIS FRIEND THOMAS,[1] ARCHBISHOP-ELECT OF THE CHURCH OF YORK, GREETING.

CANONICAL AUTHORITY prescribes that the church of a bishopric is not to remain without a pastor for more than three months.[2] Since it has pleased the King, on the advice of his barons and with our consent, that you should be elected for the archbishopric of York,[3] the time limit thus wisely ordained should not be delayed any longer by you.[4] I am therefore surprised that since your election you have not asked to be consecrated to the office to which you were elected. Accordingly I instruct you to be at your mother church of Canterbury on September sixth to do what you ought to do[5] and to receive your consecration. If you fail to do this, it is my duty to take charge and to perform the duties which belong to the episcopal office in the archbishopric of York.

Moreover I have heard[6] that you wish to have the bishop-elect of St Andrews of Scotland consecrated at York before you yourself are consecrated. You ought not to do this nor do I permit it; on the contrary I absolutely forbid it either in his case or of any other person who should be raised by the Archbishop of York for the government of souls, because you have no right to give or grant to anyone the care of souls which you have not yet received yourself. Farewell.

late August 1108.

NOTES

1. See *Ep* 442.
2. *Codex Iuris Canonici,* c. 333.
3. On 27 May 1108, *HC* 15.
4. The three-month limit would expire on 27 August 1108.
5. Anselm is demanding the profession of obedience from the archbishop-elect of York following the precedent set by Thomas I and Gerard (see *Ep* 283) which established the subjection of York to Canterbury. For the supremacy struggle, see *HC* 2–31; *HN* 12, 16, 42, 198–211; M. Dueball, 'der Suprematsstreit zwischen den Erzdiözesen Canterbury und York 1070–1126', *Historische Studien* 184 (Berlin, 1929); Barlow, *English Church,* 39–41, 61, 119–120 and passim; M. Gibson, *Lanfranc of Bec* (Oxford, 1978) 117–121, 169–170, 231–237 and passim; Fröhlich, 'Bischöfliche Kollegen', *AA* II (1970) 159–162, 167. The archbishop-elect of York was delaying his consecration in the hope that the ailing Anselm would die and thus free him from the dreaded demand of a profession of obedience to the Archbishop of Canterbury. For Thomas' prolonged delay, see *Epp* 444, 445, 451, 453, 454, 455, 456, 462, 464, 465, 471, 472 and Introduction, Volume 1: 48. In due course he made his profession at Canterbury, see Canterbury Professions, 37, just as Gerard had done, ibid 35.
6. See *Ep* 442.

444. FROM THOMAS, ARCHBISHOP-ELECT OF YORK.

Thomas, the archbishop-elect of York, gives Anselm his reasons for delaying his consecration, hopes to be at Canterbury on the appointed day but asks for a shorter period of advance notice. He begs for a letter certifying his character and election and refutes rumors that he planned to consecrate Turgot, the bishop-elect of Saint Andrews, before his own consecration.

TO HIS MOST BELOVED FATHER AND VENERABLE LORD, ANSELM, ARCHBISHOP OF THE HOLY CHURCH OF CANTERBURY: THOMAS, ELECT OF THE METROPOLITAN CHURCH OF YORK, ALTHOUGH UNWORTHY, SENDING GREETING AND THE OBEDIENCE OF AFFECTIONATE LOYALTY.

I GIVE YOU THANKS, reverend father, that you have always loved and assisted me and that your heart has rejoiced and been glad in the Lord[1] at my promotion. *May the Lord God reward you for me!*[2]

That I put off[3] coming for my consecration is due to not only one reason, nor a slight one, which has held me back. When I had collected a considerable amount of money to enable me to make the journey to you, I stayed much longer than I expected at Winchester,[4] which I had intended to leave much earlier and come to you, and so spent it all there. Since our lord the King was sending messengers to Rome on his own business, he thought it acceptable that I should send mine with them to ask for the pallium for our church. Therefore, on the King's advice, I hurriedly returned home and have been collecting money for this purpose and am still doing so; but I cannot find enough unless it is borrowed at a high rate, because lord Archbishop Gerard greatly impoverished our churches, our people and even our demesne.[5] The King promised me that he would certainly speak to you and excuse my delay to you.

With the help of God I shall be at the holy church of Canterbury on the date set by you[6] if I can conveniently do so, in order to receive and do what I ought. If I am not able to do so, since your paternity has told me to give you fifteen days' notice in advance, I beseech the holiness of your benevolence to let me give you only ten days' notice in advance. Moreover I request a letter of your paternity as evidence of our character and election such as you ought and know to be proper.[7] This your holiness owes to my lowliness; this your church ought not to refuse to ours.

Regarding what you have heard about the bishop-elect of St Andrews in Scotland,[8] these are rumors which should not be believed. It is easy to forbid what I had never planned.

Our church entreats our God that you may live healthy and happy for a long time in God. I greet the holy community of the holy church of Canterbury and pray that they may pray for me. Farewell.

August 1108.

NOTES

1. See Ps 31:11.
2. See Ps 137:8.
3. See *Ep* 443.
4. After Whitsun, 24 May 1108, Henry left Westminster for Portsmouth from where he crossed to Normandy in July, *Reg.* II, xxix. He probably went via Winchester to the coast, and Thomas with him. Anselm's demand for a profession of obedience was certainly a topic of discussion with the King, for it was with his knowledge and leave that Thomas refused to give it and thus delayed his consecration, see *HC* 15–18 and *HN* 207.
5. For Thomas' convenient excuse of a lack of money, see C. Servatius, *Paschalis II* (Stuttgart, 1979) 65.
6. 6 September 1108, see *Ep* 443.
7. Thomas would need Anselm's letter of credence in order to obtain the pallium from the Pope, see *Ep* 220.
8. See *Epp* 442, 443.

445. TO THOMAS, ARCHBISHOP OF YORK.

Anselm grants Thomas, archbishop-elect of York, a postponement of three weeks, until 27 September 1108, for coming to Canterbury. He forbids him to seek the pallium before his consecration and will provide him with the necessary certification of his election and consecration when they have met.

ANSELM, ARCHBISHOP OF CANTERBURY: TO HIS FRIEND THOMAS, ARCHBISHOP-ELECT OF YORK, GREETING.

YOU TOLD ME IN YOUR LETTER[1] that, with the help of God, you will be at Canterbury on the date I laid down for you, if you can conveniently do so, in order to receive and do what you ought. You also asked that, if you are not able to do this, I should allow you to give me only ten days' advance notice. But William, the cleric, your messenger, has begged me on your behalf to extend the date[2] of your coming a little so that you may be able to come to us more conveniently. Because of your love and convenience I willingly do this. Accordingly, so that there may be no need for you to give me any advance notice at all of your coming, I charge you to be at Canterbury on Sunday, September twenty-seventh, to do what you ought to do[3] and to receive your consecration.

Furthermore, I do not allow what you say in your letter, that you are collecting money in order to send to Rome for the pallium of your church.[4] And I consider that you would be doing this in vain because no one is entitled to have a pallium before he has been consecrated. The letter which you request as evidence of your character and election I shall gladly write for you, as I ought to do for a friend, when you have talked to me and have told me to whom I should address it. Farewell.

late August 1108.

NOTES

1. See *Ep* 444.
2. 6 September, see *Ep* 443.
3. Make his profession of obedience to the Archbishop of Canterbury as the primate of all England.
4. See *Epp* 444, 451.

446. TO GOSFRID.

Anselm encourages Gosfrid to persevere in his ascetic life but advises him to mitigate his austerity if it endangers his health, and not to despise those who do not pursue a similar way of life.

ANSELM, THE ARCHBISHOP: TO GOSFRID, SENDING THE GREETING AND BLESSING OF GOD, AND HIS OWN.

JUHEL, YOUR NEPHEW, told me about your way of life and asked me on your behalf to advise you how you should live. But having heard about your way of life I cannot think what I could add to the psalms, prayers, abstinence and bodily castigation beyond what, through the grace of God, you have begun and are doing. As long as you can continue doing what you are doing while keeping a healthy body, persevere in it. If however, you feel that you are inclining to sickness, then I advise you to restrain yourself as you see fit. For it is better for you to do something with a healthy body and in a joyful spirit than to abandon because of sickness those things which you are doing well with joy.

I advise you, therefore, to hold what you are doing as nothing and not despise in any way others who are not acting thus, nor imagine that they are of less merit before God than you. For exercise of the body is good, but God loves even more a heart full of piety, love, humility and the desire to achieve as much as it can and to enjoy the sight of God himself.[1]

May almighty God teach, strengthen and console you. I am sending you the absolution of God, and ours, if it is worth anything, from all your sins. I ask you to pray for me.

between 1100 and 1109.

NOTES

1. 1 Jn 3:2.

447. TO ASSER, ARCHBISHOP OF LUND.

Anselm congratulates Asser, Archbishop of Lund, on his elevation and exhorts him to correct the abuses in his diocese, especially not to allow anyone excluded by his own bishop to be received to ecclesiastical orders.

ANSELM, ARCHBISHOP OF CANTERBURY: TO THE REVEREND ARCHBISHOP OF THE CHURCH OF LUND, ATSER,[1] GREETING AND TRUE FRIENDSHIP IN CHRIST.

WHAT YOU ASKED ABOUT LORD ALBERIC,[2] cardinal of the Roman church, I have gladly done,[3] both for the honor of the Roman church and especially because of your love, for which I willingly wish to do anything which I perceive may please your holiness.

We give thanks to God who has raised your pious prudence and your prudent piety to the archbishopric in the kingdom of the Danes. We trust that with the help of the grace of God you will correct what is to be corrected, build what is to be built and support what is to be supported. We have heard many good things about you from the aforesaid cardinal. Therefore we have faith, and pray that God who began this within you may lead your will to a good end at all times. I ask your holiness to purify that kingdom of apostates with your holy zeal so that no foreigner may receive any ecclesiastical order there because those who have been turned away by their own bishops go there and are execrably consecrated to various orders. Farewell and pray for me.

c. 1104–1109.

NOTES

1. Atser or Asser became Bishop of Lund in 1089. In 1102 or 1103 Lund was made independent of the Archbishop of Hamburg-Bremen and raised to a metropolitan see with the suffragan bishoprics of Norway, Sweden and Iceland. About May 1104 Archbishop Asser was awarded the pallium, see C. Servatius, *Paschal II* (Stuttgart, 1979) 166; A.E. Christensen, 'Archbishop Asser, the Emperor and the Pope', *Scandinavian Journal of History* I (1976) 25–42.
2. Alberic, cardinal priest of S. Pietro in Vincoli, acted as papal legate in Denmark, 1102–1103. He brought about the separation of Lund from Hamburg-Bremen, see C. Servatius, ibid, 47, 51, 166.
3. It seems that Asser received the pallium through Anselm's mediation.

448. TO COUNTESS ATLA.

Anselm wishes a divine reward for Countess Adela's generosity and love. He hopes that what he desires for her will be fulfilled before his death.

TO HIS DEAREST LADY AND MOTHER IN GOD, THE VENERABLE COUNTESS ATLA:[1] ANSELM, SERVANT OF THE CHURCH OF CANTERBURY, WISHING HER WHATEVER MAY BE BETTER, SWEETER AND MORE AFFECTIONATE ACCORDING TO GOD.

WHENEVER I WISH TO WRITE to your Highness, I can hardly find words with which I can express the affection which my heart, before God, constantly preserves for you; perhaps I express myself better by admitting that I am not able to express myself. Reflecting in my mind on the affectionate love which I experienced in you towards me for God's sake in many different ways,[2] I cannot think of anything in myself which would be able to repay or give thanks for it sufficiently according to my will. Therefore, since I neither know any better nor am able to do any better, I turn to the Lord and pray that he himself may repay in my place your love by his love which surpasses all human merits. I do this daily and, with the help of God, shall not desist from doing it as long as I live.

You know my desire for you.[3] If only I could hear, *before I die*,[4] that this has been accomplished by the grace of God. Truly I say to you that my soul would leave my body more happily. What you desire to know about our health the bearer of this letter will adequately be able to tell you.

May the Holy Spirit always be the guardian and guide of your heart and life. Amen.

c. 1107–1109.

NOTES

1. Atla, Adala or Adela, probably the sister of Henry I, Countess of Blois and Chartres, see *Epp* 286, 340, 364, 388; *HN* 164.
2. Anselm seems to be referring to her support during his two exiles and her assistance in bringing about the meeting at l'Aigle between King Henry I and himself on 21 July 1105, see *HN* 164–165; *Epp* 364, 388, 389, 390, 397, 430.
3. Anselm wishes that Countess Adela should leave the world and enter a convent, see *Ep* 325.
4. For Anselm's growing weakness, see *Ep* 438; Gen 27:4.

449. TO HACON, EARL OF ORKNEY.

Anselm expresses to Earl Hacon of Orkney his concern that his people know very little about the Christian religion. He exhorts him to support Bishop Roger of Kirkwall in his efforts to spread the knowledge and practice of the Christian faith.

ANSELM, BY THE GRACE OF GOD, ARCHBISHOP OF CANTERBURY: TO HACON,[1] EARL OF ORKNEY, SENDING THE GREETING AND BLESSING OF GOD.

I HEAR THAT FOR WANT OF TEACHERS the people who are under your rule know and practice the Christian religion less than they should. But I rejoice because through the report of the bishop[2] you now have by the grace of God I have learned that your prudence readily accepts the word of God and the advice which pertains to salvation.

Trusting in this, therefore, I am sending your vigor my letter of admonition so that you may entrust yourself zealously to the preaching and teaching of this bishop and strive as much as you can to make your people do the same. For you can do nothing by which you can better earn the remission of your sins and the glory of eternal life than to attract your people to the practice of the Christian religion with you by admonishing them and in every other way that you can. This you will be able to carry out more effectively with God's help if, as I have just said to you, you subject yourself in devout and holy humility and with a pure intention to your bishop. If through the inspiration of God you wish to follow our advice and exhortation I shall pray almighty God that he may guide and protect you and your whole people by his grace and grant you his blessing and absolution; and as far as I can I heartily send you my blessing and absolution and the prayers of my humility.

May almighty God make you live in this world in such a way that you may be united with the blessed company of angels in the world to come. Amen.

c. 1106–1109.

NOTES

1. Hacon or Haakon or Harkon, Earl of Orkney, was married to Helga, daughter of Moddan. He succeeded Earl Paul as royal officer in 1098 and as Earl in his own right in 1106. He died in 1122 or 1123, see W. Bahnson, *Stamm- und Regententafeln zur politischen Geschichte*, Bd 3 (Berlin, 1912) Tafel 56; J. Mooney, *St Magnus - Earl of Orkney* (Kirkwall, 1935) 198–208, 312 et passim. J.F.A. Mason, 'St Anselm's Relations with Laymen', *Spicilegium Beccense* 1 (Paris, 1959) 559.
2. The bishop may have been Roger, a former monk of Whitby, who ruled c. 1101–1108. He was succeeded by Ralph Norvel, a priest of the city of York, who reigned 1109–1127, see *HC* 32, 71, 72, 74, 76, 78, 81. Bishop Ralph was succeeded by Bishop William the Old, see J. Mooney, *St Magnus - Earl of Orkney*, 217–237 et passim.

450. TO PRIOR JOHN AND THE MONKS OF BATH.

Anselm admonishes Prior John and the members of his community at Bath to maintain peace among themselves and to observe the will of God even in the smallest things.

ANSELM, THE ARCHBISHOP: TO PRIOR JOHN,[1] AND THE WHOLE COMMUNITY OF THE SERVANTS OF GOD AT BATH, SENDING THE BLESSING OF GOD AND HIS OWN, IF IT IS WORTH ANYTHING.

DOM JOHN, THE BEARER OF THIS LETTER, requested me to write your fraternity some admonition as a sign of my paternal affection. Indeed I can briefly express all the things you should avoid and all the things you should seek by saying: *Turn from evil and do good*,[2] but I consider it more appropriate to admonish your holiness about one particular virtue. Therefore I exhort you to strive wholeheartedly to keep peace among yourselves for it is said of God: *His abode has been made in peace.*[3] You will truly be the house and the temple of God if you constantly have peace among you. This you can only follow and preserve if each one of you does not try to make another carry out his will but always, as long as it is according to righteousness and the will of God, to promote the will of another. Strife among secular men is about the will of each individual, as each one says, 'Not as you will, but as I will'; true strife among monks is 'Let it not be done according to my will but according to yours'.[4] No one should expect that when he does the will of another he will repay him by acting in the same way, but he should strive never to abandon his good resolution whatever the other may do. There is something else which greatly promotes peace and love among the brothers: if no one ever tells his brother anything about another brother by which his soul might be hurt in any way; but if possible a brother should always speak about another brother so as to inflame his heart to love. Practice these things towards each other, my dearest brothers and sons.

Moreover, concerning your rule, you should be so careful that you do not violate it in the slightest way anywhere or at any time, in secret or in the sight of others. For it is written: He *who despises little things fails little by little.*[5] If therefore you want to make progress before God, never wish to despise even the smallest commands. Just as he who despises little things fails little by little, so he who does not despise little things advances, I do not say little by little, but successfully. My brothers, act so that you can say with the Prophet: *My soul is always in my hands.*[6] For in all your deeds you should consider that your soul is always in your hands because whatever anyone does his soul will receive accordingly.

May almighty God protect you from all evil[7] and having absolved you from all your sins make you persevere in your good works. Amen. I beg you to pray for me.

c. 1106–1109.

NOTES

1. John was the first prior of the cathedral priory at Bath, see *Heads*, 28. John de Villula, Bishop of Wells from 1088–1122, see *Epp* 308, 364; Fröhlich, 'Bischöfliche Kollegen', *AA* I (1969) 251–254; Barlow, *English Church*, 174 and passim, acquired the abbey of Bath in 1088 and bought the city of Bath from the King the following year, see *Reg.* I, 314.
2. Ps 36:27.
3. Cf Ps 75:2.
4. Cf Lk 22:42.
5. Si 19:1.
6. Ps 118:109.
7. Ps 121:7.

451. TO POPE PASCHAL.

Anselm beseeches Pope Paschal II not to bestow the pallium on Thomas, the archbishop-elect of York, before he has made his profession of obedience to the Archbishop of Canterbury and has received consecration from him. Moreover, he asks the Pope to refuse the pallium to Richard de Belmeis, Bishop of London, since this bishopric never had a pallium before. He enquires whether the Pope has permitted the German king the practice of investitures, since the king of England has heard this and intends to resume the practice himself.

TO HIS LORD AND FATHER PASCHAL, THE SUPREME PONTIFF, TRULY TO BE LOVED AND REVERED: ANSELM, SERVANT OF THE CHURCH OF CANTERBURY, SENDING DUE OBEDIENCE WITH FAITHFUL PRAYERS.

SINCE THE STRENGTH and order of the churches of God depend, after God, most of all on the authority of your paternity, whenever reason demands we gladly have recourse to your help and advice. The Archbishop of York, Gerard by name, has passed from this life¹ and another man, Thomas by name,² has been chosen in his place. Rumor has it³ that the pallium is being requested for him before he has been consecrated and has made his profession to me in accordance with the long-established custom of my predecessors and his.⁴ Accordingly, the principal matter of my request in this case is that he may not receive a pallium from your Highness before he is consecrated and has made, as I have said, the profession of obedience due to me, and you learn by letter from us that this has been done. I do not say this because I begrudge him the pallium but because some assert, and are even bringing it about, that if this is granted by you he may with confidence be able to refuse to make the profession of obedience he owes to me. If this should happen, you must realize that the church in England would be torn asunder and, according to the Lord's saying, *Every kingdom divided against itself will be brought to desolation*,⁵ would be made desolate and the vigor of Apostolic discipline would be greatly weakened in it. Furthermore I myself could not remain in England on any account, for I ought not nor could I permit the primacy of our church to be destroyed while I was living there.

I make the same suggestion with the same intention to your reverence about London,⁶ that if request is made by that bishop for a pallium, which he has never had, you should not give your assent to this under any circumstances. There are some people who, under pretext of doing good, are conspiring in a completely wrong manner to diminish the dignity of the primacy of Canterbury.

After Whitsuntide this year⁷ I sent your Holiness by Bernard, servant of lord Peter,⁸ your chamberlain, a letter⁹ reporting that the King of England is complaining that you are letting the German king¹⁰ grant investitures of churches without his being excommunicated, and consequently our king threatens that he will most certainly resume his investitures because the German king retains his without disturbance. Therefore your prudence should see what you should do in this matter without any delay, lest what you have established so well be irreparably destroyed.[11] For our king is enquiring diligently what you are going to do about the German king.

We pray God that he may gladden us about your prosperity for many years to come.

August 1108.

NOTES

1. Gerard, Archbishop of York, died on 21 May 1108, see *Ep* 440.
2. Thomas, son of Bishop Samson of Worcester, see *Epp* 442, 443.
3. See *Ep* 444.
4. See *Ep* 443.
5. Lk 11:17.
6. Richard de Belmeis succeeded Maurice, who died on 26 September 1107. He was raised to the see of London at Whitsun 1108, *HN* 196; Fröhlich, 'Bischöfliche Kollegen', *AA* II (1970) 155–157; Barlow, *English Church*, 81, and passim.
7. 24 May 1108.
8. Peter, the Pope's chamberlain, was the first to hold the office of administrator of papal finances; Pope Urban II had brought him from Cluny to Rome where he became a confidant of Urban's successor, Pope Paschal II. In 1106–1107 he was in France, possibly arranging Paschal's journey to France. From there he seems to have crossed to England, see K. Jordan, 'Zur Päpstlichen Finanzgeschichte im 11. und 12. Jahrhundert', *Quellen und Forschungen aus Italienischen Archiven und Bibliotheken* 25 (1933/34) 96f; C. Servatius, *Paschalis II* (Stuttgart, 1979) 63 f; *VA* 134; CS 688–689.
9. This letter is not preserved.
10. Despite the decisions of the synod of Troyes, 23 May 1107, against bishops invested by the King and those who consecrated them (see C. Hefele, *Conciliengeschichte* [Freiburg, 1886] 5:289–291), Emperor Henry V, 1106–1125, continued to invest bishops. Because of negotiations concerning the marriage of Henry I's daughter, Matilda, to the Emperor, the english king was well-informed about the activities at the imperial court; see *Epp* 424, 461.
11. Anselm is referring to the Concordat of London, 3 August 1107, see *HN* 186–187.

452. FROM POPE PASCHAL.

Pope Paschal II assures Anselm that he will not permit the honor of the church of Canterbury to be diminished and that he has not, nor will he ever tolerate investiture by Emperor Henry V of Germany.

PASCHAL, THE BISHOP, SERVANT OF THE SERVANTS OF GOD: TO HIS BELOVED BROTHER ANSELM, ARCHBISHOP OF CANTERBURY, GREETING AND APOSTOLIC BLESSING.

WE HAVE RECEIVED THE LETTER[1] of your love in which we perceive the charm of your courtesy. You have acted well and wisely by giving us warnings and cautions concerning the position and dignity of the church of Canterbury. We behold in you the venerable person of St Augustine[2] himself, the Apostle of the English, and therefore we absolutely shrink from taking anything away from the dignity of yourself or of your church. Accordingly we gladly acknowledge what you ask for, and are devoting our care and consideration towards upholding your dignity and that of your church.

Moreover, as to what you indicated in your letter, that some people are scandalized at us tolerating that the German king[3] grants investitures of churches, you ought to know that we have not at any time tolerated this nor shall we do so. We have indeed been waiting for the ferocity of that race to be subdued; however, if the King persists in the path of his father's wicked ways,[4] he will most certainly feel the sword of St Peter which we have already begun to draw.

Given at Benevento on October twelfth.

12 October 1108 at Benevento.

NOTES

1. See *Ep* 451. For the connection with the Council of Benevento, October 1108, see Blumenthal, *Paschal*, 106.

2. St Augustine was sent to England by Pope Gregory I in 596.
3. Henry V, German King and Emperor, 1106–1125.
4. Henry IV, German King and Emperor, 1056–1106.

453. FROM THOMAS, THE ARCHBISHOP-ELECT OF YORK.

Thomas, archbishop-elect of York, informs Anselm that the chapter of York has forbidden him to go to Canterbury to make a profession of obedience to the church of Canterbury. He begs Anselm for advice in his trouble.

TO HIS BELOVED LORD AND REVEREND FATHER ANSELM, BY THE GRACE OF GOD ARCHBISHOP OF THE CHURCH OF CANTERBURY: THOMAS, ARCHBISHOP-ELECT OF THE CHURCH OF YORK, ALTHOUGH UNWORTHY, SENDING GREETING AND WHATEVER SERVICE HE CAN.[1]

I HAD ARRANGED TO COME TO YOU,[2] venerable father, and had, according to my possibilities, made the necessary preparations for my journey and for other things to be done. Having obtained the permission of the chapter of our church and having summoned those whom I had thought fit to take with me, they said that from the letters[3] which your kindness had sent me and from what they had heard from other people they had lately come to the conclusion that the church of Canterbury was demanding the subjection of our church, and for that reason they were unwilling to come.[4] Moreover, they refused, in the name of God and St Peter, and by the authority of the holy Roman Church, to let me subject the church entrusted to me to that of Canterbury without just cause.[5] On the seventh day after my leaving them they furthermore repeated their refusal through an archdeacon of the church;[6] nor did this appear sufficient to them, but they followed me to Worcester[7] with a letter severely prohibiting this, saying that they would neither show me obedience, nor did they owe it to me, but that they would accuse me before the Apostolic See if I presumed to make this subjection.[8] I am thus hemmed in on both sides.[9] It would be disgraceful to go to be consecrated and return unconsecrated. To accept consecration in the face of an appeal to the Roman Church[10] and to have no one for whom one is a bishop would be dishonorable and dreadful, especially since the sacred canons say: 'Let no one be ordained bishop against his will'.[11]

Yet I fear to irritate the sweetness of your love if I defer coming to you any longer. For this reason, most serene lord, I cast upon you, in whom above all, after God, my hope rests, the task of advising me. The counsel of your blessedness and knowledge is with the Almighty and is kind and powerful. As far as my person is concerned I feel it is a great sign of honor to subject myself to your holiness in whatever you demand.

May God, and your goodness, grant that I may choose and follow the best part[12] of your advice.

early October 1108.

NOTES

1. The bearer of this letter was the monk Dom Stephen, presumably the first abbot of St Mary's, York, 1082–1112, see HC 19.
2. The date fixed by Anselm for Thomas to come to Canterbury for consecration was 6 September, *Ep* 443; it was then postponed to 24 September 1108, *Ep* 445.
3. *Epp* 443, 445.
4. F.S. Schmitt took the text of this letter from J. Raine's edition of Hugh the Chantor, 'History of Four Archbishops of York', in *Historians of the Church of York*, Rolls series (London, 1886) 2:115–116. A new edition, ed. C. Johnson (Edinburgh, 1961) 19 gives a different rendering of the Latin of this sentence: *Ad vos...dixerunt semper (=se nuper) perpendisse ex litteris ...atque ideo se velle (=nolle) venire*, see HC 19. Johnson's readings (*se nuper, nolle*) seem to be the correct ones, see the *Registrum Magnum Album* in York Minster Library, fol 5r.
5. See HC 15–18.
6. Hugh the archdeacon, HC 20.

7. HC 19: Worcester. Samson, Thomas' father was Bishop of Worcester, 1096–1122, see *Ep* 200.
8. See *Ep* 454 and the letters of Pope Urban II to Thomas I, Archbishop of York, HC 6–7, censuring him for submitting the church of York to the archbishopric of Canterbury and making a charter of profession contrary to the decree of St Gregory. For the controversy between Canterbury and York see *Ep* 443 and Introduction, Volume 1:48.
9. See Dan 13:22.
10. See *Epp* 444, 445, 451, 452, and HC 17–18, 22–23.
11. See Letter 14 of Pope Simplicius, 468–483, ed. A. Thiel, *Epistolae Rom. Pontificum*, I, (Braunsberg, 1868) 201. The text of this sentence is corrupt, see *AOO* V:402 and HC 19.
12. See Lk 10:42.

454. FROM THE CHAPTER OF THE CHURCH OF YORK.

The chapter of York informs Anselm that they fear that he called Thomas, archbishop-elect of York, to Canterbury not only to consecrate him but also to demand a profession of obedience from him. This they would find unacceptable.

TO THE LORD ANSELM, ARCHBISHOP OF CANTERBURY, TO BE REVERED FOR HIS KNOWLEDGE AND HOLINESS: THE CHAPTER OF THE CHURCH OF YORK,[1] WISHING HIM TO BE SAVED BY HIM *WHO SAVES THE UPRIGHT IN HEART*.[2]

THE FACT THAT OUR ARCHBISHOP-ELECT[3] has so long delayed his consecration is because there were also other reasons in addition to those which he told you; may we be allowed, with your permission, to speak.

You ordered him and summoned him[4] extremely severely, as it appears to us, to come to you on a date fixed by you to do and receive what he ought.

We know what he ought to receive from God by the imposition of your sacred hands, but we do not know what he ought to do. Perhaps you or your monks are saying: 'Make his profession'. We are confident about your holiness that you seek nothing in any matter but the things that are God's.⁵ We certainly grant and wish that our archbishop would show reverence and obedience by yielding, rising and bowing down to your Highness. But to subject our church to yours is to act contrary to the decrees of him⁶ who established them on the foundation of the faith, ordained archbishops on them and gave each church its privileges.⁷ Other decrees by other popes have been issued on the same point.⁸ Our church has its institutions from the Roman See, and whoever breaks them acts against sacred canons.

On account of this we have all unanimously pointed out to our elect that he should not make subjection when he receives consecration. None of us would go with him except to object to it, nor would anyone come to meet him on his return, nor obey him as archbishop. In many matters it is profitable for a wise and holy man to be his own master and to adopt his own decisions. But certain counselors, clerics as well as monks, seek to dominate rather than to be useful,⁹ aiming at and urging others to aim at preferment for self-exaltation. We are quite sure that we are doing nothing out of rivalry, self-exaltation or vainglory, but everything in the name of the Lord and with good cause.¹⁰

*May the Lord protect you from all evil; may the Lord protect your soul.*¹¹

October 1108.

NOTES

1. They sent Hugh the archdeacon with this letter to Anselm a few days after Thomas had sent *Ep* 453.
2. Ps 7:11.
3. Thomas II.
4. See *Epp* 443, 445.
5. See Ph 2:21.
6. The letter of Pope Gregory I to Augustine, 22 June 601, see Bede, *EH* I, 29.

7. For the arguments in this struggle for supremacy between Canterbury and York, see *Ep* 443.
8. M. Dueball, 'Der Suprematsstreit zwischen den Erzdiözesen Canterbury und York 1070–1126', *Historische Studien* 184 (1929) 13.
9. See Augustine, *De civ. Dei* 19, 19 et al; RB 64:8.
10. Anselm refused to answer this letter, *HN* 203.
11. Ps 120:7.

455. TO THOMAS, ARCHBISHOP-ELECT OF YORK.

Anselm for the third time instructs Thomas, the archbishop-elect of York, to come to Canterbury to make his profession of obedience and receive his consecration on 8 November. He advises him to avoid anything which might lessen the dignity of the church of Canterbury.

ANSELM, ARCHBISHOP OF CANTERBURY: TO HIS FRIEND THOMAS, ARCHBISHOP-ELECT OF YORK, GREETING.

I HAVE IN ALL CHARITY instructed you more than once[1] to come to your mother, the church of Canterbury, to receive your blessing and to do what you ought,[2] and you have not come. So, still with the same love, I once more instruct you to be with your mother on November eighth[3] to do what you ought and to receive your blessing.

Furthermore, as you ask my advice, I advise you not to begin anything which you ought not do against the church of Canterbury. You should know for sure that I shall devote myself in every possible way to see that this church loses nothing of its dignity in my time. Farewell.

October 1108.

NOTES

1. See *Epp* 443, 445.
2. Anselm is demanding Thomas' profession of obedience to the Archbishop of Canterbury.
3. 1108.

456. FROM THOMAS, ARCHBISHOP-ELECT OF YORK.

In this fragment of a letter Thomas, the archbishop-elect of York, apologizes to Anselm for the delay of his consecration, not caused by him but by the clergy of the church of York.

THOSE WHO HAVE RAISED the objection which is delaying my consecration, which no one wishes more anxiously to hasten than I, continue to uphold it.[1] In view of this, your discretion will appreciate how perilous, how shameful it would be to take possession of the government of the church over which I should preside against the common agreement of that church. How terrible a thing it would be under the appearance of a blessing to provoke a curse which should be avoided.[2]

November 1108.

NOTES

1. See *Epp* 453, 454.
2. This letter is the reply to *Ep* 455.

457. POPE PASCHAL TO HENRY, KING OF THE ENGLISH.

Pope Paschal II grants King Henry I permission to establish a new diocese at Ely, and recommends Bishop Hervey, driven from Bangor, for any vacant see.

PASCHAL, THE BISHOP, SERVANT OF THE SERVANTS OF GOD: TO HIS BELOVED SON IN CHRIST, HENRY, GLORIOUS KING OF THE ENGLISH, GREETING AND APOSTOLIC BLESSING.

WE GIVE THANKS TO ALMIGHTY GOD that he has made you such a king in our times, one who both wisely governs the earthly kingdom to the honor of God and keeps before his mind's eye the concerns of the eternal King.

You asked us in a letter[1] to set up a new bishopric by Apostolic authority in the place called Ely,[2] because the bishopric of Lincoln, as you say, is of such size that one bishop is in no way equal to carrying out all the duties pertaining to episcopal office. For this reason we both praise the devotion of your will and give our assent to your arrangement; however, it should be done in such a way that the see is established in a well-known place so that the title of bishop may not be debased—which God forbid! For a bishop is appointed in order to teach the people of God by his word and to form them by his life, and to bring back to the true shepherd, the Lord, a harvest of the souls entrusted to him. Moreover, in the matters about which you asked, although some of them appear to be irregular, yet we can in no way deny your wish.[3]

Besides, your splendor knows that the lord Bishop Hervey,[4] whose life and knowledge commend him not a little, has been driven from his see by the extreme ferocity and persecution of the barbarians and fled after many of the faithful and his brothers had been killed.[5] In order that his knowledge may bear the fruit which does not perish and his life give a good example to the people of God, we wish and we ask that, if any vacant church in your kingdom could call[6] upon him who bears the proofs of heavenly life in his knowledge and character, he should be appointed there by Apostolic authority so that he may no longer languish in fruitless silence.

May almighty God protect you and your children through the prayers of his Apostles and grant you the celestial kingdom after the earthly one.

Given on November twenty-first.[7]

21 November 1108, at Troia, Apulia.

NOTES

1. Henry's letter is not preserved, see *Epp* 379, 460.
2. See *Ep* 441, and *HN* 195.
3. The royal charter creating the see of Ely is dated 17 October 1109, *Reg.* II: 919.
4. In 1109 he became first Bishop of Ely where he ruled until his death on 30 August 1131, see *Epp* 404, 441; Barlow, *English Church*, 29, 46, 71, 117, 166.
5. See *Ep* 404.
6. After the death of Richard, Abbot of Ely (see *Ep* 422) Hervey persuaded the monks of Ely to resume the negotiations with the curia which Abbot Richard had already begun about raising the abbey to a see.
7. 1108.

458. FROM POPE PASCHAL.

Pope Paschal II informs Anselm that, at the King's request, he is ratifying the creation of the bishopric of Ely.

PASCHAL, THE BISHOP, SERVANT OF THE SERVANTS OF GOD: TO THE VENERABLE BROTHER ANSELM, ARCHBISHOP OF CANTERBURY, AND THE OTHER BISHOPS OF THE SAME PROVINCE, GREETING AND APOSTOLIC BLESSING.

THE DOCUMENTS OF THE APOSTOLIC SEE and the works of the English historians show clearly that, among the kingdoms of the world the love and obedience of the kingdom of the English has especially tied it to the Apostolic See. This fact naturally urges our solicitude even more willingly to foster the churches of that kingdom in an even more friendly way and to watch over their arrangements even more carefully.

From the letters[1] of our son the King and from you, we have learned that the bishopric of Lincoln is so large and wide-spread that one bishop is in no way equal to carrying out all the duties pertaining to episcopal office. Wherefore, according to the wish of the Bishop of Lincoln,[2] this same Henry, our dearly-beloved son and most Christian King of the English, requests us to set up a new bishopric in a part of that bishopric with the permission of the Apostolic See, namely in that place which is called Ely. Since his petitions appear to us to be devout, we gladly give our consent and through our Apostolic authority we give permission for the bishopric to be established at the aforesaid place. We hereby state that the episcopal see established in the aforesaid place should remain there henceforward for all time. It should also possess in perpetuity the area which your fraternity, together with the aforesaid brother, the Bishop of Lincoln, and the ordinance of the King shall assign to this bishopric. Furthermore, concerning the monastery in which the episcopal see is being established, the customs of the English monasteries in which bishops have been established shall be preserved.[3]

May the preservers of this constitution always enjoy the blessing of almighty God and his Apostles. Amen.

I Paschal, bishop of the catholic Church. Given at Troia by the hand of Leo,[4] cardinal deacon of the Roman Church on November twenty-first, the first indiction, in the year of the Incarnation of our Lord, 1108, in the tenth year of the pontificate of lord Pope Paschal II.

21 November 1108 at Troia, Apulia.

NOTES

1. Anselm's letter, *Ep* 441; Henry's letter is not preserved, see *Epp* 379, 457, 460.
2. Robert Bloet, Bishop of Lincoln 1094–1123, see *Ep* 311.
3. There were monastic cathedrals at Canterbury, Bath (*Ep* 450), Durham, Norwich, Rochester, Winchester, and Worcester; see M.D. Knowles, *The Monastic Order in England* (Cambridge, 1966) 65, 129–134.
4. Leo, Bishop of Ostia, originally Leo Marsicanus, offspring of the barons of Marsico, entered the monastery of Montecassino at the age of fourteen, and became the greatest historian of Italy in the middle

ages. In 1101 he was made Cardinal Bishop of Ostia by Paschal II, whom he supported loyally. He died on 22 May 1115, see C. Servatius, *Paschalis II* (Stuttgart, 1979) 43–45, 242, 247, 299, 301.

459. FROM POPE PASCHAL.

Pope Paschal recommends that Anselm appoint Bishop Hervey of Bangor to any church asking for him.

PASCHAL, THE BISHOP, SERVANT OF THE SERVANTS OF GOD: TO THE VENERABLE BROTHER ANSELM, ARCHBISHOP OF CANTERBURY, GREETING AND APOSTOLIC BLESSING.

YOUR FRATERNITY KNOWS that as emphasized by Apostolic statement *Every high priest* is *chosen from among men, and appointed for men in things pertaining to God*.[1] Your brother, this Hervey, who is recommended by his life and knowledge, could not fulfil the episcopal office in the church to which he was appointed because of the ferocity of the barbarians which they cruelly inflicted on his brothers and other Christians.[2] But lest the office laid on him remain without fruit we instruct your love and ask you to provide for him most attentively; and if any vacant church in your province should call him[3] you should appoint him to it by the authority of the Apostolic See, so that he may be able to serve God there, and by the Lord's generosity fulfil the episcopal office so that he who bears the proofs of heavenly life in his knowledge and character may no longer remain idle in fruitless silence. In the meantime however, hold him recommended in all things, for he has shown himself zealous in representing your affairs at our court competently and faithfully.[4]

May divine power keep your fraternity safe for a long time. Given on November twenty-first.

21 November 1108 at Troia, Apulia.

NOTES

1. Heb 5:1.
2. See *Epp* 404, 418, 425, 441, 457.
3. See *Ep* 457.
4. See *Ep* 460; Eadmer judges Hervey less favorably when he writes: 'Bishop Hervey of Bangor who had left his own church was in fact translated and was enthroned as bishop in the new bishopric which the king and the princes had sometime before resolved to have established in Ely. This preferment sought by much asking, by much promising of many kinds and by performing many services, he finally succeeded in obtaining as soon as ever Anselm, that most active father, was dead.' *HN* 211.

460. POPE PASCHAL TO HENRY, KING OF THE ENGLISH.

Pope Paschal II informs King Henry of the English that he will consider his secret information; he permits the exchange the King has sought through Bishop Hervey and the chamberlain Peter and once more recommends Hervey to the King's favor.

PASCHAL, THE BISHOP, SERVANT OF THE SERVANTS OF GOD: TO HIS BELOVED SON HENRY, GLORIOUS KING OF THE ENGLISH, GREETING AND BENEDICTION.

WE HAVE RECEIVED THE LETTER[1] of your kindest love to us which shows the sweetness of affection you bear for St Peter and for us, his servant. We rejoiced greatly about this because we perceive the love for the heavenly home in the heart of an earthly king. Therefore, we give our assent to your petition the more gladly and readily as we with greater certainty perceive that you are seeking what is pleasing to the heavenly king.

With regard to that matter[2] about which your affection was anxious to inform us secretly, we shall take care to give it as much attention as we can and in all other matters we gladly seek to do everything possible for the honor of God and the excellence and exaltation of your glory. As to the exchange[3] about which your love asked us through our brothers, Bishop Hervey and the chamberlain Peter,[4] if it can be done for the good of the Church as you say, we give our assent to your petitions. We recommend most attentively to your honor that same brother, Bishop Hervey, whom we know to be dear to you.[5]

21 November 1108 at Troia, Apulia.

NOTES

1. Henry's letter is not preserved, see *Epp* 379, 457, 458.
2. Paschal may be referring to Henry's request for the pallium for Thomas, the archbishop-elect of York, *HC* 22–23. Anselm successfully prevented the Pope from granting it to Thomas before he made his profession of obedience to the Archbishop of Canterbury and received his consecration at Canterbury, see *Epp* 451, 452.
3. Paschal is probably referring to Hervey's translation from the see of Bangor to the newly-created see of Ely, see *Epp* 457, 459.
4. See *Ep* 451, note 8.
5. Sent on the same date as *Epp* 457, 458, 459.

461. FROM HENRY, KING OF THE ENGLISH.

Henry, King of the English, rejoices in Anselm's good health and informs him about his meeting with King Louis VI of France. He entrusts to Anselm the care of his kingdom and of his son William and daughter Matilda during his absence.

HENRY, BY THE GRACE OF GOD, KING OF THE
ENGLISH: TO ANSELM, ARCHBISHOP OF CANTERBURY,
HIS DEAREST FATHER, GREETING AND LOVE.

KNOW, MY FATHER, that by the grace of God I am healthy and safe and all my affairs progress and prosper.[1] You should know that I rejoice with you not a little at what I have heard about you and your health through Anfrid, your cleric, and others, and also about the matters going on around you being furthered by the felicity of good health[2] and prosperity.

Lest it remain hidden from the knowledge of your benevolence how the conversation[3] between me and Louis of France[4] took place you should know that we held a conversation, I with a large number of my troops and he with his army gathered from every side. Employing reason and impartiality, together with moderate humility, while still observing royal rigor I remained calm and collected until by his exceedingly presumptuous and proud haughtiness he demanded too much of me. Thus, under the guidance of the grace of the Holy Spirit, I brought our discussion to an end so that, accompanied by my barons I could withdraw with reason and justice. So it is that even those people whom Louis himself had given to me as hostages on his behalf agree with my case and defend it and weaken and criticize the case of Louis.

Moreover, you should know that in the matter[5] which was being discussed between myself and the Emperor of the Romans, we brought it to a good end by the grace of God, to the honor of God and ourselves, and the honor of holy Church and the Christian people.

About the other matters[6] which exist in England and are being discussed there, I wish that they should be subject to your will and be settled on your advice. I have informed our justiciars[7] about this. I entrust to you my son[8] and my daughter,[9] so that you may cherish them with paternal love and care for them with parental love.

Witnessed by Ranulf,[10] the chancellor, at Rouen.[11]

c. autumn 1108.

NOTES

1. Henry crossed to Normandy from Bosham, near Chichester, in July 1108 and returned to England on 31 May 1109. Anselm intended to

give him his blessing, but the night before the departure Anselm was taken ill and was unfit to go to the King, *HN* 197-198.
2. Henry seems to be referring to Anselm's improved health in August and September 1108; for his periods of sickness, see *Ep* 438.
3. Since 911 the Normans were vassals of the king of France. After the battle of Tinchebrai on 28 September 1106, which put the duchy of Normandy into the possession of the English king, Henry I strove to shed the overlordship of the French king. Louis' demand to retain the vassalage over the duchy of Normandy led to a period of wars, see A.L. Poole, *From Domesday Book to Magna Carta* (Oxford, 1958) 122-127; F. Barlow, *Feudal Kingdom of England* (London, 1955) 195-199; C.W. Hollister, 'Normandy, France and the Anglo-Norman Regnum', *Speculum* 51 (1976) 202-242.
4. Philip I, King of France, died on 29 July 1108 and was succeeded by his son Louis VI le Gros who reigned until 1137, see *Epp* 341, 342.
5. Henry's daughter Matilda was to become the wife of Emperor Henry V, see *Epp* 424, 451, note 10.
6. These were the carrying out of the decrees of the Westminster synod of Whitsun 1108 demanding a celibate clergy (*Ep* 422), the struggle of supremacy between Canterbury and York (*Epp* 442-445, 451-456), and the establishment of the new bishopric of Ely (*Epp* 441, 457-460).
7. See J.F.J. West, *The Justiciarship in England 1066-1232* (Cambridge, 1966).
8. William, born August 1103, *HN* 197; *Epp* 305, 320, 321.
9. Matilda or Maud, born in summer 1102, *Ep* 424.
10. Ranulf succeeded Waldric as chancellor in spring 1107, see *Reg.* II, ix, x.
11. Anselm's serious illness of July 1108 improved in late summer/autumn. From winter 1108-1109 his health deteriorated until his death on 21 April 1109. Therefore the date of this letter is rather autumn 1108 than March 1109, see *Reg.* II: 910; see also *Epp* 407, 438.

462. TO HENRY, KING OF THE ENGLISH.

Anselm rejoices about King Henry's successes in Normandy and thanks him for his concern about his health and for the trust displayed by appointing him viceroy of England; he begs Henry's help in the case of Thomas, the archbishop-elect of York.

TO HIS DEAREST LORD HENRY, BY THE GRACE OF GOD, GLORIOUS KING OF THE ENGLISH: ANSELM, ARCHBISHOP OF CANTERBURY, SENDING FAITHFUL SERVICE WITH PRAYERS AND THE BLESSING OF GOD, AND HIS OWN, FOR WHAT IT IS WORTH.

I GIVE THANKS TO ALMIGHTY GOD from the bottom of my heart for all the prosperity and successes which God, through his grace, kindly allowed you to receive; and I pray to him that he may make your Highness always to progress to greater and better things, and may lead you through continuing prosperity of the earthly kingdom to the happiness of the heavenly one.

I also give thanks to your honor who has amicably made known to me by your letter[1] as to a faithful and truly loving friend how things are with you, and has rejoiced my heart by the report of your joy and prosperity. I give thanks that you so lovingly commend your son and daughter to my care and love and that you entrust your kingdom and the affairs of your kingdom to my will: although for this purpose there is not sufficient wisdom in me, nevertheless, because I know your immense benevolence and gratitude towards me I gratefully accept, as far as I can, and what you commit to me I commend to the disposition and help of God, through whom everything is well disposed.

I inform your Highness by word of mouth through Dom Baldwin,[2] your faithful and loving servant, how the case regarding the archbishop-elect of the church of York[3] stands. For this matter I beseech your help and support from the bottom of my heart that you should not allow the dignity of the church of Canterbury, which was preserved by your predecessors and entrusted to your care by God, and whose honor is yours, to be diminished. As far as I am concerned I tell you for certain that I would be prepared to die[4] in order that its dignity be preserved unharmed rather than to let it be violated through any negligence of mine.[5]

May almighty God always guide and protect you and yours. Amen.

winter 1108.

NOTES

1. Anselm's reply to *Ep* 461.
2. See *Epp* 129, 151.
3. See *Ep* 461.
4. 2 Macc 7:2.
5. Compare Anselm's determination expressed here with *Ep* 451 to Pope Paschal.

463. TO POPE PASCHAL.

Anselm recommends to Pope Paschal II the case of the bearer of this letter.

TO PASCHAL, THE SUPREME PONTIFF, WITH REVERENT LOVE AND LOVING REVERENCE: ANSELM, SERVANT OF THE CHURCH OF CANTERBURY, SENDING DUE SUBJECTION WITH THE CONSTANCY OF PRAYERS.

ALTHOUGH THROUGH NO MERIT of my own, some people, seeing that I always have your benevolence present in my affairs, think that I, like a faithful servant, can obtain anything from you in those matters proper to your Highness. Therefore, pressed by the petitions of others I presume to beseech your majesty to deign to listen to the request of the bearer[1] of this letter and to decide on it as your wisdom pleases.

May almighty God preserve your holiness for us in long-lasting prosperity. Amen.

1100–1109.

NOTES

1. For a possible identification see M. Brett, *The English Church under Henry I* (Oxford, 1975) 237.

464. TO SAMSON, BISHOP OF WORCESTER.

Anselm writes to his friend, Bishop Samson of Worcester, who made his profession of obedience to the church of Canterbury, to assist him against the archbishop-elect of York, his son. Thomas had been invited three times to come to make his profession but had excused himself on the grounds that he was awaiting the return of his envoys from Rome and Normandy. Anselm begs Samson to support the mission of the bishops of Rochester and Norwich to gain the King's support.

ANSELM, ARCHBISHOP OF CANTERBURY: TO
SAMSON, BISHOP OF WORCESTER, GREETING.

YOU KNOW WHAT THE CHURCH OF YORK owes to the church of Canterbury and in what way the former ought to be subject to the latter.[1] After Thomas[2] was elected archbishop of York he should have sought his consecration and professed the obedience which the archbishop of York owes to the archbishop and church of Canterbury. He scorned to do what he should have done.[3] Nevertheless, out of the abundance of charity I invited him twice[4] by our clerics and a third time by two bishops[5] to come to his mother, the church of Canterbury, and to me, to whom this office is entrusted, and to do and receive what he ought. He has disregarded to do what he should have done and he answers that he has sent his messengers to Rome and to Normandy;[6] when they return he will do what he learns through their advice. We consider that such an answer in this matter is not acceptable.

I therefore ask you as a friend and one who has made his profession to our church[7] that against this injury, which affects not only me but all the bishops and churches of our archdiocese and primacy, and moreover also the kingdom of England, to be a help to me in checking such an intolerable presumption. Your reverence may be assured that I shall not fail to do anything I can, either as regards God or men, in order to suppress this irregular presumption of his. He ought to remember that he received the major orders which he holds in my archdiocese, and the priesthood at my command, and that his election came about by my favor.[8] Wherefore, if he considered it in the right light, he would not rise up irregularly against me, nay rather, above me. I crave your advice in this matter. Since, on the advice of the other bishops who are involved in this injury, I shall be sending in the near future two bishops, namely Rochester and Thetford,[9] to our lord the King on my behalf and theirs to ask his help in carrying out what I canonically have to do and wish to do in this matter: inform these bishops so that they may carry out this legation on your behalf as well as on that of the other bishops. Farewell.

c. December 1108.

NOTES

1. Profession of obedience to the archbishop of Canterbury recognizing him as primate and superior; see *Epp* 442, 443, 444, 445, 451–456, 461.
2. Thomas is Samson's son, see *Ep* 442.
3. See *Epp* 444, 453, 454, 456.
4. See *Epp* 443, 445, 455.
5. Anselm had sent Richard, Bishop of London, consecrated on 26 July 1108, and Dean of the church of Canterbury, and Ralph, Bishop of Rochester, consecrated on 9 August 1108, the private and domestic vicar of Canterbury, see *HN* 204; *HC* 21–22.
6. See *HC* 22–23.

7. *Ego Samson, Wigorniensis ecclesiae electus et a te, reverende pater Anselme, sancte Cantuariensis ecclesiae archiepiscope et totius Britanniae primas, antistes consecrandus, tibi et obedientiam me per omnia servaturum esse promitto.* This is Samson's profession from the Canterbury Professions, ed. M. Richter, 34–35.
8. See *Ep* 444.
9. Bishops Ralph of Rochester and Herbert of Norwich-Thetford.

465. FROM SAMSON, BISHOP OF WORCESTER.

Samson, Bishop of Worcester, confirms his profession of obedience to Anselm and advises him not to become excessively upset about this case. He believes that Thomas has only good intentions towards Anselm and that Anselm cannot be blamed for the delay in this matter.

TO HIS LORD AND DEAREST FATHER ANSELM, THE VENERABLE ARCHBISHOP OF CANTERBURY: SAMSON, PRIEST OF THE CHURCH OF WORCESTER, SENDING GREETING, SERVICE AND FAITHFUL PRAYERS.

YOU ASKED[1] ME, MY LORD, having reminded me of my profession of obedience to your church and to you, to come to the help of you and your church, namely Canterbury, in the matter between you and Thomas, the elect of the church of York. I beseech your excellency not to doubt that I would ever wish to break the profession which I made and still continue to make, and want to keep under all circumstances because of any matter or of any person. For I consider that in your case you will have no helper more faithful than me nor, according to my powers, more devoted.

About the advice you asked of me, if I knew truly what was more expedient for you and for us I would not hesitate to tell you. This only I say, that I think it unworthy for you to be so angry about this matter. Since we have so many bishops, so many abbots and such a number of important men as witnesses, I think that there should be no difficulty in refuting clerics of so little or of no authority. I cannot see any problem in bringing the presumptuous audacity of those who caused such a great controversy to nothing. As regards that elect, I have believed and do believe, and if one can believe him I affirm truly, that he only has good intentions towards you and that as long as you live he will be most devoutly subject to you and your church in all things. I am pleased, however, that you did what you had to do, guiding by good intentions and commanding by due authority, because if there be any sin in delaying consecration it is not your fault but that of someone else.[2]

December 1108 or January 1109.

NOTES

1. In *Ep* 464.
2. At the Whitsun court on 13 June 1109, after Anselm's death, Samson confirmed his statement that the archbishop of York was bound to make profession of obedience to the archbishop of Canterbury before his consecration, see *HN* 208.

466. TO COUNT ELIAS.

Anselm tells Helias, Count of Maine, through Dom Hardus, the way to certain bliss and sends him the absolution he asked for.

ANSELM, SERVANT OF THE CHURCH OF CANTERBURY: TO HIS LORD AND DEARLY-BELOVED FRIEND IN GOD, COUNT ELIAS,[1] SENDING GREETING AND WISHING THAT HE MAY ALWAYS BE GUIDED AND PROTECTED BY THE GRACE OF GOD.

I REJOICE AND GIVE THANKS to almighty God, from whom all good comes, who has so filled your heart with good will and a holy intention that you are most eagerly seeking advice about the path and way of life by which you can more certainly and effectively reach the kingdom of heaven and the blessed company of the angels. Since you asked me this I am telling it to you through our beloved brother, Dom Hardus, your friend and confidant, as indeed I can best understand it; and in what manner this is you can clearly learn from him personally.

Our absolution, which you begged from me through the same brother, as he told me, I am sending to your affection by heart, mouth and in writing, and I pray daily for you. May almighty God inflame your holy desire more and more and lead it to a blessed end. Amen.[2]

1100-1109.

NOTES

1. Helias or Elias, son of John of la Flèche, Count of Maine, was a loyal supporter of Kings William II and Henry I, see OV IV: 154, 194, 198; V: 226, 228–238, 242, 246, 248, 254–258, 304–306; VI: 78, 84, 88–90, 94–98, 172. He died on 3 July 1110.
2. In MS L this is letter 384, possibly written during the winter of 1108–1109.

467. TO ROBERT, COUNT OF MEULAN.

Anselm solemnly entreats Robert, Count of Meulan, chief advisor to the King, on no account to allow the injury which Thomas, the archbishop-elect of York, is trying to inflict on the church of Canterbury.

ANSELM, ARCHBISHOP OF CANTERBURY: TO HIS DEAREST LORD AND FRIEND ROBERT, COUNT OF MEULAN, SENDING THE GREETING AND BLESSING OF GOD, AND HIS OWN, FOR WHAT IT IS WORTH.

REGARDING THE CASE[1] which exists between myself and Thomas, the elect of York, I ask and beseech you as a true friend and son of the mother church of Canterbury and I advise you as a faithful Christian and one who faithfully loves the honor and dignity of the King and the whole kingdom of England, to consider most diligently and carefully the importance of the great evil that Thomas is trying to commit, and to suppress with all your strength his intention which is an injury and ignominy to the King, the whole kingdom of England, your mother church and the Archbishop of Canterbury. As regards myself I affirm in the hope of God's help that it will never be through me; and if I knew I was to die tomorrow, before his breach of law was abolished, I would pass my judgement on him with the greatest severity I can think of. Your love can be certain of this, that no one can maintain this presumption of his in any way without grave sin and the wrath of God.[2]

May the Holy Spirit guide your heart in truth. Amen.

early 1109.

NOTES

1. See *Epp* 442–445, 451–456, 461, 462, 464, 465; *HN* 199–211; *HC* 15–31.
2. Robert of Meulan opposed Anselm's condemnation of Thomas, the archbishop-elect of York, see *Ep* 472; *HN* 207–209.

468. TO WILLIAM, ABBOT OF BEC.

Anselm instructs Abbot William of Bec that vows made in the world are fulfilled within the monastic profession and are therefore at the abbot's discretion.

ANSELM, MONK OF BEC AND PRIEST OF THE CHURCH OF CANTERBURY: TO HIS BELOVED FRIEND, THE REVEREND ABBOT WILLIAM[1] OF BEC, GREETING.

YOU WISHED TO HEAR our advice concerning the vow of the monk who vowed never to drink wine any more[2] before he came to our order. It seems to me that what was done by the forefathers of our order, and above all at Cluny, is to be done, namely that vows of this kind which are made without a promise of faith or an oath[3] are judged to be fulfilled within the vow of the monastic order in which a man offers God everything belonging to him and the whole of himself.[4] It lies within the disposition of the superior whether to allow them to be observed within reason or to change them. You can, if you wish, allow this monk about whom we are speaking to continue for a time what he has begun. If you ever perceive, however, that this is not expedient, order him to observe faithfully what the brothers observe in common.

early 1109.

NOTES

1. See *Epp* 157, 163.
2. For Anselm's position on lesser vows, see also *Ep* 188.
3. A solemn vow was considered an act similar to a public oath. It was pronounced in front of the abbot or bishop as representative of Christ, see RB 58:17–20.
4. See RB 58:24–25.

469. TO RALPH, BISHOP OF CHICHESTER.

Anselm commands Ralph, Bishop of Chichester, to free the hostages his archdeacon had arrested illegally and render him satisfaction for the injustice. He will treat his own men as he thinks fit.

ANSELM, ARCHBISHOP OF CANTERBURY: TO
RALPH,[1] BISHOP OF CHICHESTER, GREETING.

I HAVE HEARD that your archdeacon has arrested[2] my people as a penalty for the breaking of a feast day and took hostages from them, nor was he willing to free them before he had the hostages. Neither he nor anybody else has power over my people. Therefore I instruct you that these hostages should be left in peace and that you should render me justice for your archdeacon who presumed to exercise such power over my people. I give you thanks that you asked me to punish our men, lest anybody should take bad example from them, and with God's approval I shall do what I have to do. Farewell.

possibly early 1109.

NOTES

1. Ralph Luffa, Bishop of Chichester, 1091–1123, see Fröhlich, 'Bischöfliche Kollegen', *AA* I (1969) 254–255.
2. For matters of episcopal jurisdiction, see M. Brett, *The English Church under Henry I* (Oxford, 1975) 148–161.

470. FROM KING HENRY.

Henry, King of the English, asks Anselm to defer the consecration of the Archbishop of York until Easter 1109, so that he can settle the dispute between the two metropolitans after his return to England.

HENRY, BY THE GRACE OF GOD, KING OF THE ENGLISH: TO HIS DEAR FATHER ANSELM,[1] ARCHBISHOP OF CANTERBURY, GREETING AND FRIENDSHIP.

I ASK YOU TO DEFER with serenity and good will the blessing of Thomas, Archbishop of York, and whatever has taken place between you on this matter, until Easter.[2] If I return to England[3] before the aforesaid date I will then reconcile you justly and honorably on the advice of my bishops and barons. If I do not return so soon I will then act in such a way that there will be fraternal peace and good harmony between you.[4] Farewell.

December 1108 or January 1109.

NOTES

1. Henry here replies to the embassy of Bishops Ralph of Rochester and Herbert of Norwich, as representatives of the other bishops, *Ep* 464.
2. Easter was on 25 April 1109; Anselm died on 21 April 1109, the Wednesday of Holy Week, see *VA* 141–143.
3. Henry was in Normandy from July 1108 until 31 May or 2 June 1109, *Ep* 464.
4. Anselm's reply was taken to Normandy by Odo, Dean of the church of Chichester, and Athbold, monk of Bec. He informed the King about his dispute with Thomas, begged him to use his authority to avoid a split in the church and kingdom of England, and stated that 'He would sooner let his whole body be cut to pieces limb by limb than he would ever for a single hour grant Thomas such a truce in this dispute', see *HN* 205. The envoys returned with the message that the King had received Anselm's reasons well and that he also desired the unity of the Christian Church in England.

471. TO BISHOP R.

Anselm individually commands every bishop to act in future towards Thomas, the archbishop-elect of York, as he has laid down in the letter sent to Thomas, of which a copy is attached.

ANSELM, ARCHBISHOP OF CANTERBURY: TO HIS
BELOVED FRIEND, THE REVEREND BISHOP R., GREETING.

I INSTRUCT[1] AND ORDER you through the holy obedience you owe to the church of Canterbury and myself that you henceforth maintain towards Thomas the elect of the church of York[2] what is written in the accompanying letter[3] which I have sent to Thomas.

March or April 1109.

NOTES

1. Not long before his death on 21 April 1109 Anselm had *Epp* 471 and 472 sent to all the bishops of England. The initial 'R' applies to eight of the fifteen bishops of England, see Volume 1:351.

2. This letter is the penultimate one in MS L = L 388, which would justify the date March or April 1109.
3. See *Ep* 472.

472. TO THOMAS, ARCHBISHOP-ELECT OF YORK.

Anselm suspends Thomas, the archbishop-elect of York, from his priestly office until he has subjected himself to the church of Canterbury or has renounced the episcopacy. He forbids all the bishops of England to consecrate him or to receive him if he should be consecrated by foreign bishops.

ANSELM, MINISTER OF THE CHURCH OF CANTERBURY:
TO THOMAS,[1] ARCHBISHOP-ELECT OF YORK.

TO YOU THOMAS, in the sight of almighty God, I, Anselm, Archbishop of Canterbury and primate of all Britain, speak. Speaking in the name of God himself I now forbid you the priestly office which you undertook at my bidding in my diocese as my suffragan, and I command you not to presume to meddle in any way in any pastoral responsibility until you abandon the rebellion which you have started against the church of Canterbury and profess the subjection to that church which your predecessors Archbishops Thomas and Gerard made following the old-established custom of their predecessors.[2]

If you choose to persist any longer in this course upon which you have started rather than abandon it, I forbid all the bishops of the whole of Britain, under the curse of perpetual anathema, that no one of them is to lay his hand upon you in order to promote you to the episcopate, or if you should be so promoted by bishops from abroad, to receive you as bishop or in any Christian fellowship. I also forbid you, Thomas, under the same anathema in the name of God, ever to accept the blessing as bishop of York without first making the profession which your predecessors Thomas and Gerard made to the church of Canterbury.[3]

If, however, you entirely relinquish the bishopric of York, then I permit you to perform the priestly office which you have already received.⁴

March or April 1109.

NOTES

1. Anselm sent a copy of this letter with *Ep* 471 to all the bishops of England.
2. See *Ep* 442.
3. Anselm's injunction on Thomas was discussed by the Whitsun court on 13 June 1109 at Westminster, *HN* 207–209. Despite the attack of Robert of Meulan (*HN* 207–209; *Ep* 467) the bishops unanimously abided by Anselm's demand that Thomas should make his profession of obedience to the church of Canterbury before being allowed to receive consecration. According to Eadmer, 'the King sided with the bishops because he had no wish at all to bring upon himself the excommunication of Father Anselm', *HN* 207–209. Finally the King decided that Thomas was to follow the example of his predecessors or give up the archbishopric of York. Thomas gave in and his consecration was fixed for Sunday, 27 July 1109, at Canterbury. During the service Thomas made his profession of subjugation and obedience (*HN* 210 and Canterbury Professions, ed. M. Richter, 37) and was consecrated by Richard, Bishop of London.
4. This is the last letter in MS L = 389.

473. TO ROBERT, BISHOP OF LINCOLN, AND OTHERS.

Anselm testifies to Bishop Robert of Lincoln that when he was Abbot of Bec he had seen the remains of St Neot and had taken a small piece of the relic and the key of the shrine. He encourages the faithful to build a church in honor of the saint.

ANSELM, BY THE GRACE OF GOD, ARCHBISHOP OF CANTERBURY: TO ROBERT,¹ REVEREND BISHOP OF LINCOLN, AND TO ALL WHO WISH TO KNOW THE TRUTH ABOUT THE BODY OF SAINT NEOT, THE CONFESSOR, GREETING.

MAY YOU KNOW FOR CERTAIN that I myself, when I was abbot of Bec, made investigations at St Neot's² and found in a box which they call a shrine the bones of the holy and treasured confessor, Neot. I immediately replaced them in the same box except for one arm which is said to be in Cornwall and a small part which I kept for myself as a memorial and in veneration of that saint. Having carefully shut up this box with the same bones inside, I took the key back with me to the church of Bec, where it is carefully preserved to this day.[3]

Now I pray that all those to whom God will give the opportunity and who have made enquiries, should bestow some help—as God will deign to inspire them—either in deed or in word for the construction of a church for this holy confessor. Let no one hinder in any way those who provide labor for this church or seek help for this purpose; rather let God reward each one in eternal life and let the saint intercede for them before God as he knows to be expedient for them.[4]

We indeed, as far as we can, devoutly beseech God that he may grant his blessing and the absolution from sin to all those who give any assistance to that church. Farewell.

c. 1094–1097.

NOTES

1. Robert Bloet, Bishop of Lincoln, 1094–1123, see *Ep* 311.
2. See *Epp* 90–94; this investigation took place during Anselm's first visit to England as Abbot of Bec in 1080, see M. Chibnall, 'The Relations of St Anselm with the English Dependencies of Bec, 1079–1093', *Spicilegium Beccense* 1 (Paris, 1959) 524–527.
3. A list of the relics at Bec was drawn up in 1134; it mentions the relic of St Neot, see *VA* 57.
4. For the slowly growing welfare of the community of St Neots through benefactions, see M. Chibnall, ibid., 525.

474. TO THE MONKS OF CANTERBURY.

Anselm returns half the offerings at the high altar and the manor of Stisted to his monks.

I, ANSELM, Archbishop of the holy church of Canterbury, return to the monks of Christ Church half of the revenues of the altar of Christ which I held in my possession after the death of my predecessor, Archbishop Lanfranc, who had given them the other half during his lifetime, knowing in fact that it belonged to them.[1] Similarly, I restore to the same monks the manor called Stisted[2] because it is known to belong and to have belonged to their possessions.

Witnesses:
William, Archdeacon of Christ Church[3]
Haimo, the sheriff[4]
Haimo, son of Vitel[5]
Robert, son of Watson
Wimundus, man of the sheriff
Radulph,[6] nephew of Bishop Gundulf
and several others.

c. 1093–1097.

NOTES

1. For the bishop's revenues, see M. Brett, *The English Church under Henry I* (Oxford, 1975) 161–173; Southern, *Anselm*, 256–259.
2. The estate of Stisted in Essex.
3. See *Epp* 208, 257, 360, 374.
4. For Haimo, see *Epp* 356, 359, and *Reg.* II: xii.
5. Vitalis, a knight who fought in the battle of Hastings, see *Bayeux Tapestry*, ed. F.M. Stenton (London, 1957) plates 55, 56, 57; *The Bayeux Tapestry*, ed. D.M. Wilson (London, 1985) plates 54, 55, pp. 190, 199. For his holdings, see W. Urry, 'The Normans in Canterbury', *Annales de Normandie*, 8 (1958) 130–131. For his son Haimo, see Urry, 131–134.
6. For Radulf, see Urry, 124–125.

475. TO ALL THE FAITHFUL OF CHRIST CHURCH.

Anselm informs all the faithful of Christ Church Canterbury that he has granted in perpetuity to the monks of Christ Church the lands at Saltwood and Hythe which came into his possession after the death of Robert of Montfort.

ANSELM, BISHOP OF THE HOLY CHRUCH OF CANTERBURY: TO ALL THE FAITHFUL OF CHRIST CHURCH, GREETING AND THE BLESSING OF GOD, AND HIS OWN.

LET IT BE KNOWN TO YOU that by the recent death of Robert of Montfort[1] on his way to Jerusalem the lands at Saltwood and Hythe[2] have come into my possession and I have handed them over to Christ Church and the monks for their sustenance. I therefore ask my successors, namely all archbishops, to allow the aforesaid lands to remain in the possession of the church as I put them.

c. 1109.

NOTES

1. Robert, son of Hugh of Montfort, held the honor of constable and commanded the armies of William Rufus, *OV* V, 246, 258. His allegiance remained uncertain. After serving Henry I for some years (*OV* VI, 56, 84; *Ep* 299) he was exiled for breach of faith in 1107 and asked for and obtained leave to go to Jerusalem, *OV* VI: 100. Robert joined Bohemond, and they landed at Avlona on the Greek coast opposite Brindisi on 9 October 1107. The following September 1108, Bohemond had to sign the Treaty of Devol which made him subject to Emperor Alexius, see S. Runciman, *History of the Crusades* (London, 1965) 2:49–51. Soon after this Robert died, *OV* VI, 104.
2. See Southern, *Anselm*, 257.

SELECTED BIBLIOGRAPHY

Anselmi Opera Omnia [=AOO], ed. F.S. Schmitt, vols 1-6. Edinburgh 1946-1963, reprinted with 'Prolegomena seu ratio editionis', Stuttgart, 1968.

The Memorials of Saint Anselm, edd., R.W. Southern and F.S. Schmitt. London, 1969.

A Concordance to the Works of St. Anselm, 4 vols, ed. G.R. Evans. Millwood, New York 1984.

TRANSLATIONS

by M. Charlesworth:
Proslogion (Oxford 1965)

by Sidney Norton Deane:
Proslogium; Monologium; An Appendix on Behalf of the Fool by Gaunilon; and Cur Deus Homo. Lasalle, Illinois, 1903, 1962.

by Jasper Hopkins and Herbert Richardson:
Anselm of Canterbury: Truth, Freedom, and Evil: Three Philosophical Dialogues [*De veritate, De libertate arbitrii, De casu diaboli*] (Cambridge 1965; New York, 1967).
Complete Treatises, 4 vol. (Toronto-New York 1974-1976).

by Jasper Hopkins:
A New Interpretive Translation of St. Anselm's Monologion *and* Proslogion. Minneapolis, 1986.

by B. Ward:
The Prayers and Meditations of Saint Anselm. Penguin, Classics; rpt. with Proslogion, 1973, 1979.

by F.S. Schmitt:
Monologion (Stuttgart-Bad Cannstatt, 1964)
Proslogion (Stuttgart-Bad Cannstatt, 1962)
De veritate (Stuttgart-Bad Cannstatt, 1966)
Cur Deus Homo (Munich 1956)

by H. Verweyen:
De veritate, De libertate arbitrii, De casu diaboli, De concordia (Einsiedeln, 1982)

by L. Helbing:
Gebete (Einsiedeln, 1965).

Councils and Synods, with other documents relating to the English Church [CS], 871-1204, 2 vols., ed. D. Whitelock, M. Brett and C.N.L. Brooke. Oxford, 1981.

Eadmer, *Historia Novorum in Anglia*, (HN), ed. M. Rule, in Rolls Series. London, 1884: translation of books 1-4 by G. Bosanquet. London, 1964.

Eadmer, *Vita Anselmi* (VA), ed. and trans. by R.W. Southern. Edinburgh, 1962, reprinted Oxford, 1972.

Florence of Worcester, *Chronicon ex Chronicis*, ed. B. Thorpe, 2 vols. London, 1848/9.

Herbert de Losinga, *Epistolae*, ed. A.R. Anstruther. Brussels, 1846.

Herbert de Losinga, *The Life, Letters and Sermons of Bishop Herbert de Losinga*, ed. E.M. Goulburn and H. Symonds, 2 vols. London, 1884.
Hugh the Cantor [HC], *The History of the Church of York, 1066-1127*, ed. and trans. C. Johnson, Edinburgh, 1960.
Lanfranc of Canterbury, *The Letters of Lanfranc Archbishop of Canterbury*, ed. and trans. H. Clover and M. Gibson. Oxford, 1979.
Ordericus Vitalis, *The Ecclesiastical History of Ordericus Vitalis* [OV], 6 vols. ed. and trans. M. Chibnall. Oxford, 1969-1980.
Regesta Regum Anglorum-Normannorum [Reg] vol. I, 1066-1100, ed. H.W.C. Davis. Oxford, 1913; vol. 2, 1100-1135, ed. C. Johnson and H.A. Cronne. Oxford, 1956.
William of Jumièges, *Gesta Normannorum Ducum*, ed. E. van Hout. Volume 1. Oxford, 1992. Volume 2. Oxford, 1993.
William of Malmesbury, *De Gestis Pontificum Anglorum*, ed. N.E.S.A. Hamilton. London, 1870.

ANSELMIAN STUDIES collected in:

Spicilegium Beccense I (Papers read at the Congrès International du IXème centenaire de l'arrivée d'Anselme au Bec), Paris, 1959.
Sola ratione, Anselm-Studien für F.S. Schmitt, ed. H. Kohlenberger. Stuttgart-Bad Cannstatt, 1970.
Analecta Anselmiana I (1969)-V (1976)
  1st International Anselm Congress (Die Wirkungsgeschichte Anselms von Canterbury) at Bad Wimpfen in 1970, proceedings published in *Analecta Anselmiana* IV/1 (1975) and IV/2 (1975).
  2nd International Anselm Congress (Saint Anselme: ses Précurseurs et ses Contemporains) at Aosta in 1973, proceedings published in *Analecta Anselmiana* V (1976).

3rd International Anselm Congress (Anselm at Canterbury) at Canterbury in 1979, a selection of the proceedings published in *Anselm Studies* 1 (1983).

4th International Anselm Congress (Les Mutations socio-culturelles au tournant des XIe-XIIe siècle) at Bec in 1982, proceedings published in *Spicilegium Beccense* II, Paris, 1984.

5th International Anselm Congress (Episcopi ad Saecula— St Anselm and St Augustine) at Villanova, Pennsylvania, in 1985, proceedings published in *Anselm Studies* 2 (1988).

Saint Anselme. Penseur d'hier et d'aujourd' hui. Colloque international du CNRS. Paris 1993 (forthcoming).

BIBLIOGRAPHIES or works by/on Anselm are in:

J. Hopkins. *A Companion to the Study of St Anselm.* Minneapolis, 1972. Pp. 260-275.

———. *A New Interpretive Translation* (above, p. 338) 331-342.

Analecta Anselmiana I (1969) 269-331, II (1970) 223-252.

Internationale Anselm-Bibliographie, herausgegeben von K. Kienzler unter Mitarbeit von H. Kohlenberger, J. Biffi, E. Briancesco, M. Corbin, W. Fröhlich und F. Van Fleteren. New York, 1993.

STUDIES

R. Allers. *Anselm von Canterbury.* Vienna, 1936.
F. Barlow. *The English Church 1066-1154.* London, 1979.
———. *William Rufus.* London, 1983.
D. Bates. *Normandy before 1066.* London, 1982.
———. *William the Conqueror.* London, 1989.
H. Böhmer. *Kirche und Staat in England und in der Normandie im 11. und 12. Jahrhundert.* Leipzig, 1899, reprinted Aalen, 1968.

Selected Bibliography

M. Brett. *The English Church under Henry I*. Oxford, 1975.

Z. Brooke. *The English Church and the Papacy*. Cambridge, 1931, 1952.

R.A. Brown. *The Normans and the Norman Conquest*. Woodbridge, 1969.

R. Campbell. *From Belief to Understanding*. Canberra, 1976.

———. *From God to Understanding*. Toronto, 1987.

Giles Constable. *Letters and Letter-Collections*. Turnhout, 1976.

R.W. Church. *Saint Anselm*. London, 1870.

G.R. Evans. *Anselm and Talking about God*. Oxford, 1978.

———. *Anselm and the New Generation*. Oxford, 1980.

E.A. Freeman. *The Reign of William Rufus and the Accession of Henry I*, 2 vols. Oxford, 1882.

W. Fröhlich. *Die bischöflichen Kollegen Erzbischof Anselms von Canterbury*. Munich, 1971.

———. 'Anselm and the Bishops of the Province of Canterbury', *Spicilegium Beccense* 2 (1984) 125–145.

———. 'Bischof Walram von Naumburg, der einzige deutsche Korrespondent Anselms von Canterbury', *Analecta Anselmiana* 5 (1976) 261–282.

———. 'Saint Anselm's Weltbild as Revealed in his Letters', *Anselm Studies* 2 (1988) 483-525.

———. 'St Anselm's Special Relationship with William the Conqueror', *Anglo-Norman Studies* 10 (1988) 101-110.

———. 'The Letters omitted from Anselm's Collection of Letters', *Anglo-Norman Studies* 6 (1984) 58-71.

———. 'The Genesis of the Collections of St Anselm's Letters', *American Benedictine Review* 35 (1984) 249-266.

———. 'Anselm's Concept of Kingship', *Saint Anselme. Penseur d'hier et d'aujourd'hui*. Colloque international du CNRS. Paris 1993 (forthcoming)

A. Gransden. *Historical Writing in England c. 550-c. 1307*. London, 1974.

F.R. Hasse. *Anselm von Canterbury*, 2 vols. Leipzig, 1843-52, reprinted 1965.

R. Heinzmann. 'Anselm von Canterbury', in *Klassiker der Theologie*, vol. I. Munich, 1981: 165–180.
D. Henry. *The Logic of Saint Anselm*. Oxford, 1967.
J. Hopkins. *A Companion to the Study of St Anselm*. Minneapolis, 1972.
K. Kienzler. *Glauben und Denken bei Anselm von Canterbury*. Freiburg, 1981.
M. David Knowles. *The Monastic Order in England*. Cambridge, 1940.
J. Loughlin. *Saint Anselm as Letter Writer*. Washington-Ann Arbor, 1968.
Brian P. McGuire. *Friendship and Community. The Monastic Experience, 350-1250*. Cistercian Studies Series No. 95. Kalamazoo, 1988.
M. Morgan. *The English Lands of the Abbey of Bec*. Oxford, 1946, reprinted 1968.
A. Porée. *Histoire de L'Abbaye du Bec*, 2 vols. Evreux, 1901, reprinted Brussels, 1980.
H. Richter. *Englische Geschichtsschreiber des 12. Jahrhunderts*. Berlin, 1938.
M. Rule. *The Life and Times of St Anselm of Canterbury*, 2 vols. London, 1883.
R.W. Southern. *St Anselm and his Biographer*. Cambridge, 1963.
———. *Saint Anselm. A Portrait in A Landscape*. Cambridge, 1990.
A. Stolz. *Anselm von Canterbury*. Munich, 1937.
S.N. Vaughn. *The Abbey of Bec and the Anglo-Norman State 1034-1136*, Woodbridge, 1981.
———. *Anselm of Bec and Robert of Meulan, The Innocence of the Dove and the Wisdom of the Serpent*. Berkeley, 1987.

ABBREVIATIONS

Abbreviations of works frequently referred to in the footnotes.

AA	*Analecta Anselmiana.* Frankfurt, 1969–
AEp	*Anselmi Epistola*
AOO	*Anselmi Opera Omnia*, ed. F.S. Schmitt. Edinburgh 1946–1961. Stuttgart, [2] 1968 containing the editor's *Prolegomena seu Ratio editionis*, pages marked with an asterisk *.
ASC	Anglo-Saxon Chronicle
Barlow, *English Church*	F. Barlow, *The English Church 1066–1154.* London, 1979.
Bec profession-roll	in Rule I: 394–396.
Bede, *EH*	Bede's *Ecclesiastical History of the English People*, ed. B. Colgrave and R.A.B. Mynors. Oxford, [2]1972.
Blumenthal, *Paschal*	U.-R., Blumenthal, *The Early Councils of Pope Paschal II, 1100–1110*, Studies

	and Texts of the Pontifical Institute of Medieval Studies, vol. 43. Toronto, 1978.
Canterbury Professions	*Canterbury Professions*, ed. M. Richter, Canterbury and York Society, 67 (1973).
Chibnall, Relations	M. Chibnall, 'The Relations of St Anselm with the English Dependencies of the Abbey of Bec 1079-1093', in *Spicilegium Beccense*. Paris, 1959. Pp. 521–530.
CS	*Councils and Synods with other documents relating to the English Church*, I, 871–1204, ed. D. Whitelock, M. Brett, C.N.L. Brooke. Oxford, 1981.
CSEL	*Corpus scriptorum ecclesiasticorum latinorum* series. Vienna, 1866–.
Douglas, William	D.C. Douglas, *William the Conqueror*. London, 1964.
EHD II	*English Historical Documents*, ed. D.C. Douglas, vol. II, 1042–1189. London, 1961.
EHR	*English Historical Review*.
Fröhlich, 'Bischöfliche Kollegen'	W. Fröhlich, 'Die bischöflichen Kollegen des hl. Erzbischof Anselm von Canterbury', *AA* 1(1969) 223–267; 2 (1970) 117–168.
GC	*Gallia Christiana in provincias ecclesiasticas distributa*, 16 vols. Paris, 1856–1899.
Heads	*The Heads of Religious Houses, England and Wales 940–1216*, ed. D. Knowles, C.N.L. Brooke, V.C. London. Cambridge, 1972.
HC	Hugh the Chantor, *The History of the Church of York 1066–1127*, ed. C. Johnson. Oxford, 1961.
HN	*Eadmeri Historia Novorum in Anglia*, ed. M. Rule. London, 1884, Repr. 1965; transl. by G. Bosanquet. London, 1964.

IER	*Irish Ecclesiastical Records.*
Mansi	*Sacrorum Conciliorum Nova Collectio,* 31 vols. Venice 1757–1798, repr. Graz, 1960.
MARS	*Medieval and Renaissance Studies*
Mason, *Laymen*	J.F.A. Mason, 'Saint Anselm's Relations with Laymen: Selected Letters', *Spicilegium Beccense,* Paris, 1959. Pp 547–560.
MS L	Manuscript Lambeth Palace Library 59, London.
OV	*The Ecclesiastical History of Orderic Vitalis,* ed. M. Chibnall, 6 vols. Oxford, 1969–1980.
RB	*Regula monachorum sancti Benedicti; Rule of St Benedict*
Reg	*Regesta Regum Anglo-Normannorum 1066–1154,* Vol I, 1066–1100, ed. H.W.C. Davis and R.J. Whitwell, Oxford, 1913; Vol II, 1100–1135, ed. C. Johnson and H.A. Cronne, Oxford, 1956.
Rule	M. Rule, *The Life and Times of St Anselm,* 2 vols, London, 1883.
Southern, *Anselm*	R.W. Southern, *Saint Anselm and his Biographer,* Cambridge, 1963.
Tillmann, *Legaten*	H. Tillmann, *Die päpstlichen Legaten in England bis zur Beendigung der Legation Gualas (1218),* Bonn, 1926.
VA	*Eadmeri Vita Sancti Anselmi,* ed. R.W. Southern, Edinburgh, 1962; Oxford, 1972.

ERRATA

The Letters of Saint Anselm of Canterbury: volume 2

p. 3 line 20: *for* 1988 *read* 1987
p. 36 line 5: *for* nominem *read* nomen
p. 62 line 1: *for* logic *read* dialectic
p. 92 line 2: *for* shöfliche *read* schöfliche
p. 99 line 17: *for* 1115 *read* 1116
p. 108 line 35: *for* Rheims *read* Reims
p. 143 line 34: *for* Quicunque *read* Quicumque
p. 171 line 37: *for* seinem *read* seinen
p. 238 line 25: *for* Dicitum *read* Dictum
p. 243 line 26: *for* Liber Magistrum *read* Liber ad Magistrum
p. 254 line 7: *for* Hughues *read* Hugues
p. 257 line 11: *for* 1102 *read* 1100
line 12: *for* court at *read* court in 1102
p. 339 line 19: *for* Congres *read* Congrès
p. 340 line 2: *for* siecle *read* siecles
line 9: *for* Sainte *read* Saint
p. 341 line 16: *for* in Letters *read* in his Letters
line 24: *for* Sainte *read* Saint

INDICES

The numbers following the place names refer to the number of the letter and not to page or volume. Bec and Canterbury are not listed in the index of place names.

INDEX OF PERSONS

Aaron, 281
Achab, 284
Adela, countess of Flanders, 86
Adela, daughter of William the Conqueror, countess of Blois, 286, 287, 340, 388
Adelaide, daughter of William the Conqueror, 10
Adrian, apostate monk of Canterbury, 431
Aedulf, 384, 385
Agatho, Pope (678 - 681), 149
Agnes, saint, 184
Airard, runaway monk of Canterbury, 431
Aivertus, brother of Girard of Arras, 15
Alan Niger, count of Brittany and lord of Richmond, younger brother of Count Alan Rufus, 168, 169
Alan Rufus, count of Brittany and lord of Richmond, 168, 169
Alberic of Canterbury, 287
Alberic, cardinal priest of S. Pietro in Vincoli, 447
Albert, physician at Canterbury, 32, 33, 34, 36, 39, 44
Alexander, King of the Scots, 413
Alexander, monk of Canterbury, 223, 284, 311, 325
Ambrosius, saint, bishop of Milan, doctor of the Church, 23, 216, 310
Amos, 284
Anastasius, monk of Mont Saint Michel, 3
Andrew, apostle, 149
Anfrid, clerk of King Henry, 461
Anselm
   abbot, 97
   archbishop, 172
   archbishop of the first prime see of the English, and primate of

all the Irish and of the North, which is called Orkney, 242
bishop of the church of Canterbury, 475
brother of Bec, 2
metropolitan bishop, 193, 194, 198
nephew, 211, 264, 268, 289, 290, 291, 292, 309, 320, 321, 328
sinner and monk, 2
primate of all Britain, 472
prior, 25
Ansfrid, Anselm's envoy, 287
Ansfrid, Anselm's servant, 173
Antistenes, 242
Antony, subprior of Canterbury, 182, 313
Arnulf, monk of Beauvais, 38, 64
Athelits, abbess of Romsey, 236, 237
Athelits, abbess of Winchester, 276
Atla/Adela, countess of Blois and Chartres, daughter of William the Conqueror, 448
Atser, archbishop of Lund, 447
Augustine, saint, bishop of Hippo, doctor of the Church, 77, 83, 128, 204, 384
Augustine, saint, of Canterbury, 351
Avesgot, 19, 20

Baldric, prior of Bec, 147, 156, 157, 164, 179
Baldwin of Tournai, 124, 151, 223, 284, 338, 339, 349, 367, 371, 377, 378, 390, 397, 430, 438, 462
Baldwin, abbot of Bury St Edmunds, 92
Baldwin, king of Jerusalem, 235, 324

Basilia, wife of Hugh of Gournay, 68, 147, 420
Bayeux, bishop, 123
Bede, 42
Benedict, 227
Benedict, monk of Saint Pierre-sur-Dives, 104, 105
Benedict, saint, 139, 156
Benjamin, monk of Canterbury, 355
Bernard de Neufmarché, 270
Bernard, monk of Saint Werburgh, Chester, 233
Bernard, prior of Saint Albans, 203, 204
Bernard, servant of Peter, the pope's chamberlain, 451
Boniface IV, pope (608 - 615), 149
Boso, monk of Bec, 4th abbot of Bec, 146, 174, 209
Burgundius, husband of Richeza, Anselm's sister, 211, 258, 264

Calixtus, pope (217 - 222), 65
Canons of York, 255, 453, 545
Cassian, 425
Cicero, 242, 384
Clementia, countess of Flanders, 180, 248, 249
Constantine, emperor (306 - 337), 216
Conus of Arras, 285
Crispin family adopting Anselm, 22, 98
Cyril, bishop of Alexandria, 223

Danes, 447
Daniel, prophet, 227, 242
David, king of Israel, 216, 249, 413
Dermeth, Irish duke, father of King Muirchertach, 201
Diacus, bishop of Santiago di Compostella, 263

Dirgit, nun, 414; see also Seit
Dofnaldus, see Domnaldus
Domnaldus, bishop of Cashel, 198, 201
Donatus, bishop of Dublin, 198, 278; see also Samuel
Dunstan, archbishop of Canterbury, 39, 42, 149, 170
Durand, abbot of La Chaise-Dieu, 70, 71

Edit, nun, see Robert, see Seit
Edmer/Eadmer, monk of Canterbury, 208, 209, 311
Elferus, prior of Bury St Edmunds, 267, 382, 408; see also Bury St Edmunds
Elias, prophet, 242, 248
Elias/Helias, count of Maine, 466
Eliseus, prophet, 242
Elmer, monk of Canterbury, 69
Elured, 260
Engelard, 15
Engelard, monk, 86
Engelram, cleric of the bishop of Lincoln, 440
Ermengard, 136
Ernulf, Robert's brother, 270
Ernulf, abbot of Troarn, 123, 425
Ernulf, chaplain of the bishop of Rochester, 330
Ernulf, prior of Canterbury, 182, 286, 289, 291, 292, 295, 306, 307, 308, 310, 311, 312, 328, 330, 332, 349, 355, 357, 359, 364, 374, 376, 380
Ernulf/Arnulf of Montgomery, Earl of Pembroke and Holderness, 426
Eudo/Odo, the king's steward, 163, 371
Eulalia, abbess of Saint Edwards, Shaftesbury, 183, 208, 337, 403
Eustachius, Geoffrey's father, 297
Eustachius, Robert's brother, 298
Eve, wife of William Crispin, 22, 98, 118, 147
Everard, 307, 330, 331
Evremer, 21

Farman, monk of Canterbury, 173, 355
Ferdomnach, bishop of Kildare-Leinster, 201
Folcerald, Anselm's uncle, 22, 54
Folcerald/Fulcherald, Anselm's cousin, 55, 56, 110, 209
Frodelina, 45
Fronto, Marcus Cornelius, 384
Fulbert, cleric of Liveth, 89
Fulco, abbot of Saint Pierre-sur-Dives, 61, 88, 105
Fulco, bishop of Beauvais, 125, 126, 127, 136, 193

Galenus, 60
Geoffrey, William's brother, 135
Geoffrey, monk of Bec, 297
Gerard, bishop of Hereford and archbishop of York, 212, 214, 220, 238, 250, 253, 255, 256, 299, 326, 331, 354, 362, 363, 373, 386, 440, 444, 472
Gerbert, abbot of Saint Wandrille, 11, 85
German king (Henry V 1105 - 1125), 451, 452
German people, 452
Geront, abbot of Saint Benigne of Dijon, 302
Gervinus, bishop of Amiens, 187
Giezi, 317
Gilbert Crispin, monk of Bec and abbot of Westminster, 84, 103, 106, 130, 142, 147, 191, 366

Gilbert, abbot of Saint Etienne of Caen, 139
Gilbert, bishop of Evreux, 159
Gilbert, bishop of Limerick, 428, 429
Gilbert, brother of Robert of Bec, 122
Gilbert, monk of Bec, 165, 378
Girard, bishop of Thérouanne, 144
Girard, moneyer of Arras, monk of Bec, 14, 15, 23, 98, 164
Godefrid of Malling, 287, 331
Godefrid, prior of Winchester, 202
Godit, nun, see also Seit
Gosfrido, 446
Gosfrid, bishop of Paris, 161, 162
Gosfrid, sacristan of Cluny, 259
Greeks, 204, 239
Gregory I, pope (590 - 604), 23, 25, 26, 65, 149, 161, 162, 222, 225, 227, 239, 242, 284, 384, 454
Gregory VII, pope, (1073 - 1085) 102, 125
Guido/Guy, archbishop of Vienne, papal legate, 214
Gundulf/Gondulf Anselm's father, 4
Gundulf/Gondulf, monk of Bec and bishop of Rochester, 4, 5, 7, 8, 16, 28, 34, 41, 42, 43, 51, 58, 59, 68, 78, 91, 96, 141, 150, 286, 287, 291, 292, 293, 299, 300, 306, 314, 316, 319, 330, 331, 355, 359, 374, 381, 464, 474
Gunfrid, brother of abbot Roger of Lessay, 48
Gunhilda, nun, daughter of King Harold 168, 169
Gunther, canon of Saint Quentin of Beauvais, 345

Habbacuc, 242

Hacon, count of Orkney, 449
Haimo, Anselm's cousin, 120
Haimo, Robert's father, 212
Haimo, Vitalis' son, 474
Haimo, sheriff, 356, 359, 474
Haimo, steward, 212
Hardus, monk of Canterbury, 466
Harold, King of the English 168, 169
Helgot, prior of Saint Etienne of Caen and abbot of Saint Ouen of Rouen, 25, 29, 48, 407
Helinand, 101
Henry, 121
Henry V, king of the Germans, emperor (1105 - 1125), 415, 416, 451, 452
Henry of Gournay, monk of Bec, 96
Henry, abbot of Folcerald 55, 110
Henry, earl of Warwick, 212
Henry, king of the English, 212, 214, 215, 216, 217, 219, 221, 224, 227, 228, 251, 265, 280, 292, 294, 301, 305, 306, 308, 315, 316, 318, 319, 320, 321, 322, 330, 347, 348, 349, 351, 352, 353, 354, 367, 368, 369, 370, 371, 372, 373, 377, 378, 388, 391, 392, 393, 394, 396, 397, 399, 401, 402, 404, 406, 407, 422, 424, 430, 444, 451, 457, 460, 461, 462, 464, 470
Henry, monk of Bec, 96
Henry, monk of Bec, prior of Canterbury, 4, 5, 7, 17, 24, 33, 40, 42, 50, 58, 63, 64, 67, 73, 93, 140, 141, 182
Herbert de Losinga, bishop of Thetford/Norwich, 254, 386, 464
Herbert, abbot of Fontenay, 89

Indices

Herengod, father of Radulf, 300
Herluin, founder abbot of Bec, 5, 12, 17, 25, 27, 55, 63, 73, 89
Herluin, monk of Bec, 5, 7, 8, 17, 35, 43, 51, 60, 69, 74
Hervey, bishop of Bangor, 404, 457, 459, 460
Herward, bishop of Wales, 175
Hieronymus/Ieronimus, saint, doctor of the Church, 23, 384
Hildebert of Lavardin, bishop of Le Mans, archbishop of Tours, 239, 240, 241
Holvard/Hulvard/Hulward, monk of Canterbury, 33, 69, 74
Honorius I, pope (625 - 638), 149
Horace, 31, 384
Hubert, cardinal deacon, papal legate, 102, 125
Hugh de Gournay, monk of Bec, 68, 118
Hugh, abbot of Cluny, 259, 328, 409, 411
Hugh, archbishop of Lyon, 100, 109, 176, 208, 210, 260, 261, 322, 389, 390, 409
Hugh, archdeacon of Canterbury, 208
Hugh, bishop of Lisieux, 89
Hugh, earl of Chester, 251, 266, 271, 412
Hugh, monk of Bec, 118
Hugh, son of Mabilia, 300
Hugh, the hermit, 112
Hugh, young monk of Saint Werburgh, 232
Humbert, see Umbert
Hunfrid, 81

Ida, countess of Boulogne sur Mer, 82, 114, 131, 167, 244, 247

Idunan, bishop of Meath, 201
Isaias, prophet, 284
Ivo, bishop of Chartres, 181

James, apostle, 284
James, patriarch, 284
Jeroboam, king of Israel, 284
Job, 425
Joffridus/Geoffrey, monk of Bec, 165
John, 247
John, archbishop of Rouen, 89
John, bishop of Bath, 195
John, cardinal, 284, 339
John, cleric of Rome, monk of Bec, abbot of Telese, cardinal bishop of Frascti (Tusculum), 125, 128, 129, 213, 339
John, monk of Bec, 145, 146
John, prior of Bath, 450
John, provost of the canons regular of Mont Saint Eloi, 234
Jonathan, 386
Joseph, 331
Jotseran, archbishop of Lyon, 432
Judas Machabaeus, 386
Juhel, nephew of Gosfred, 446
Julian Apostate, 415, 416
Julius Caesar, 415
Justinian, 216

King of the French, 126

Lambert, 133
Lambert, Anselm's uncle, 22, 54; see also Folcerald
Lambert, abbot of Saint Bertin, 197, 421
Lambert, bishop of Arras, 285, 437, 438, 439
Lambert, canon, chaplain of Countess Ida, 244
Lambert, teacher of William and Roger of Bayeux, 21

Lanfranc, monk and prior of Bec, abbot of Saint Etienne of Caen, archbishop of Canterbury, 1, 4, 7, 13, 14, 15, 19, 20, 23, 25, 26, 27, 30, 31, 32, 39, 40, 42, 44, 49, 51, 57, 60, 63, 66, 69, 72, 73, 74, 77, 79, 89, 90, 96, 98, 103, 124, 128, 136, 152, 176, 182, 198, 206, 277, 278, 283, 304, 315, 319, 329, 330, 364

Lanfranc, monk of Bec, nephew of Lanfranc, archbishop of Canterbury, 4, 25, 30, 31, 32, 39, 66, 72, 75, 130, 138, 155

Lanfrid, abbot of Saint Wulmar, 144, 186

Langobards, 124

Lanscelinus, father of Radulf, 115

Lanzo, novice and prior of Saint Pancras of Lewes, 2, 37, 335

Lawrence, archbishop of Canterbury, 149

Leo I, pope (440 - 461), 453

Leo, cardinal deacon, 458

Levi, 284

Louis, king of the French 342, 461; see also Philip, king of the French

Lwerun, nun, 414; see also Seit

M, nun, possible daughter Richard and Rohais of Clare, 94, 184

Mabilia, mother of Hugh, 300

Mabilia, nun, 405

Mainer, abbot of Saint Evroul, 108

Malchus, monk of Winchester, bishop of Waterford, 201, 202, 207, 277

Malcolm III, king of the Scots, 177

Martin, saint and abbot, 156

Mary Magdalen, 242

Mary, holy, mother of God, 28, 94, 156, 331

Mathathias, 386

Matilda, abbess of Caen, 298

Matilda, abbess of Wilton, 185, 208

Matilda, countess of Tuscany, 325, 350

Matilda/Eadgyth daughter of King Malcolm III of Scotland, queen of the English, 177, 242, 243, 246, 288, 296, 317, 319, 320, 321, 323, 329, 346, 347, 352, 384, 385, 395, 397, 400, 406

Maurice, bishop of London, 170, 200, 331, 451

Maurice, monk of Bec, 32, 33, 34, 35, 36, 40, 42, 43, 47, 51, 60, 64, 69, 72, 74, 79, 97, 104, 147

Mortain, count of, 401

Moses, monk of Canterbury, 140, 141

Moses, prophet, 242, 416

Muirchertach Ua Briain, king of the Irish, 201, 426, 427, 435

Naboth, 284

Neot, saint, 90, 91, 92, 93, 94, 96, 473

Nero, emperor, 415, 416

Nicodemus, 416

Nicolas, monk of Troarn, 123

Norman, canon regular, 187, 234

O, abbot, 26

Odo, 2, 118

Odo of London, monk of Canterbury, 357, 359

Odo, cellerar, 436

Odo, father of William the servant, 18

Odo, half-brother of William the

Conqueror, bishop of Bayeux, 87
Odo, provost of Saint Quentin of Beauvais, also called abbot, 345
Ordwin, monk of Canterbury, 327, 336, 355
Osbern, bishop of Exeter, 172, 195, 226
Osbern, father of William 89
Osbern, monk of Bec 4, 5, 17, 58
Osbern, monk of Bec who died, 4, 5, 7
Osbern, monk of Canterbury, 39, 69, 74, 149, 182
Osbern, who died, 87
Osmund, bishop of Salisbury (Old Sarum), 177, 185, 190, 195
Ovid, 373
Ozias, 281, 284

P, monk of Saint Martin of Séez, 410
Paschal II, pope (1099 - 1118), 210, 213, 214, 215, 216, 217, 218, 219, 220, 221, 222, 223, 224, 225, 226, 272, 280, 281, 282, 283, 301, 303, 304, 305, 315, 338, 340, 348, 349, 350, 351, 352, 353, 361, 362, 378, 388, 397, 398, 422, 423, 430, 441, 451, 452, 457, 458, 459, 460, 463, 464
Paul, abbot of Saint Albans, 80
Paul, saint and apostle, 66, 70, 149, 242, 317, 335, 384
Persius, 19, 20
Peter and Salome, 360
Peter, abbot of Ivry, 113
Peter, pope's chamberlain, 451, 460
Peter, saint and apostle, 149, 154, 156, 248, 262, 351, 373, 382

Philip de Briouze, 270
Philipp, king of the French, 3451; see also Louis
Philipp, monk of Canterbury, 333
Pytagoras, 242

Quintillian, 384

R, bishop, 471, 472
Radulf/Ralph de Mortimer, 270
Radulf/Ralph, nephew of bishop Gundulf, 474
Radulf/Ralph, son of Herengod, 300
Radulf/Ralph/Rodulf, bishop of Chichester, 386, 496
Rainald, Anselm's cousin, see Haimo
Rainald, monk of Bec, 174
Rainald, resigned bishop of Hereford, 343
Rainald/Reginald, abbot of Saint Cyprian of Poitiers, 83
Rainer, abbot of Mont Saint Trinité, 122
Rainer, clerc of countess Ida, 167
Ranulf Flambard, bishop of Durham, 214, 223, 225, 373, 442, 461
Reiner, bearer of letter, 235
Richard of Clare, son of Osbern, father of Richard, young monk of Bec, 94, 96
Richard of Reviers, 430
Richard, abbot of Saint Werburgh of Chester, 231, 232
Richard, monk of Bec, 114, 131
Richard, monk of Bec, 196
Richard, monk of Bec, 78
Richard, monk of Canterbury, 188
Richard, servant of abbot Gilbert of Westminster, 142
Richard, son of Richard and Rohais of Clare, monk of Bec,

abbot of Ely, 94, 96, 397, 422
Richeza, Anselm's sister, 264, 268, 328; see also Burgundius
Ricoard, 107
Riculf, monk of Bec, 107
Robert Beaumont, count of Meulan, earl of Leicester, 353, 354, 364, 369, 371, 377, 430, 467
Robert Bloet, bishop of Lincoln, 311, 318, 441, 473
Robert de Montfort, 299, 475
Robert of Brionne, monk of Saint Wandrille, 119
Robert of Canterbury, 331
Robert of Lyminge, 331
Robert of Montgomery, lord of Belléme and earl of Shrewsbury, 270
Robert of Mowbray, earl of Northumbria, 423
Robert of Stuteville, 401
Robert, abbot of Bury St Edmunds, 408
Robert, abbot of Séez, 132
Robert, brother of Eustace, 298
Robert, chaplain to Seit, Edith, 230, 414
Robert, convert from Judaism, 380, 381
Robert, count of Flanders, 180, 248, 249; see also Clementia
Robert, duke of the Normans, 153, 159, 163, 164, 165, 322, 396, 401
Robert, monk of Bec, 7, 14, 30, 74, 122
Robert, monk of Canterbury, 289, 331
Robert, monk of Mont Saint Michel, 3
Robert, oblate of Bishop Gundulf, 299, 330, 331

Robert, royal cleric, 377
Robert, son of Earl Hugh of Chester, 251, 266, 271
Robert, son of Haimo, 212
Robert, son of Watso, 474
Rodbert/Robert de Limsey, bishop of Chester, 386
Rodulf, father of William, 359
Rodulf, monk, 29, 55, 104
Rodulf, prior of Saint Etienne of Caen, 12, 13
Rodulf, reeve of Harrow, 299
Rodulf, son of Lanscelin, 99, 115, 117, 133
Rodulf/Ralph d'Escures, abbot of Saint Martin of Séez, 145, 146, 175
Roger Puntel, 331
Roger le Poer, bishop of Salisbury, 373
Roger le Sap, abbot of Saint Evroul, 251, 266, 271
Roger of Caen, 74
Roger, abbot of Lessay, 158
Roger, cleric of the Roman Church, 125
Roger, monk of Canterbury, 307
Roger, recommended to William Giffard, elect of Winchester, 275
Roger, runaway monk of Bec, 76
Roger, young man of Bayeux, 21, 70
Rohais, wife of Richard of Clare, see Richard
Roscelin, cleric of Compigne, 128, 129, 136, 146, 147
Rothard, canon, 181

Saint Arnulf, abbot of, 62
Salome, see Peter
Salvius, monk of Canterbury, 58

Samson, bishop of Worcester, 386, 464, 465
Samuel, 351
Samuel, bishop of Dublin, 201, 277, 278
Samuel, monk of Caen, 74
Saracens, 263; see also Diacus
Saul, king of Israel, 351
Saul, who becomes St Paul, the apostle, 416
Scholastica, saint, 184
Scolland, knight, 442
Secundinus, hermit, 69
Seit, nun, with Edith, Thydit, Lwerun, Dirigit, Godit, 414
Serlo, monk of Saint Evroul, 108
Severus, saint, 271
Simon Magus, 149
Simon of Thasi, 386
Simon, pharisee, 242
Simplicius, pope (468 - 483), 453
Socrates, 242
Sorech, 284
Stephen, archdeacon of Winchester, 236
Stephen, monk of Mont Saint Trinité, 122
Stigand, archbishop of Canterbury, 171

Tezo, monk of Bec, 151
Theard, monk of Cluny, 411
Theduin, monk of Bec, 97
Theodor, friend of Anselm. Anselm's nephew, 309
Theodosius, emperor, 310
Thidric/Thidiric, monk and scribe of Canterbury, 334, 379
Thomas I, archbishop of York, 283, 472
Thomas II, elect of York, 442, 443, 444, 445, 451, 453, 454, 455, 456, 464, 465, 467, 470, 471

Thydit, nun, see Seit
Tiberius, cadinal, 213, 299, 301
Timotheus/Thimotheus, 242, 317
Tullius, see Cicero
Turold, elect of Saint Andrews, 442, 443, 444
Turold, monk of Bec, 418

Ulfric, monk of Canterbury, 333
Urban II, pope (1088 - 1099), 125, 126, 127, 176, 192, 193, 206, 210, 214, 226, 280, 282, 329, 397
Ursio/Ursus, cleric, 113
Ursio/Ursus, prior of Saint Martin de Champs, 104, 162
Ursus, friend of Lanzo, 37

Virgil, 2, 64
Vitalis of Caen, 74
Vitalis, abbot of Bernay, 27
Vitalis, duke, 121
Vitilian, pope (657 - 672), 149
Vulgar, servant of Lyminge, 330, 331
Vulmar/Wulmar, saint, 144, 186

Walchelin, bishop of Winchester, 122, 191, 201, 202
Waldric/Wandric, royal chancellor, 370, 371, 392, 394, 396, 399, 401
Waleran, cantor of the church of Paris, 161, 162
Walo, regular canon and provost of Saint Quentin of Beauvais, 272
Walram, bishop of Naumburg, 415, 416, 417
Walter, abbot of La Trinité-du-Mont of Rouen or Saint Martin of Pontoise, 62
Walter, cardinal, archbishop of Albano and papal legate, 191, 192, 194

Walter, monk of Bury St Edmunds, 433, 434
Walter, monk of Saint Wandrille, 85
Walter, prior of Saint Wandrille, 138, 143
Walter, teacher of Anselm, the nephew, 309, 328
Waltheof, earl, 236, 237
Warner, monk of Canterbury, 331, 335
Warner, novice of Canterbury, 375
Watso, father of Robert, 474
Welsh bishop, 223, 280, 282
Wibert, archbishop of Ravenna, antipope Clement III (1084 - 1100), 176
Wido, monk, 383
Wido, monk of Bec, 31, 39, 69, 75
Wido, monk of Saint Etienne of Caen, 279
Wilencus, 115
Wilfrid, bishop of Saint David, 270
William, 46
William Beaumont, abbot of Bec, 157, 163, 468
William Calvellus, 358, 359
William Crispin, 401
William Giffard, chancellor of King William II, elect of Winchester, 212, 229, 236, 265, 273, 274, 275, 276, 322, 344, 386, 404
William II Rufus, king of the English, 147, 176, 178, 190, 191, 192, 206, 209, 210, 212, 214, 251, 362
William de Rots, abbot of Fécamp, 65
William de Warelwast, royal cleric, bishop of Exeter, 212, 214, 219, 220, 305, 306, 308, 310, 315, 318, 330, 367, 370, 371, 377, 378, 396, 397, 398, 422, 430
William of Ferrers, 401
William of Maidstone, 299
William of Warenne, earl of Surrey, 424
William, the chamberlain, 419
William, archdeacon of Canterbury, 208, 257, 360, 374, 380, 474
William, brother of Geoffrey, 135
William, cleric of York, 445
William, monk 230, 414
William, monk of Bec or Canterbury, 173
William, monk of Canterbury, 182
William, monk of Saint Werburgh of Chester, 189, 245
William, son of Godefred of Malling, 287
William, son of King Henry, 305
William, son of Nio, 287
William, son of Osbern, 89
William, son of Rodulf, 359
William, the Conqueror, duke of the Normans and king of the English, 27, 55, 89, 96, 329, 330, 364
William, young man, 117
William, young man of Bayeux, 21, 70
William, monk of abbot Robert of Séez, 132
Wimund, man of the sheriff, 474
Wimund, monk of Saint Ouen and archbishop of Aversa, 19, 20

Wulfstan, saint, bishop of
  Worcester, 170, 171
Wulmar, see Vulmar

Zachaeus, publican, 242
Zacharias, prophet, 57

INDEX OF PLACES

Amiens, 187
Arras, 14, 15, 23, 285, 437, 438, 439
Aversa, 19, 20
Avranches, 89

Bangor, 404, 457, 459, 460
Bari, 239
Bath, 195, 450
Battle, 172, 175, 226; see also Saint Martin
Bayeux, 21, 70, 87, 123
Beauvais, 74, 99, 115, 117, 125, 126, 127, 133, 136, 160, 193, 272, 331, 345
Bec, 89, 126, 163, 164
Bernay, 27
Boulogne, 82, 114, 131, 167, 244, 247
Bourges, 315
Brionne, 89
Bristol, 202
Britain, 472
Bury St Edmunds, 251, 252, 266, 267, 269, 271, 382, 408, 433, 434

Caen, 12, 13, 18, 23, 25, 26, 48, 52, 74, 139, 146, 279, 298
Canterbury, 182, 191, 293, 295, 310, 312, 331, 332, 349, 356, 474
Cerne, 195
Chaise-Dieu, 70, 71
Chartres, 181, 287, 302, 340, 345
Chester, 386
Chichester, 386, 469
Chiusa, St Michael, 328

Cluny, 259, 328, 409, 411, 412, 421, 468
Compostella, Saint James of, 263
Conflans, Sainte Honorine, 97, 104

Denmark, 447
Dorobernia, old name for Canterbury, 303, 308, 431, 474, 475
Dublin, 201, 277, 278
Durham, 214, 223, 225, 373, 442, 461

Elbeuf, 401
Ely, 397, 422, 441, 457, 458
England, 30, 42, 90, 91, 92, 93, 94, 98, 116, 147, 191, 193, 210, 214, 261, 366
Evreux, 159
Exeter, 172, 195, 226

Fécamp, 65
Flanders, 180, 248, 249
Fontenay, 89
Fordwich, 356
France, 55, 341, 342, 461
Frascati, 339

Harrow, 170, 171, 200, 299
Hereford, 214, 343
Hythe, 475

Ireland, 201, 202, 366, 426, 427, 429, 435
Ivry, 113

Jerusalem, 117, 195, 235, 260, 261, 263, 264, 268, 324, 410, 475

L'Aigle, 368, 369
La Chaise-Dieu, see Chaise-Dieu
La-Trinité-du-Mont at Rouen, 62, 122
Lateran, see Rome
Le Mans, 239, 240, 241
Leinster, 201
Lessay, 48, 158
Limerick, 428, 429
Lincoln, 311, 318, 377, 441, 457, 458, 473
Lisieux, 89, 404
Liveth, 89
London, 170, 200, 253, 254, 255, 256, 257, 331, 357, 391, 451
Lund, 447
Lyminge, 98, 331
Lyon, 100, 109, 176, 208, 260, 261, 322, 389, 390, 409, 432

Maidstone, 299
Malling, 287, 331
Malmesbury, 168, 384, 385
Marcigny, 328
Meath, 201
Meulan, 353, 354, 364, 388, 369, 371, 377, 430, 467
Molesmes, 181
Mont Saint Eloi, 234
Mont Saint Michel, 3
Mortain, 401
Muchelney, 228

Naumburg, 415, 416, 417
Normandy, 153, 159, 163, 165, 273, 322, 401
Norwich, 254, 386, 464

Orkney, 449
Paris, 161, 162, 345
Poissy, 181
Pont Authou, 89

Ramsonetum, a tract of land close to Bec, 89

Rochester, 4, 7, 16, 28, 34, 41, 42, 43, 51, 56, 59, 78, 91, 141, 150, 286, 287, 291, 292, 293, 299, 300, 306, 314, 316, 319, 330, 331, 355, 359, 374, 381, 464
Rockingham, 192, 198
Roginge, 300
Rome, 308, 318, 367, 371, 378
Romsey, 236
Rouen, 89, 126, 154, 266, 269, 271, 274, 279, 388, 397, 398, 419

Saint Albans, 80, 203, 204
Saint Andrews, Scotland, 442, 443, 444
Saint Arnulf, 62
Saint Bertin, 197, 421
Saint Botolph's, Colchester, 187, 234
Saint Cyprian at Portiers, 83
Saint David, 270
Saint Edward, Shaftesbury, 183, 208, 337, 403
Saint Evroul, 108, 251, 266, 269, 271
Saint Giles, 188
Saint Magloire, monastery, 104
Saint Martin at Battle, 172, 175, 226
Saint Martin at Pontoise, 62
Saint Martin at Séez, 108, 132, 145, 146, 175, 410
Saint Martin des Champs, 104, 161, 162
Saint Neots, 90, 91, 92, 93, 94, 96, 473
Saint Ouen at Rouen, 19, 20
Saint Pancras at Lewes, 2, 37, 335
Saint Peter at Muchelney, 228
Saint Peter of Westminster, 130, 142
Saint Pierre-sur-Dives, 61, 88, 104, 105

Saint Wandrille, 85, 119, 137, 138, 143
Saint Werburgh at Chester, 189, 231, 232
Saint Wulmar, 144, 186
Salisbury, 177, 185, 190, 195
Saltwood, 475
Sandwich, 356
Savoy, 262
Stisted, 474
Susa, 262, 409

Thérouanne, 144
Tinchebrai, 401, 402
Toledo, 161, 162
Tonbridge, 392
Tournai, 124, 151, 223, 284, 338, 339, 349, 367, 371, 377, 378, 390, 397, 430, 438, 462
Troarn, 123, 425

Tuscany, 325, 350
Tusculum, see Frascati

Vermand, 151
Vienne, 214

Wales, 175
Waterford, 201 202, 207, 277
Wilton, 168, 169, 185, 208
Winchester, 122, 191, 201, 202, 207, 212, 236, 265, 273, 274, 275, 276, 322, 344, 386, 404
Worcester, 170, 171, 195, 386, 453, 464, 465

York, 212, 214, 220, 238, 250, 253, 255, 256, 283, 299, 326, 331, 354, 362, 363, 373, 386, 440, 442, 443, 444, 445, 451, 453, 454, 455, 456, 465, 467, 470, 471, 472

SUBJECT INDEX

Proper Names

Anselm's works:
  Prayers and Meditations (1072 - 1074, later additions), 10, 28, 55, 70, 71, 120, 147, 325
  Monologion (1076), 72, 74, 75, 83, 100, 109
  Proslogion (1077), 100, 109, 112
  De conceptu virginali (1099–110), 334 (insertion of Rm 8:1), 349
  Cur Deus Homo (1098), 209, 349
  tract on evil, 97 (*De casu diaboli*, after 1082)
  De processione spiritus sancti (1102), 83, 239, 240, 415
  De incarnatione verbi (1093/1094), 146, 207
  tract on intention and evil, 132

Anglo-Saxon ladies, 168, 169, 414
Anselm's absence, 310, 326, 327, 336, 363, 365, 373, 386, 391
Austin/Augustinian Canons, 234, 244

Bec
  dependency, 97, 104
  familia, 98, 118, 147, 420
  gifts for, 1, 7, 14, 16, 25, 34, 47, 49, 58, 66, 68, 73, 84, 89, 90, 94, 107, 114, 118, 131, 141
  monastery, 89, 126, 159, 163, 164
  monks, 98, 116, 148, 150, 151, 155, 156, 157, 159, 165, 173, 178, 181, 199, 205
  monks at Caen, 48

monks at Canterbury, 1, 4, 5, 7, 9, 16, 17, 32, 33, 34, 35, 36, 40, 42, 43, 44, 47, 51, 58, 60, 64, 69, 72, 74, 75, 78, 84, 103, 124
monks at Conflans Sainte-Honorine, 97, 104
monks at Séez, 146
monks returning to, 60, 69, 72, 74, 75, 79, 110
monks to England, 90, 91, 92, 93, 94
needs, 89, 90, 124
orphaned, 158, 159
papal protection, 126
people coming to, 55, 56, 76, 85, 114, 115, 117, 120
property in England, 118, 147
properties, 89, 118

Caen monks at Canterbury, 5, 8, 74
Caen monks at Saint Albans, 80
Canterbury, see also feudal responsibility; primacy
 accepting boys and young men to, 331, 357
 admission to, 295, 307, 331, 333
 cathedral, 293
 church, 149, 303, 431, 474, 475
 church, papal legation in England, 214, 222, 303, 451, 452, 453, 454, 455
 division of property between archbishopric and monastery, 349, 359
 income to monks of, 474, 475
 increase of monks' revenue, 192, 474, 475
 lands, 176, 304, 475
 lands, alienation of 176, 206, 210, 223, 356, 357, 358, 359
 legateship to, 214, 222
 monks at Bec, 30, 31, 32, 33, 39, 40, 58, 66, 67, 69, 74, 140, 141
 possessions, see also reinvestiture
 possessions, seizure of, 210, 310, 319, 320, 321, 327, 338, 339, 348, 339, 348, 349, 355, 356, 363
 revenues from possessions, 293, 294, 299, 300, 304, 314, 316, 318, 319, 321, 356, 357, 358, 359, 390, 392
 revenues of the archdeaconate of, 380, 381
 vacancy of, 149

Emperor Henry IV, 299, 415, 417
Emperor Henry V, 451, 452, 461
Ernulf, acting as Anselm's abbatial representative, 311, 312, 328, 330, 331, 332, 335, 355, 357, 381

German race, 452
Gundulf, acting as Anselm's representative, 287, 299, 293, 300, 306, 314, 316, 330, 331, 355, 359, 365, 374, 381

Irish church, 198, 201, 202, 242; see also primacy of Canterbury

Judaism, 380

L'Aigle, agreement of (22 July 1104), 364, 365, 367, 368, 369, 370, 371, 372, 376, 384, 385, 388, 389, 390, 391, 394, 397, 399, 402, 407, 409, 411, 430, 448, 451; see also synod of London; Hugh of Lyon; homage; investiture

Normandy
 conquest of, 394, 396, 400, 401
 successes in, 461, 462

Peter's pence, 125, 213, 215, 287, 299; see also romescot
Pope, royal respect for, 213, 215
Rome, journey to
  (1st journey January 1098), 206, 208, 210
  (2nd journey summer 1103), 286, 287, 288, 289, 294, 296, 299, 300, 301, 307, 308
York, chapter of, 453, 454, 456

General Index

abbacy, giving up, 156
abbatial absolution and blessing, 166
abbot, on electing a new, 156, 157, 163, 164
abbots/bishops, choice of, 78, 126, 127, 137, 138, 156, 157, 163, 164, 165, 272, 430, 443
absolution from excommunication, 364, 365, 369, 373, 397, 408, 422
absolution of sins, 382, 383, 397, 414, 425, 446
ad liminas visit, 125
advice
  from Hugh of Lyon, 100, 109, 176, 208, 210, 260, 261, 322, 389, 390; see also Hugh of Lyon
  on becoming a nun, 325, 337
  on spiritual progress, 166, 178, 179, 183, 184, 185, 189, 231, 232, 285, 286, 289, 291
  to abbot, 62, 175, 186, 425
  to a lapsed nun, 168, 169, 177, 238
  to hold out in office, 186, 298, 436
  to lay persons, 10, 45, 131, 134, 167, 180, 235, 258, 273, 296, 297, 320, 325, 346, 347, 420
  to monks of Bec, 151, 156, 157, 199
  to novice, 37, 335
  to repentent monk, 333, 355, 450
  to runaway monk, 62, 130, 331, 333, 431
  to successor, 165
affection for monks, 151, 156, 158, 159, 160, 163, 164, 165, 166, 173, 174, 178, 199, 205, 209
age, sickness, feebleness of body, 51, 104, 106, 124, 139, 142, 193, 206, 242, 243, 286, 291, 301, 399, 400, 407, 430, 438, 439, 448, 461
almsgiving, 380, 381
anathema, 136
angel, 230, 337
appeal to pope, 206, 210
archbishopric
  consent to election, 148, 150, 151, 153, 154, 155, 157, 159, 176, 198
  delay in acceptance of, 149, 152
  dispossession, 316, 318, 319, 320, 321, 327, 338, 339, 348, 349
  election to, 148, 149, 150, 151, 156, 158, 159, 176, 198, 206
  no greed for, 148, 156, 158, 159, 160
ascetic life, 446
authority, legal, 453
authority, theological, 19, 70, 102, 207, 239, 240, 305, 351, 416

barbarians, 80, 103, 222, 223, 282, 457, 459
beating, 233
bishopric of Bayeux, advice on giving up, 418

bishops, 210, 216, 222, 261, 270, 272, 280, 281, 372, 386, 387, 393, 394; see also episcopal colleagues blasphemy, 136
books
  lending, 2, 23, 25, 26, 42, 70, 146
  return/exchange of, 12, 23, 26, 66, 70
brevity, 1, 2, 5, 6, 7, 13, 17, 23, 28, 37, 38, 45, 54, 61, 99, 101, 103, 109, 112, 121, 127, 129, 132, 138, 160, 161, 165, 173, 175, 180, 192, 205, 208, 217, 242, 308, 312, 314, 346, 388, 415, 450
burden of office, 6, 25, 39, 42

canon law, 65, 304, 310, 316, 319, 321, 331, 351, 391, 404, 412, 425, 427, 428, 435, 441, 442, 443, 453, 454, 456, 457, 458, 459, 464, 472
care of souls entrusted to Prior Ernulf, 312
celibacy, 65, 126, 223, 254, 255, 256, 257, 282, 310, 331, 364, 365, 374, 389, 391, 392, 393, 394, 422
chrism, 359
church, 191, 192, 224, 243, 248, 249, 262, 281, 288, 323, 327, 331, 336, 351, 355, 357, 363, 365, 420
classical authors, 2, 19, 20, 64, 216, 242, 373, 384, 425, 453
cleric, 101, 161, 162, 223, 227, 257, 307, 331
  becoming monk, 113, 125, 331
clerical attire, 101
cloister, 101, 178, 333, 418
cluniac monks, 411, 412, 421
communion resumed, 408

concordat of London, 430, 443, 451
concubine, 223, 255
confessions, 313
constitutions of Bec and Canterbury, 178
copying manuscripts, 23, 29, 39, 42, 43, 55, 60, 66, 70, 232, 334, 349, 379
council
  of Bari (3 - 10 October 1098), 239
  of Benevent (12 October 1108), 452
  of Guastalla (22 October 1106), 409
  of Rome (Lateran April 1099), 214, 353, 354; see also decrees of lenten synod
  of Toledo, IV council, (633), 161, 162
  of Westminster (1102), 253, 254, 255, 256, 257, 307
  of Westminster (1108), 441; see also new see of Ely
  plans for general, 176
cowl, 113, 425; see also habit
criticism of bishops, 161, 162, 172, 177, 187, 195, 278
creed, apostolic, 136
creed of Nicaea, 136
creed of Athanasius, 136, 204
crusade, 117, 195, 235, 260, 261, 263, 264, 268, 410, 475; see also Jerusalem
curia regis meeting (1 - 3 August 1107), 430; see also synod of London

death, 53, 211, 264, 268
debts, paying of, 15, 23, 140, 287
decrees of lenten synod in Rome (1099), 213, 214, 216, 217, 218,

Indices

220, 222, 223, 246, 248, 249, 262, 265, 280, 281, 284, 286, 305, 306, 308, 310, 311, 317, 323, 327, 329, 330, 346, 349, 351, 352, 353, 361, 364, 365, 368, 369, 370, 373, 388, 389, 397, 417, 428
  decrees, mitigation of, 265, 281, 286, 306, 308, 323, 338, 348
demand for Anselm to write, 74, 97
demand for Anselm's presence in England, 310, 320, 323, 351, 353, 365, 366, 373, 375, 384, 386, 395
disagreement/quarrel with King Henry, 314, 315, 318, 319, 320, 321, 323, 331, 332, 338, 339, 351, 362
diseases
  headache, 32, 33, 34, 36, 39, 44
  high blood pressure, 39
  vertigo, 39, 72, 75
disobedience to rule, 97, 104, 137
dispensation, 223
dispute between church of Chartres and Countess Adela, 340; see also Adela, Chartres
dispute between monasteries, 181
drinking in public places, 96

election (after 1107 on the basis of concordat of London), 430, 435, 443
envoys to Rome: royal, 212, 214, 215, 216, 217, 218, 222, 223, 224, 225, 226, 250, 280, 281, 283, 284, 305, 318, 364, 367, 368, 369, 370, 371, 377 422
  archiepiscopal, 217, 218, 219, 220, 221, 223, 247, 253, 280, 284, 331, 367
  joint, 376, 378, 387, 388, 389, 390, 396, 397, 422, 430
episcopal
  colleagues, 192, 198, 206, 210, 217, 219, 253, 261, 265, 274, 284, 286, 306, 307, 308, 326, 386, 387, 397, 464, 465, 471, 472; see also bishops
  consecration, 161, 164, 176, 229, 261, 265, 322, 354, 362, 363, 373, 397, 427, 428, 435, 443, 444, 447
  duties, 354, 429, 447, 449, 457, 458, 459
  election, 281, 428, 430, 435, 443
  jurisdiction, 469
esteem
  as letter writer, 384
  as religious, 70
  as teacher, 19
evil counsellors, 351, 352, 353, 354, 397
evil influence, 326, 329, 360, 361, 369
evils in England, 30, 206, 210, 217, 260, 310, 311, 317, 365, 366
excommunication, 65, 210, 280, 281, 308 310, 311, 315, 327, 348, 349, 351, 352, 353, 354, 355, 358, 361, 363, 364, 365, 369, 373, 374, 388, 397, 408, 422, 431, 452
exile
  (1st: 9 November 1097 - 23 September 1100), 206, 207, 208, 209, 210, 212, 213, 214, 217, 219
  (2nd: 20 December 1103 - September 1106), 260, 261, 305, 306, 307, 308, 310, 311, 312, 314, 315, 317, 326, 327, 329, 331, 332, 336, 337, 338, 339, 341, 342, 343, 348, 349, 350, 351, 352, 353, 355, 362,

363, 390, 403, 428, 448
eyesight, failing, 164

fasting, 49, 196 242, 243, 446
fellowship between monasteries, 70
feudal/military responsibility, 191, 209
financial demands from King Henry I, 292, 293
flores psalmorum, 10
friendship, 7, 12, 13, 16, 17, 20, 28, 36, 64, 75, 100, 259, 358, 371, 417, 434

grammar, 19, 64, 328
greed, 148, 156, 158, 159, 160, 164
guardian of King Henry's children, 461

habit, 113, 168, 169, 177, 238, 425
hair, long, 257, 365
heresy, 83, 373
homage, 214, 222, 223, 322, 388, 389, 397
humility, 2, 3, 10, 11, 13, 20, 45, 46, 61, 65, 66, 71, 72, 85, 86, 87, 88, 92, 96, 100, 106, 112, 160, 161, 189, 193, 321, 340, 411, 421, 430

illegally invested persons, 280, 305, 306, 310, 352, 389, 397; see also homage; see also investiture
illiteracy of King Muirchertach, 435
insult to Anselm, 360
intercession for others, 11, 18, 27, 31, 48, 70, 86, 100, 103, 105, 107, 114, 122, 125, 126, 131, 140, 141, 142, 144, 197, 315, 321, 350, 388, 397, 406
invasion
of England, 191, 193
of monastery, 251, 252, 266, 267, 269, 271
investiture by laymen, 192 213, 214, 215, 216, 217, 218, 219, 220, 222, 223, 224, 227, 228, 246, 248, 260, 261, 268, 280, 281, 282, 284, 305, 308, 311, 314, 315, 322, 327, 343, 344, 346, 348, 351, 352, 353, 354, 355, 361, 364, 365, 373, 386, 388, 389, 397, 415, 423, 428, 430, 451, 452; see also homage

Jew, conversion of a, 380, 381
journey
dangerous, 355
safe, 325

kingship, 176, 180, 190, 212, 215, 216, 222, 223, 224, 228, 235, 243, 246, 248, 249, 251, 262, 270, 281, 288, 296, 305, 319, 324, 346, 348, 351, 352, 354, 355, 365, 368, 369, 373, 378, 389, 402, 413, 427, 435, 449

law of God, 319, 329, 391
lay influence in church matters, 126, 127, 386
laymen, 223, 254, 281, 365
legate, 102, 125, 191, 192, 193, 194
legateship to Canterbury, 214, 222
letter of recommendation, 279, 444, 463
letter, secret, 127, 326
letters
collection and preservation of, 104, 147, 299, 306, 307, 357, 364, 379
dictating, 6, 39, 100, 101, 116, 156
reference to his, 335, 381
returned, 104, 147
libertas ecclesiae, 338, 351, 352, 353, 389, 402

life, shortness of, 2, 13, 35
love
  fraternal, 96, 113
  of God 2, 37, 112, 418, 434
  paternal, 96, 99, 101, 113, 384, 403, 450
  spiritual 2, 3, 4, 5, 6, 7, 9, 11, 12, 13, 16, 31, 37, 51, 43, 44, 46, 47, 51, 54, 59, 60, 65, 68, 69, 74, 75, 79, 84, 85, 92, 115, 117, 120, 121, 133, 321, 337, 418, 434

marriage cases, 177, 238, 242, 243, 297, 365, 415, 419, 423, 424, 427, 435
mitigation of decrees, 265, 281, 286, 306, 308, 323, 338, 348
monasteries, quarrel between, 113, 122, 182, 251, 266, 267, 269, 271, 302, 450
monastery of Saint Augustine, 351
monastic
  discipline, 97, 104, 119, 137, 195, 312
  life, 2, 4, 5, 8, 9, 13, 16, 17, 29, 30, 31, 35, 36, 37, 38, 42, 43, 44, 46, 49, 51, 56, 66, 67, 75, 79, 96, 98, 100, 101, 112, 118, 121, 132, 161, 162, 166, 172, 178, 195, 199, 203, 205, 231, 232, 254, 312, 322, 331, 332, 333, 335
  paradise of the cloister, 375, 376, 382, 383, 403, 405, 414, 418, 431, 450, 458
money sent, 89, 287
monk
  affection for Anselm, 148, 155, 166, 173, 174
  apostate, 331, 333, 431
  arrested, 412
  becoming a monk/nun shortly before death, 29, 86, 328, 331, 412, 448
  burial, 226, 412
  changing monastery, 55, 100, 110, 111, 113, 355; see also *stabilitas loci*
  encouragement to become a, 2, 15, 30, 36, 37, 44, 56, 76, 81, 95, 99, 101, 114, 115, 117, 120, 121, 133, 132, 335, 448, 466
  oblate, 106, 195
  profession, 123, 156, 188, 468
  returns to monastery, 143, 331, 333, 431
  sent to England, 90, 91, 92, 93, 94
  sent to Scotland, 413
morals in England, 30
music, 146
mutual love, 4, 5, 7, 11, 13, 16, 23, 28, 31, 34, 37, 41, 42, 45, 46, 48, 50, 59, 60, 65, 68, 69, 74, 84, 87, 91, 93, 119, 125, 130, 141, 142, 146, 209, 245, 334

new see: Ely 441, 457, 458, 459, 460
novice, 2, 37, 38, 99, 113, 335, 375
nuns, 169, 183, 230, 314, 330, 405, 414; see also Malling

obedience, 5, 17, 73, 88, 196, 231, 232, 233, 311, 313, 373, 403, 421, 436
  to Apostolic See, 280, 338, 350, 351, 361, 388, 390, 397, 408, 410, 441
  to Canterbury, 172, 177, 185, 190, 192, 195, 198, 207, 226, 236, 237, 242, 277, 278, 363, 373, 403, 405, 413, 426, 427, 429, 435, 443, 451, 464, 465
  to superiors, 6, 13, 38, 73, 74, 79, 312, 403, 408, 410, 421

obeying the rule, 123, 203, 425, 436
office, demands of, 20, 21 30, 39, 42, 50, 85, 100, 106, 125, 126, 129, 132, 139, 144
opposition to royal injustice, 354
pallium, 14, 176, 192, 193, 214, 220, 221, 278, 304, 445, 447, 451
papal
    admonition, 305, 323, 348, 351, 352, 354, 362, 363, 397
    advice sought, 315
    confirmation of the rights of the church of Canterbury, 304, 452
    vicar, 397, 398, 411, 422, 440, 459; see also William Bona Anima, archbishop of Rouen
paradise of the cloister, 333, 418
pastor, 323, 373
paternal admonition, 360, 384, 403, 405, 449
perversity of former life, 67
plea for Anselm's return, 310, 317, 323, 347, 351, 352, 353, 363, 365, 366, 373, 375, 384, 386, 395
poem of praise on Anselm, 189, 227
pope
    Roman, universal pontififf, successor and vicar of Christ and Peter, 126, 127, 218, 221, 223, 248, 262, 278, 323, 373
    royal respect for, 213, 215
prayers for King William II, 190
precedence, setting an example, 78, 80, 106, 137, 156, 160, 168, 169, 176, 186, 206, 208, 210, 238, 248, 281, 293, 308, 311, 314, 322, 324, 326, 328, 339, 355, 391, 422, 451, 455, 462, 464, 467, 470
preferment
    advice on, 52, 61, 88, 78, 80, 106, 148, 149, 156, 345, 421
    resenting, 125, 148, 156, 160, 165, 176, 193, 194, 198, 206
pride, 285
priests
    non-celibate, royal taxation, 364, 389, 391, 392, 393, 394; see also celibacy
    sons, 126, 222, 255, 282, 422
primacy of Canterbury, 198, 201, 202, 222, 242, 303, 304, 307, 319, 373, 471, 472; see also obedience to Canterbury
primatial authority, 200, 201, 202, 222, 229 236, 237, 242, 251, 255, 261, 265, 270, 277, 278, 282, 303, 304, 319, 426, 427, 428, 429, 435, 449, 451, 452, 453, 455, 464, 465, 467, 471, 472
primatial controversy: Canterbury - York, 442, 443, 444, 445, 453, 454, 455, 456, 462, 464, 465, 467, 470, 471, 472
prior, office of, 6, 25, 39, 42
profession of obedience to archbishop of Canterbury, 283, 443, 444, 445, 451, 452, 453, 454, 455, 456, 464, 465, 467, 469, 471, 472, 473
profession, vow, 113
propriety church, 170, 171, 270

qualities for a bishop, 201, 202, 225, 457
quarrel with King William II, 176, 178, 206

reconciliation with King Henry, I 364, 373, 376, 384, 385, 388,

Indices

391, 397, 402, 411, 448
reinvestiture, 364, 388, 391, 392, 399, 400; see also Canterbury
respite between King Henry and Anselm, 265
responsibilty, accusation of fleeing, 310, 311, 327, 336, 365, 366
return
  (1100), 212, 214, 217, 218, 219, 222
  (1105/1106), 365, 366, 386, 387, 389, 395, 397, 399, 400, 403, 411
  after second exile, 355, 364, 365, 366, 368, 369, 370, 373, 375, 376, 387, 395, 400, 403, 407, 433
  delay of, 310, 311, 312, 314, 336, 364, 365, 366, 368, 369, 375, 407; see also accusation of fleeing resposibility
returning churches, 270
roads, uncertain, 55
royal favour, 151, 163, 164, 165
rule, 113, 123, 137, 156, 163, 251, 267, 375, 403, 450
rumors, 311, 322, 327, 336, 357, 362, 377

sacraments, 63, 223, 254, 255, 311, 415, 416, 417, 468
  non-celibate priests, 223, 254, 255, 256, 257, 282; see also celibacy
safe conduct, 124, 176, 193, 206, 315, 437
scandal, 169
schism in Rome, 377, 378
schismatic, accused of being, 192
scribe, 25, 334, 379
sex, preoccupation with, 310
sheriff's duties, 356, 359

sickness, feebleness, old age, 51, 53, 104, 106, 124, 139, 142, 193, 206, 242, 243, 286, 291, 301, 399, 400, 407, 430 438, 448, 461
simony, 222, 255, 285, 322, 385
sodomy, 257, 365
spiritual care, 125, 312
stabilitas loci, 6, 17, 37, 38, 55, 105, 113, 119, 178, 188, 195, 226, 355, 405, 410, 431, 433
substance = person in God, 204
successor, blessing and advice, 165
suitabilty for office, 156, 160, 193, 198, 206
support from fellow bishops, 429, 447, 449, 457, 458, 459
synod, Lateran (1105), 348, 349
synod of London (1 - 3 August 1107), 430; see also curia regis meeting
synod of Soissons (24 May 1089), 136
synod of Westminster (1102), 336, 348

teaching, 64
thoroughness of conveying thoughts, 28
training/education of monks, 30, 32, 33, 34, 35, 39, 42, 64, 66, 72, 328
training, thankful for, 22
trial of bishop by fellow bishop, 225
tribulation, 138, 217, 219, 310, 311, 312, 331, 332, 349, 357, 365, 366, 372, 382, 387, 425, 432
trinity, 128, 129, 136, 204, 207
tyrannus, 126, 176, 192, 193, 198, 206, 208, 209, 210, 213, 216,

222, 224, 235, 248, 262, 310, 351, 352, 354, 415, 416

usus atque leges, 176, 191, 192, 193, 206, 209, 210, 214, 215, 216, 221, 246, 310, 315, 317, 318, 319, 323, 329

vacancies, 206, 310, 443
veneration, Anselm forbids undue, 236, 237
viceroy in England, 407, 461, 462
virginity/chastity, 134, 168
visits to England
  (1st visit 1079/80), 98, 99
  (2nd visit 1086), 155, 116, 117, 188, 119, 120, 121, 130
  (3rd visit 26 October 1092 - 6 March 1093), 147
voyage to England, 98

wealth, 49
wife, provide for, 264
will of God, 150, 151, 154, 155, 156, 157, 158, 159, 160, 166, 176, 193, 198
will, making a, 264

Synchronous chart of Anselm's episcopal colleagues I

Anselm 1093–1109

See	Bishops
Canterbury	Lanfranc; Anselm 1093–1109
Bath & Wells	John of Tours
Chichester	Ralph Luffa; William Warelwast
Exeter	Osbern fitzOsbern; Reinhelm
Hereford	Robert de Losinga; Gerard; Robert Bloeth
Chester	Robert de Limesey
Lincoln	
London	Maurice; Richard
Norwich	Herbert de Losinga
Rochester	Gundulf; Ralph
Salisbury	Osmund; Roger
Winchester	Walkelin; William Giffard
Worcester	Wulfstan; Samson; Thomas II
York	Thomas I; Gerard
Durham	William St. Calais; Rannulf Flambard

1093 · 1097 · 1100 · 1103 · 1106 · 1109

monachus ++++   capellanus regis ———   cancellarius regis ――――   cancellarius reginae ------

The Letters of St. Anselm

Synchronous chart of Anselm's episcopal colleagues II

		country of origin*	monk	capella regis	relationship to roy. family	cathedral new / rebuilt	diocesan activities	usus atque leges +/-/0 1094-1097	roy. investiture +/-/0 1100-1107	church reform 1102, 1108	supremacy of Canterbury 1108/1109
1. Bath and Wells, John	1088-1122	F Tours		C	friend of W II	new	fulfills ep. duties	+	+		
2. Chichester, Ralph Luffa	1091-1123	N		C	friend of W II	rebuilt	freq. visitations	0	0 −		for Cant.
3. Durham, William of St. Calais	1081-1096	N Bayeux	St. Calais St. Vincent		confidant of W II	new		+			for Cant.
4. Ranulf Flambard	1099-1128	N Bayeux		C		new		+			0
5. Exeter, Osbern fitzOsbern	1072-1103	N		C	cousin of W I		blameless	0		married, 2 sons	
6. William de Warelwast	1107-1137	N		C			estab. canons regulars, active	+	+		for Cant.
7. Hereford, Robert Losinga	1079-1095			C		new		+			
8. Gerard	1096-1101	N		C ch. 1085-1091	nephew of Walkelin, (rel. of W I)		little known		+ ↑ −		for York
9. Roger	1102	N		ch. queen					−		
10. Reinhelm	1107-1115	N		C			active		−		for Cant.
11. Lichfield, Robert de Limesey	1086-1117	N		C					+ ↑ −		for Cant.
12. Lincoln, Robert Bloet	1093/4-1123	N Ivry		C ch. 1091-94		consecrated new cath.		+	+		for Cant.
13. London, Maurice	1085/6-1107	F Le Mans		ch. 1078-85		new					
14. Richard Beaumais	1108-1127	N								addicted to women for health reasons	
15. Norwich, Herbert Losinga	1091-1119	N	Fécamp Ramsey	C	friend W II	new	exemplary bp.		+ ↑ −	married, dynasty St. Paul's	for Cant.
16. Rochester, Gundulf	1076-1108	F/It	Bec Caen			new	freq. visitations	0	−	active in reforms	for Cant.
17. Ralph d'Escures	1108-1114	N Sées								active in reforms	for Cant.
18. Salisbury, Osmund	1078-1099	N		ch. 1070-78	nephew W I	new	liturgical reform	+			for Cant.
19. Roger le Poer	1107-1139	N Caen		ch. 1101-03			efficient bp.		+	married, 2 sons	
20. Winchester, Walkelin	1070-1098	N		C	relative to W I	new		+			for Cant.
21. William Giffard	1107-1129	N Rouen		C ch. 1094-1101			active		−		
22. Worcester, Wulfstan	1062-1095	AS	Worcester			new	freq. visitations				for Cant.
23. Samson	1096-1112	N Bayeux		C				0	0	mon. reform	for Cant.
24. York, Thomas I	1070-1100	N Bayeux		C		new		0		married, 2 sons, 2 daughters	for Cant.
25/8. Gerard	1101-1108										for York
26. Thomas II	11089-1114	N Bayeux		C			bp. above average		+ ↑ −		for York

* F = France, N = Normandy, It = Italy, AS = Anglo Saxon, C = member of capella regis, ch = king's chancellor

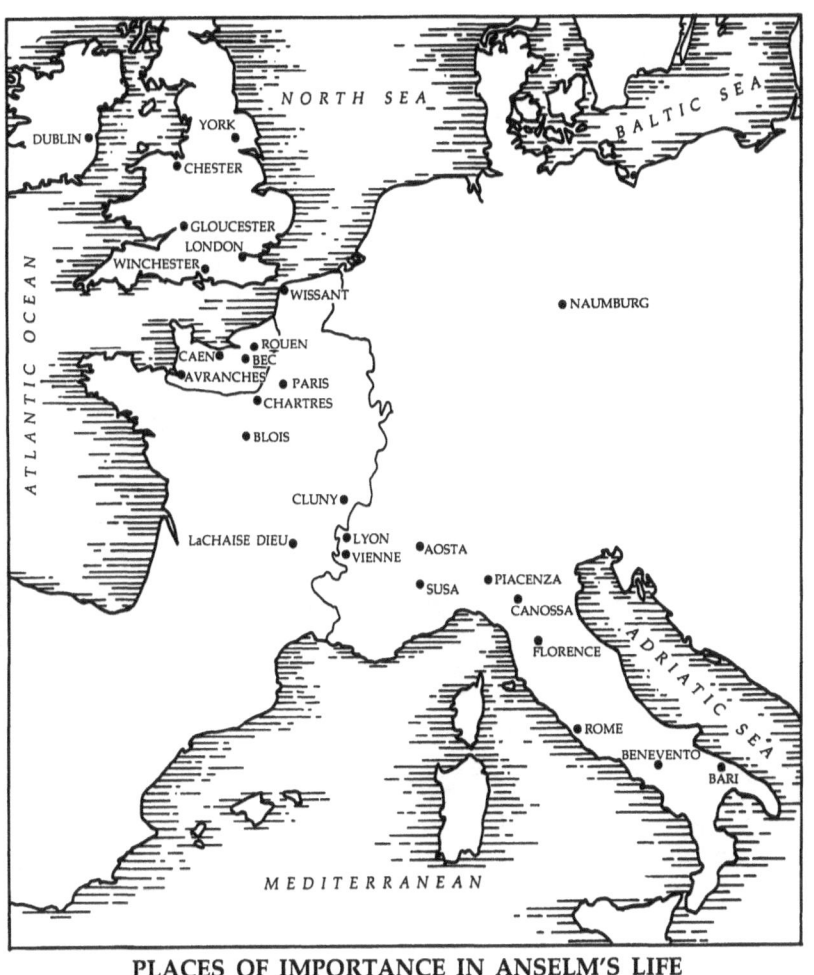

PLACES OF IMPORTANCE IN ANSELM'S LIFE

THE CHURCH IN ENGLAND IN 1100

The sees of these bishoprics were translated: from Wells to *Bath* in 1090; from Lichfield to *Chester* in 1073, from there to *Coventry* in 1087; from Selsey to *Chichester* in 1075; from Crediton to *Exeter* in 1050; from Dorchester to *Lincoln* in 1072; from Elmham to Thetford in 1075, from there to *Norwich* in 1094/1095; in 1058 Ramsbury was united with Sherborne, translated from there to *Old Sarum* in 1078 and again in 1218 to Salisbury.